BRITISH

POLITICAL ISSUES

VOLUME I

BRITISH
POLITICAL ISSUES

VOLUME I

E. LIGGETT

Tutor-organizer
Workers' Educational Association

PERGAMON PRESS
OXFORD · LONDON · EDINBURGH · NEW YORK
PARIS · FRANKFURT

PERGAMON PRESS LTD.	Headington Hill Hall, Oxford
	4 & 5 Fitzroy Square, London W.1
PERGAMON PRESS (SCOTLAND) LTD.	2 & 3 Teviot Place, Edinburgh 1
PERGAMON PRESS INC.	122 East 55th Street, New York 22, N.Y
GAUTHIER-VILLARS ED.	55 Quai des Grands-Augustins, Paris 6
PERGAMON PRESS G.m.b.H.	Kaiserstrasse 75, Frankfurt am Main
FEDERAL PUBLICATIONS LTD.	Times House
	River Valley Road, Singapore
SAMCAX BOOK SERVICES LTD.	Queensway, P.O. Box 2720
	Nairobi, Kenya

First edition 1964

Copyright © 1964 PERGAMON PRESS LTD.

Library of Congress Catalog Card No. 64-8868

Set in 11 on 12 pt Bembo   Printed in Great Britain by
BLACKIE & SON LTD., GLASGOW

CONTENTS

To the
WORKERS' EDUCATIONAL ASSOCIATION

PREFACE

The table of contents of this book will reveal that it attempts to provide a conspectus of British political issues—a ground-plan of political debate. It seeks to present a sound factual framework for the study of political programmes and political parties. I have tried to provide not an academic study of any one aspect of politics but a comprehensive survey of the questions of the day, of all those problems which have recently 'risen to the surface of politics'.

My justification for writing this book is that it brings together information which, otherwise, is available only from widely scattered sources—from numerous books, pamphlets, leaflets, magazines, journals, and newspapers. I hope that it will be of use to adult students, freshers at university (before they become immersed in their various specialisms), trade unionists, teachers and students of social studies in schools and colleges.

The arrangement of the sections of 'British Political Issues' has caused me much thought. The notes—for example, on Nationalization or on Law and Justice—are not short explanatory insertions but are coherent passages of supporting material. The note matter, inserted at appropriate points, is 'relegated' in this way so as not to impede the development of lines of study in each of the book's parts. An annotated table of contents has been provided to make the material of the book more accessible.

The book is the result of six years' work as a full-time tutor with the Workers' Educational Association and, I hope, reflects the practical needs of adult students who are not content to observe the divisions of study commonly found in academic institutions.

E. LIGGETT

Swing Gate, Gressingham,
Hornby, Lancaster
April 1964

ACKNOWLEDGEMENTS

This book would not have been written without the stimulus provided by the many adult students with whom I have worked. I am particularly indebted to those people who have read the various sections of my script—Mr. Werner Burmeister, of the Department of Extra-Mural Studies, University of London; Professor Peter Campbell, of the Department of Political Economy, University of Reading; Mr. Norman Cunningham, of the Department of Economics, University of Liverpool; Mr. Arthur Marsh, of the Delegacy for Extra-Mural Studies, University of Oxford; Dr. Malcolm Pittock, of the Workers' Educational Association, West Lancashire and Cheshire District; and Mrs. Barbara N. Rodgers of the Department of Social Administration, University of Manchester. While these have given invaluable help with the detail and manner of presentation of my material they are absolved from any responsibility for deficiencies of the final work. My thanks are also due to my wife, Sheila, for her practical help and moral support during the last six years.

E. L.

SHORT TABLE OF CONTENTS

VOLUMES ONE AND TWO

VOLUME ONE

VOLUME TWO

ANNOTATED TABLE OF CONTENTS

VOLUME ONE

INTRODUCTION

Historical Background to the Political Debate

The scope of politics: nineteenth century reforms and reformers. Origins of problems: growth of towns; growth of political awareness. Violence and civil disobedience.

Attitude of the State. The political party—the engine of modern government. Advent of Labour: deficiencies of Liberals and Conservatives. All parties remain progressive.

Origins of conservatism: maintenance of institutions; amelioration of the condition of the people. End of the 19th Century: Conservatives and the united support of the moneyed classes—the compromising of principles. Inter-war years: discontent with the party's attitude to social and economic affairs—the 'Y.M.C.A.'. Conservative liberalism: British and Continental conservatism.

Origins of liberalism: individual judgement in religion; opposition to authoritarianism. Conditional obedience to government: social contract theories of government. Nineteenth Century electoral reform. The co-ownership of liberalism: a common mental stock.

The State as a policeman: Conservative and Liberal failure; Socialists and the enlargement of state action. The 'Lib-Lab' alliance: the gradual break of Liberals with the workers. Workers' discontent the essential driving-force of politics during the first half of the Twentieth Century. Independent Labour Party: a voice for the workers' aspirations.

The Labour Party: cautious Socialism and liberal trade unionism. Reformism and respectability. Workers and electoral politics: the chronology. Development of the Labour Party: Coalition Government; 1918, 'Labour and the

The New Liberalism

The Political Divide

The 'political slump' of the early and mid-'fifties: Butskellism or Macrossmanism. Macleod on the political divide: the centripetal tendencies of British politics.

Factors of moderation: 'Welfare Capitalism'—economics replaces politics; pluralist stagnation. The Lobby: the Government's need of co-operation. Political philosophy a political liability.

The political revival of the late 'fifties: new thinking on pensions, nationalization, economic development; defence and the Campaign for Nuclear Disarmament; political television; Europe.

Political borderlines.

The Current Political Scene: a Preview

The status and efficiency of Parliament. Growth of interest in the central administration and in the machinery of government: discontent with the amateur approach. Local and Regional Government. Inadequacy of political information and democratic participation: suppression of the facts.

The Parties: Wilson and extroverting of Labour's energies; Conservative introspection; a vigorous Liberalism. Party finance: demands for a definition of political activity and a limit to electoral expenditure.

Constitutional government: control of state power—the Ombudsman.

The economic position: confidence and balance. Trade. Controls and 'forward-looks'. Government spending.

Wages policy: union and employer resistance. Price competition, monopolies, mergers, restrictive practices, and consumer protection.

Economic planning: doubting Conservatives; Liberals—a balance of individualism and collectivism. The machinery of investigation: 'Big Neddy' and 'Little Neddies'. Regionalism. A science-based economy. The problems within planning: the 'brain-drain' and the question of individual incentives; the weight of taxation—a tax on capital?; railways closures—hard choices and the balance of economic advantage; use of manpower; business schools.

The European Economic Community and party positions. Shrewd electoral calculation and party philosophy. Exclusion a blessing?

The industrial front. The pressure for trade union reorganization—T.U.C. initiatives. Employers' organizations: illogical division of competence. Shop-stewards. Strikes. Industrial democracy. Efforts of Conservative Ministers of Labour.

The Welfare State reconsidered. Conservatives and Tories. The Conservative 'One Nation'. A slogan for the 'sixties.—'Expansion!'. Misgivings

ONE: POLITICAL

I. *Government and Parties*

1. *Parliament*

(i) *The Sickness of Parliament*

Decline of Parliament: growth of business; shortage of time; universal suffrage; party discipline. Parliamentary government, to Cabinet government, to 'Presidential' government. Crossman: the Cabinet now part of the 'dignified façade' of government.

Inadequacies of parliamentary control—national finance, the nationalized industries. Delegated legislation: statutory instruments.

Rubber-stamp Parliament and robot M.P.s? Press, radio and television: the alternative forums. Strong government and fixed responsibility. Ministerial evasion of Questions.

Function of Parliament: Amery on consent and coercion; Laski on necessary limits to debate.

Adequacy of opposition: time and political will. Alternating party-government a myth? Keynes plus public relations equals perpetual office? Fixed-term elections? 1963 Wilson and Labour: opposition not dead. Representative and responsible government.

(ii) *The Backbencher*

M.P.'s pay and working conditions: the strain of stewardship. Committee of Inquiry into pay: Holford Plan for the Palace of Westminster.

Commanding intellects at Westminster, or high average ability? Overwork or underwork? M.P.s attendances. Importance of the backbencher —Crichel Down, Waters Case, Suez. Scope for initiative.

Discipline of the party-controlled House: advantages and disadvantages. Crossman 1955: the alternating party oligarchy and the systematic abuse of majority rule. How far should collective responsibility extend? Labour's Standing Orders: 1959 'Chairman's Statement'.

Labour: natural rebelliousness and tight discipline. Labour's public sanctions: Conservatives' unobtrusive 'trap-door' sanctions. Backbench opinion: Labour and coherent revolt, Conservative isolated protest.

Note (a). Reform of Parliament

(i) *Institutional Reform*

A smaller Commons? Functional representation: a House of Industry; National Economic Development Council. Regional Government: Scotland, Wales, and the North-east.

(ii) *The Lords*

Composition. Life Peerages Act 1958: non-hereditary peerages and the revitalizing of the Upper House. Debate on composition continues. Wedgwood Benn case 1961. Peerages Act 1963: renunciation for a lifetime.

Powers. Government use of Lords. Wasteful duplication? Socialist attitudes: Bevan versus Morrison.

(iii) *Procedural Reform*

Waste of time: discussion of trivia; divisions. Report of the Select Committee on Procedure March 1959; attendance; printed speeches; proxy-voting; Questions; shorter speeches, etc.

The Committee System: clearing the floor of specialist business— the Finance Bill. Specialist committees. Government caution: dislike

III. *Political Information*

8. *The Press*

INTRODUCTION

HISTORICAL BACKGROUND TO THE POLITICAL DEBATE

A review of British domestic politics over the last 200 years would involve discussion of social, economic, industrial, and electoral problems. Social problems in the fields of housing, public health, and education first attracted individual reformers and reforming groups which were not organized along party lines as we know them today. Industrial problems such as the granting of legal immunities to trade unions were tackled by the unions themselves although, in the earlier part of the nineteenth century when the unions were not yet well organized, humanitarian reformers gave significant help to the workers in the movement for factory reform. For the solution, or an attempt at the beginnings of a solution, of the problems of unemployment and economic control we had to wait until the twentieth century, for the writings of Keynes. Political problems such as the granting of the vote to ever greater sections of the population were dealt with by the systematic work of political associations, ultimately by political parties competing for electoral support.

The problems mentioned above came with the growth of the towns, the concentration of workers into factories, and with the arrival at self-consciousness first of the middle-class, then the working-class. Violence and riot accompanied the work of reform in many cases: in the 1960s we still have occasional scuffles between demonstrators and police and civil disobedience is not entirely unpopular.

In the last 200 years the attitude of the State towards social, economic and industrial matters has undergone considerable change: the Gladstones of the nineteenth century were 'loth to take into the hands of the State the business of the individual', but the Charles Booths, the Rowntrees, the Keir Hardies and the Beveridges were less reluctant. The engine of modern government is the political party: in the twentieth century race to extend the protection of the State to the individual, the Liberal Party won the first sprint but were overtaken by the new Labour Party, which offered more thoroughly radical solutions to our political ills. It is important, at the outset, to examine the deficiencies of the old Conservative and Liberal Parties which permitted the advent of a third party. While one studies the failure of the Liberals to maintain their position as the radical left of British politics one has to look at the proposition that all three major political parties of the twentieth century became, in varying degrees, radical, progressive, or liberal.

A central strand of Conservative thinking has always been the support of existing institutions—the party had its early roots in the support of the Crown, the Church and the Constitution. In the nineteenth century Disraeli declared that the party should preserve institutions, maintain the Empire, and ameliorate the condition of the people. In fact, nineteenth century Tories were not identified with the 'bosses' and were often champions of the underdog. Enemies say that, once the party of the underdog, at the end of the century the Conservatives became the voice of land, finance and industry—the united support of the moneyed made the party compromise its principles. In the years between the two world wars some Conservatives were deeply distressed by their party's attitude to economic and social affairs—unless the party listened to the voice of conscience, they said, it would be destroyed. Macmillan, Boothby and Oliver Stanley formed a group of young theorists—known as the 'Y.M.C.A.'—which called for the rationalization of industries such as those of housing, fuel and power, and for the creation of welfare services which would make extreme poverty impossible.

Nevertheless, the Conservative Party can claim to have participated in the building of the Welfare State, to have helped in the introduction of piecemeal reform before 1945. While the Conservatives, at the beginning of the century, provided a logical home for opponents of the Socialist threat, they became, also, a party of 'progress'. Nominally the nation's right-wing party, the Conservatives are very different from the conservative parties of the continent, which are often violently reactionary, indifferent and even hostile to democracy and social progress. In real terms, most British Conservatives are liberals. Their opponents neither seek to assassinate Conservative leaders nor do they retire from the electoral battle in despair.

Historians trace the origins of liberalism to the growth of individualism of judgement in religious matters in the sixteenth century and to the growth of opposition to authoritarian government in the seventeenth. In the eighteenth century, with the secularization of political issues and the strengthening of the commercial middle class, belief that the subject should give only conditional obedience to the State led to the acceptance of social contract theories of government. In the nineteenth century, with the agitation for the extension of the franchise, which led to the Reform Bill of 1831 and the Reform Act of the following year, the liberal position was consolidated. Political and religious privilege was virtually ended in the nineteenth century and the belief in liberty, tolerance and opposition to authoritarianism became so general as to be part of the mental stock of all major parties.

Today, Grimond quotes with approval a statement made by Walter Lippman: 'the State may well be a useful policeman, its care may let the citizens arrive safely at their destinations; the State should not say what time the citizen should depart or arrive, it should not say what route he ought to take, or specify the destination.' (*Political Quarterly*, July–Sept. 1953.) In fact, the nineteenth-century British parties, long wedded to a *laissez-faire* attitude towards commercial and industrial freedom, failed to be efficient policemen. Grimond has said that the Liberal Party failed because it did not stick to its empiricism—it failed to examine the results of *laissez-faire* and to reinterpret the meaning of freedom. It was left largely to the Webbs, Wallas, Tawney, and Laski to examine the results of *laissez-faire* and to swing political thinking towards an enlargement of the field of State action.

At the beginning of the twentieth century Liberal Party leaders were divided in their attitude to State action: one element was prepared to mobilize the forces of the State for great programmes of social welfare, the other not. One historian of the Liberal Party, Sir Henry Slessor, has interpreted the party's failure as a failure of leadership. The Liberal Party's break with the workers was slow in coming—in 1906, when the Lloyd George and the Asquithian elements of the party were fused under Campbell-Bannerman, relations were still friendly. (Philip P. Poirier's book, 'The Advent of the Labour Party' 1958, discusses the unavowed 'Lib-Lab' alliance which contributed much to the great electoral victory of 1906. The alliance was the work of MacDonald and Herbert Gladstone, the Liberal Chief Whip.) If Campbell-Bannerman had lived (he died in 1908) a concordat with Labour might have been achieved: Asquith, the new leader, was far less radical, far less appreciative of the workers' aspirations.

In the 1960s we have become accustomed to the cries of distress of the 'white-collared'—the teachers, the bank clerks and the bank managers, the doctors and the dentists. While this discontent is not an entirely new phenomenon its earlier existence was not crucial—the essential driving-force of the first half of the twentieth century was that which aimed at the amelioration of the social condition of the workers. The arrival of the Independent Labour Party in 1893, a voice for the workers' radical aims, was an indictment of the Conservatives as it was of the Liberals—both the old parties were deficient. Both essentially middle-class parties, Conservatives and Liberals failed to provide a means of expressing working-class aspirations—neither was able to move sufficiently quickly towards a progressive social welfare programme, or to lead an attack on economic privilege. In the event, the Labour Party established itself as the radical left of British politics and the Conservative Party became the home of those who feared an aggressive working class.

The Labour Party was the offspring of a cautious Socialism and a liberal-minded trade unionism, and it is still an alliance of these elements. Socialism in Britain did not become revolutionary—the milder, reformist type prevailed, its exponents the Fabian Society and the Independent Labour Party. As with Socialism, the milder form of trade unionism prevailed. During the nineteenth century union attitudes towards politics varied. Early, in the Owenite period after the French War, the newly formed mass unions made a show of revolution. (In the years immediately before 1914 a revolutionary atmosphere attached to the actions of some unionists who leaned away from conventional political methods of expression towards direct action for the securing of workers' control of industry.) In the mid-Victorian period the respectable craft unions were content to play a conservative part in the existing political system: nevertheless, during this period, the union leaders entered electoral politics.

In 1874 the first workmen M.P.s were elected and associated themselves with the Liberals—they did not represent an independent workers' voice. The desire for an independent working-class voice in Parliament led to the election, in 1892, of Keir Hardie—and of two others who later went over to the Liberals—and to the founding of the I.L.P. in the following year. The trade unions, concerned about economic conditions, were eventually persuaded by the Socialists to help establish a Labour group in Parliament: in 1900 the Labour Representation Committee was formed. In 1906 the L.R.C. became the Labour Party, which gained 30 seats in the election of that year. As seen above, the founding of the new party did not involve an immediate break away from Liberalism: trade union M.P.s were Liberal in outlook.

Labour took part in the coalition governments of the First World War. There was a great increase in the national affiliations of trade unions to the party and profit was also gained from the beginning of the break-up of the Liberals. After the war, with the publication of its moderate programme, 'Labour and the New Social Order', Labour became avowedly Socialist for the first time. A nation-wide network of constituency parties was formed. The Labour Party formed two minority governments in the 'twenties: the life of these was brief because of the party's inexperience in government and its lack of firm purpose, and because of the terrible economic conditions prevailing on both occasions. Labour played a significant part in the coalition government of the Second World War and came to power, not simply to office, in 1945.

The year 1945 represents the culmination of a long history of political demands for a redefinition of social justice in Britain. The Labour Government built on the achievements of previous governments, and the work which began in 1945 followed the campaigning of people of various political persuasions. The Liberal Beveridge was identified with the major preparatory work for the provision of comprehensive insurance and the maintenance of full employment (the Socialists soon departed from the 'Beveridge Principle', see Vol. II, p. 171); the

Conservative Butler, sharing honours with the Socialist Chuter Ede, had planned educational reconstruction; the Independent Eleanor Rathbone (Member for the Combined Universities from 1929) had campaigned for Family Allowances, while the Fabian Socialists, as far back as 1907, had demanded a national health service—an aim which appeared in the Labour Party programme of 1934.

The Labour Government of 1945, in addition to its concern for the building of a Welfare State, was intent on establishing a wide measure of collective ownership—of railways, road haulage, civil aviation, coal, gas, electricity, steel, and the Bank of England. It also held to the stern wartime egalitarianism, as seen in the long continuation of the rationing of food and clothing, and continued a tax policy, established during the war, which involved a substantial redistribution of incomes.

It must be noted that the Socialism of the Labour Government was moderate and reformist in character, not revolutionary—nationalization, for example, did not carry with it expropriation. Gaitskell once referred to Keir Hardie's Socialism as being idealistic in character, drawing more from Methodism and from Robert Burns, than from men like Karl Marx. In this spirit the Third Labour Government worked—accepting a class struggle, rejecting a class war.

CONSERVATISM IN THEORY AND PRACTICE

In the post-war world the Conservative Party has been remarkable for the vigour of its opposition to the Labour Governments of 1945 and 1950, and for the revival of its fortunes during the 'fifties, seen in three successive electoral victories, during the second and third of which its majorities were increased. The Conservative Party as a whole continues to show a traditional respect for the party leadership and the regular extra-parliamentary forums of party debate continue to show a high degree of docility. Conservative disputes—for example, that relating to the Central Africa Federation in Parliament, and that relating to Nicolson's Suez stand in Bournemouth East and Christchurch—when they do occur show a degree of bitterness equal to anything Labour can show. However, a high degree of cohesion in the parliamentary party has enabled it to survive such 'crises' as the Suez episode, the Thorneycroft resignation, the massive Cabinet reshuffle of 1962, and the Profumo Affair and leadership battle of 1963.

The Conservatives have enjoyed extensive periods in office. Between 1918 and 1945 the party was in power, either alone or in coalition, save for the two short periods of Labour rule. The electorate has long held to the belief that the Conservatives, of the educated and aristocratic party, 'know how to rule'. During the inter-war years the Conservatives were helped by the fact that the Liberals were in decline, and by the fact that the Socialists had not yet matured. Positive factors have helped the party. The Conservatives have not been hampered by the strong pacifist element which, for some people, renders Labour suspect. The party, despite criticisms of its lack of social conscience, can claim to have helped in the building of the Welfare State—for example, tributes have been paid to the work of Neville Chamberlain at the Ministry of Health between 1924 and 1929. (The Ministry of Health was created in 1919. Chamberlain may have made it 'a leading department of State' but it is severely criticized today for its lack of firm direction of the National Health Service. See Vol. II, p. 191.)

Disraeli said of the Conservative Party, 'Unless it is a national party, it is nothing'. Similar assertions are heard today. Conservatives declare that theirs is a national party, a party which believes in a common heritage and in 'One Nation' and rejects the idea of class-war. The claim to be a national party is one any party organized to work in the British system of universal suffrage must make: the Labour Party, as its experience in office has increased, has become much more a 'national' party than it was as a minority government in the 'twenties. However, the claim to be a national party is most commonly made by the Conservatives—the party is, they say, much nearer to being an even balance of social classes in its supporters than Labour. (See, for example, 'Some Principles of Conservatism' 1956, Peter Goldman, p. 5). Conservatives also boast of the diversity of shades of opinion among their M.P.s: there are people of the left, right and centre; those of 'advanced' views, 'standpatters', Tories, liberals, and anti-socialists.

In addition to being a national and a tolerant party, the Conservatives claim to be flexible in their willingness to accept change. Although the Conservatives have enjoyed long periods in office they have also frequently participated in coalitions, which makes it difficult to follow the track of a pure Conservative tradition—as one writer asks, 'Can the Catering Wages Act of 1943, for example, be properly described as a Conservative measure?' (Burn, p. 48 'Law and Opinion in England in the Twentieth Century' ed. Ginsberg). When in office alone Conservatives are prodded into action by their opponents: prior to the National Insurance Act of 1959 which modified our pensions scheme, one Bow-Grouper admitted that 'it was a race to the statute book'. Speaking of the welfare field as a whole, it is the 'Innovators' of the party, and not the parliamentary leaders, who are carrying Conservative tradition forward in demanding an empirical approach to welfare spending. (See Vol. II, p. 222.)

Conservative compromise has led critics to say that Conservatism has ceased to exist, that the party has abandoned its tradition in order to gain votes—that the party, since 1900, has been time-serving, acting from electoral expediency and not from inner conviction. Conservatives should rule, and they should rule in a Conservative manner—the first principle is important, the second may be abandoned if necessary. Since 1900 the momentum of politics has increased (and seems to be still increasing): with the two world wars and the building of the Welfare State the functions of governments have multiplied. To judge whether the charge that Conservative compromise has meant the abandonment of Conservatism one must ask how far politicians mould events, and how far they themselves are moulded. Political situations are not static and Conservatives may plead that Conservatism cannot remain static: in dealing with unemployment, inflation and the balance-of-payments in the twentieth century 'compromise' has meant nothing less than political realism. (With regard to the management of balance-of-payments and economic planning, it must be said that the party has been very tardy in facing realities. Only a few months before the July 1961 watershed Conservatives were sneering at planning as Socialist nonsense: since this date they have been anxious to foster support for planning, while propagating the idea that Conservative and Socialist planning are totally different products.)

In 1910 Conservative leaders allowed the party's opponents to go to the people on the 'People versus Peers' question: usually, and not merely in respect of the powers of the House of Lords, Conservatives have not chosen to meet demands for constitutional change with total opposition. Further, Conservatives do not put the constitutional clock back:

> It is the duty of every Englishman and of every English party to accept a political defeat cordially, and to lend their best endeavours to secure the success, or to neutralize the evils, of the principles to which they have been forced to succumb. (Burn, p. 44, *op. cit.*, quoting Salisbury 1867.)

When the Conservative Party came to power in 1951 it was with the intention of bringing about the denationalization of the steel and long-distance road haulage industries: they accepted the fact that the other nationalized industries should continue as they were. The Conservatives did not seek to restore the University Constituencies, as they had said they would when the Socialists abolished them, nor have they instituted any legislation to circumscribe the freedom gained by the trade unions under the 1945 Labour Government. Though under strong pressure from the party outside Parliament, they have not given a fillip to private medical practice by introducing the provision of free drugs for private patients—promised when Labour was in power.

> The maintenance of domestic peace can exact heavy sacrifices from individual consciences and the line which divides duplicity from magnanimity is not always clear. (Burn, *op. cit.*, p. 44.)

As the electorate has grown bigger, a State bureaucracy has developed to administer an ever-growing body of legislation. Some political philosophers express profound dislike for the nature and extent of modern governmental activity with its over-concern for the individual and the group interest (e.g. Walter Lippman, 'The Public Philosophy' 1955). Government, they hold, has degenerated because governments are slaves to mass sentiment—we have 'government by Gallup Poll'. Parties compete for public favour by offering more and more 'gifts', they swim with the electoral tide. The public interest, say the critics of modern democratic government, necessitates hard decisions: the public interest demands that governments should tax, conscript, command and prohibit. Good government does not come from the melting-pot of private interests. (See below, 'Pluralist stagnation', p. 35, and 'The Lobby', p. 36.)

The Conservative Party is the chief propagandist in Britain for the 'he governs best who governs least' line of reasoning. In their theoretical writings Conservatives stress the importance of the individual and the family and declare that politics are of secondary importance. Conservative philosophy stresses a high regard for the 'permanent values'—for religion, the family, and so on—and rejects revolutionary utopian ideas based on a belief in the perfectibility of man.

Butler has remarked that he would rather have been a painter than a Cabinet Minister: he is only one of a legion of Conservatives who have pronounced on the secondary importance of politics. Politics are secondary and government powers should be limited because politics and government are merely means to the attainment of other things. The things most wrong in the world are not touched by politics:

> The things that are most wrong in our world and always have been, the things that make people most unhappy, and always have done, are things that can scarcely be touched by political action. This is the case, because they are not defects in laws or in institutions, but defects in human nature; and it is in human nature that the remedies must be sought. To comprehend this limitation upon politics is the beginning of political wisdom. (Peter Goldman, 'Some Principles of Conservatism', p. 12.)

And:

> The great dividing line in British politics has always been between those who regard politics as supremely important and those who conceive it to be the handmaid of religion, art, science and society. The Left are in the first category, Conservatives are in the second. (Burn, *op. cit.*, p. 50, quoting Utley.)

Yet Conservatives, like Socialists, practise 'big government' and, since the war, have wooed the electorate with their programmes at election time—not so many years ago programmes were taboo, a Socialist heresy. In practice, Conservative Governments do not contract out of the welfare and economic planning business: the party does not hearken to its Enoch Powells or its Thorneycrofts. The student, noting the extent of government activity under the Conservatives and hearing declaration of political faith about the true nature of the State and the proper (limited) sphere of government, might be forgiven for feeling somewhat confused.

Conservative statements as to the secondary importance of politics involve considerable exaggeration but part of the strength of the Conservative Party does come from its appeal to non-political or even anti-political elements in society—to those who doubt the powers of the 'magic wand of the Act of Parliament', who believe that 'the laws reach but a very little way'. Legislation by itself achieves little—the State cannot make men better or wiser. Thinking only of one of the fruits of legislation, the National Health Service, one is tempted to take issue with this last view. (Yet it is argued that our medical services would have been as good, if not better, if the State scheme had never been. See Vol. II, p. 190.)

Essentially, Conservative politicians cannot and do not think that politics are unimportant: political problems are not solved by turning one's back (even though, as in economic planning, one may try this solution): non-political values must be defended through political action. There is no real dilemma: the Conservative politician is not really in the position of saying that his chosen profession is unimportant.

In Socialist pronouncements one sees a desire for a greater measure of interference in certain spheres of life, stemming from a belief in an ordered society. In dealing with newspaper closures, monopolies, the revision of company law, improvement of standards of television advertising, the control of land values, the Socialists demand the radical reform. Conservatives talk constantly of the need to provide the individual with opportunity rather than equality: while they have not wished to deprive people of benefits once granted, they have been less ready than the Socialists to promise new benefits.

In the positive act of imposing controls on the citizen the Socialists are more severe than Conservatives. This difference is shown in attitudes towards economic planning, although not to the degree sometimes imagined—the Labour Party is very conscious of the limitation it must observe in imposing controls. (See Vol. II, p. 49, '1945–51: limitations of planning and control'.) During the 'fifties the Conservatives failed to introduce radical economic measures to meet the problem of inflation: since July 1961 measures have been introduced which, if late and clumsily introduced (was it necessary to introduce a wages pause and target planning at the same time, and at a time of economic crisis?) are forward-looking, if not bold.

Neither party sails the political seas without a rudder. To the Conservative the art of politics or statesmanship involves empiricism, action from observation and experiment and not from mere theory. This does not mean that Conservatives act without reference to theory but it does mean that they reject utopianism. The demand for sweeping change which comes easily to Socialist lips is indicative of a definite difference in political temperament—Socialists do not make their wide demands only when in opposition. While the Conservatives *tend* to be empirical, Socialists *tend* to be utopian. (See below, p. 34, 'Factors of Moderation'.)

Socialists favour the grand gesture. On the question of the school-leaving age, for example, the Labour Party would raise the minimum leaving-age and then deal with the administrative difficulties—the supply of teachers, accommodation, and so on. The Conservatives, until very recently, have taken the line that is better to encourage voluntary late-staying and to leave the raising of the minimum leaving-age until the administrative difficulties involved are less severe. A similar difference of approach revealed itself during the debate preceding the 1959 Mental Health Act when the question of the provision of mental welfare services arose. Socialists said that it should be mandatory on local authorities to supply such services: Conservatives said that, given the shortage of social workers in the field, it would be wiser to make the provision of welfare services permissive and work for gradual improvement.

Conservatives regard the State as a growth of nature, like the family, the Church, and like voluntary associations. From this belief stems a respect for history: Conservatives are bound to believe that the accumulated wisdom and experience of all generations that have gone before is more likely to be right and to give good guidance than the fashions and fads of the passing hour:

> To discover the order which inheres in things rather than to impose an order upon them; to strengthen and perpetuate that order rather than to dispose things anew according to some formula which may be nothing more than a fashion; to legislate along the grain of human nature rather than against it; to pursue limited objectives with a watchful eye; to amend here, to prune there; in short, to preserve the method of nature in the conduct of the State . . . this is Conservatism. (White, 'The Conservative Tradition', p. 3.)

The Conservative view of change is the organic view—it embraces a disposition to preserve and an ability to improve it, it accepts grafting but rejects axing, welcomes evolution and fears revolution. To the Conservative, change can be dignified with the name progress only if it is in harmony with the environment and customs of the people—and the onus of proof is on the proposer of change. Conservatives reject the shallowness of doctrinaire reasoning.

If Socialists are prisoners of words, Conservatives are in danger of being prisoners of scepticism: one right-wing commentator has spoken of the Conservative need of release from their 'thraldom to moral scepticism in politics' which would give them greater scope in showing their latent idealism. Conservative scepticism, with its emphasis on man's imperfections and its useful insight into man's limitations, runs the risk of becoming an ideology in its own right: scepticism, ceasing to be merely a realistic reaction to excessive radical optimism, may become a positive force actually making human beings less altruistic, less loving than if left to themselves.

> When Conservatives begin to argue that reformers are the real menace, rather than the evils which reformers seek to correct, it is surely time to begin to feel that Conservative thinking has lost all touch with reality, and has become as doctrinairely blind as the doctrinaire it seeks to debunk. (Peregrine Worsthorne, *Sunday Telegraph*, 18th June 1961.)

SOCIALISM AND THE LABOUR PARTY

Barbara Castle has said: 'It is very difficult to fight a general election against a party which has announced its conversion to the main points of your own policy. Is it surprising that the Labour Party should be a little breathless?' (*Manchester Guardian*, 23rd June 1955). The Conservatives may or may not have been the best pupils of Socialism in the last twenty years, but, as a party which regards itself, and is apparently often so regarded by a substantial part of the electorate, as naturally the best fitted to rule Britain, it certainly possesses considerable powers of adaptation. The voyage of the Conservative Party into the 'sixties has been less troubled than that of Labour—the 'fifties and early 'sixties were a time of severe internal crisis for the Socialists. However, before commenting on the bitter party battles which divided the party from 1950 onwards, one should make brief note of the impressive size of the legislative programme of the 1945 Government, and of the workmanlike rethinking of policy during the period after the 1955 election defeat.

Labour's difficulties in the 'fifties stemmed from two factors—the need to plan a programme for a 'second stage of Socialism', and secondly the existence of a party machine which provided ample opportunities for dissentients to raise their voices. We here concentrate on the first factor, leaving the second until later. (See below, p. 125, 'Centres of Power'.) As far as a programme was concerned, Labour had achieved much and was undecided about the direction of advance. Economic planning was implicit in Socialism but Labour had still to work out methods of economic control. (The task remains. See Balogh, 'Planning for Progress', Fabian Society 1963.) Ample evidence of the existence of social evils was to be found in the Britain of the early 'fifties, but these were less obvious to the elector than had been the ill-health, poverty and unemployment of the 'thirties. The electorate, in the years of Tory prosperity, had less patience than in former times with a party of change (one should not exaggerate the size of the victories of Labour's opponents—see voting figures, p. 25): Labour had not yet worked out its plans for wage-related insurance benefits in the age of affluence—the Titmuss Era did not dawn until 1957. (For an interesting account of how Titmuss was introduced—by chance?—to Labour Conference see Crossman, 'The Thought Barrier', *The Guardian*, 5th April 1963.)

The questions, discussed elsewhere, relating to Labour's decision-making machinery were not wholly new in the 'fifties: the question relating to the party's rethinking of aims and to the possibility of its capturing the imagination of the newly affluent electors was new. However, the questions of party democracy and the questions of Labour's position in the affluent society could not be separated—those who attacked and those who defended Labour as a proletarian party had to work through normal party channels.

The battle within the Labour Party in the 'fifties was between the Socialists, who wished to challenge the economic and social system, and the Reformists, who were content to modify or tinker with the existing society. The conflict was an inevitable result of the nature of the party, made up as it was of Marxists, Christian idealists, and reforming liberals. In 1958 the *New Statesman* said:

> The Labour Party stands in principle for a new social order and in practice for a reformed capitalism: its record over the last thirty years is a dialogue between these two objectives and this, fundamentally, is what all the rows between floor and platform have been about at one conference after another. (23rd Aug. 1958.)

To the Fundamentalists it was evident that the party had to offer a clear alternative to 'people's capitalism' and travel on from the 'stalemate state'. The complaints were variously expressed: 'If we want a moderate policy we can get it from the Tories'; 'Labour is merely offering less glossy versions of Tory policies'; 'Labour fights skirmishes and avoids pitched battles'; 'The party is suffering from acute anaemia'; and, 'Gaitskell, in his care for the floating-voter, has forgotten the idealists of the party'. The view of the Fundamentalists was that a narrow election victory on a moderate policy would be disastrous to the party's long-term interests—the telling of Socialist truth counted for more than a false victory. The *New Statesman*, *Tribune*, the Bevanites and the 'Victory for Socialism' group were the chief propagandists for a renewed expression of Socialism: among the issues they argued over were education and social policy, further nationalization, and the unilateral renunciation of nuclear weapons.

Socialism meant more than material welfare, freedom of opportunity, and the competition of man with man—it meant human fellowship and social equality. 'People's Capitalism' had to be rejected because the ethical conversion of capitalists, and capitalist apologists, could not be expected within such a system. It was unrealistic to expect the conversion of a capitalist society to a code of conduct consistent with a socialist ideal without a change of institutions, ethical conversion would not come with mere preaching. Thus, there had to be no compromise for the sake of expediency—Socialist ends and Socialist means went together.

An affluent society with Labour in power was not the desire of the Fundamentalists, the True Believers, or the Old Socialists: they deplored Labour's lack of commitment to radical measures in the fields of education, the organization of industry, and defence. Opposed to this type of thinking were the Trimmers or the Reformists who declared that it stood in the way of the formulation of sensible programmes and confused political discussion appropriate to the day's needs. While Socialist slogans, admittedly, gave the party drive, they nevertheless obscured thinking on defensible means to practicable ends. The slogans, '... atavistic growls belonging to the distant springtime of the Socialist movement', were a liability.

The Trimmers accepted the new and prosperous society and subscribed to the Conservative aim of doubling the standard-of-living in 25 years—Socialists should not be shocked puritans resentful of the comfort of the television age, ostriches denying change. In an age of full-employment the provision of equality of opportunity was the party's rightful aim—the modification of the educational system was legitimate, the modification of the ownership of industry redundant. For their pains, Trimmers like Crosland earned the sneers of the Fundamentalists who dubbed them blatant opportunists and cheerleaders of the affluent society.

We can date Labour's internal battles from 1950, when the party served the nation with a government of 'tired old men and inexperienced young men' (Crossman). The Korean War caused an economic crisis—the rearmament programme was imposed on an already overemployed economy:

> But the rearmament programme had not only produced financial disaster: it had also precipitated a political crisis which was to divide and lame the Labour Party for the whole of the next decade. Ten days after Mr. Gaitskell's Budget, Aneurin Bevan resigned, and two days later Harold Wilson and John Freeman followed suit. The famous Bevanite split had begun. As so often happens in political crisis, the breaking-point was such a trivial issue that it seems incredible in retrospect that serious men, all of them lifelong Socialists, could have found it impossible to settle it sensibly. Mr. Gaitskell insisted on imposing a charge on teeth and spectacles prescribed under the Health Service, and although the sum involved was ridiculously small he insisted that it was essential as a sign that the country was prepared to make the sacrifices in the social services necessary for the sake of rearmament. The Cabinet supported Mr. Gaitskell, whereupon Aneurin Bevan resigned. But, like Wilson and Freeman, he was soon arguing that the enlarged rearmament programme—not teeth and spectacles—was the real ground for his resignation; and demanding—as his Bevanite alternative policy—the imposition of full-scale Socialist planning, including steadying

prices by consumer subsidies, and stopping the dollar drain by rigid import controls. (Crossman, 'Who Was Right in 1951', *The Listener*, 18th April 1963.)

Bevan resigned as Minister of Labour in 1951.

(R. T. McKenzie writes: 'It is difficult not to conclude that the real reason for Bevan's resignation in 1951 was that he had been passed over by Attlee when the offices of Chancellor of the Exchequer and Foreign Secretary in turn fell vacant. [Cripps resigned in 1950 and was succeeded by Gaitskell; in the following year Bevin was replaced by Morrison. The two who were thus promoted were Bevan's only possible rivals for the Leadership.] 'British Political Parties', revised edition 1963, Note 2, p. 597.)

In 1954 he resigned from the Shadow Cabinet, the Committee of the Parliamentary Labour Party, on the issues of German rearmament and the formation of a 'Pacific N.A.T.O.' (Bevan attacked Attlee in the House on the South-east Asia Treaty issue.) On 16th March 1955 the Parliamentary Labour Party accepted the recommendation of the Shadow Cabinet to withdraw the whip from Bevan, by 141 votes to 112. (On 2nd March in the House in the vote on the Opposition's amendment at the end of a defence debate sixty-two Labour Members abstained. In the debate, Bevan had asked whether the hydrogen bomb would be used against any attack by conventional forces. He had challenged his leader to say that this was not Labour's policy and had declared that, without this assurance, he could not vote for the Opposition amendment. Attlee had given no direct reply.)

The Bevanites, with their 'Tribune' pamphlets and their 'brains trusts', became something of a party within a party. In domestic affairs they campaigned against cuts in Health Service expenditure and for further large-scale nationalization. Bevanism, according to one commentator, was a 'mood rather than a movement', and a mood based on no coherent principles. One must reject this estimate: both the Bevanites and their successors expressed their opposition to official party policies from strong moral convictions. (The hostility of Bevan towards the party leadership may have been heightened by personal animosities—it has been suggested that he felt deep social resentment towards his middle-class colleagues.)

In demanding more Socialism of the Labour Party Bevan once inquired if he had been asked to join a rugby team merely to play tiddly-winks. Bevan ranged himself with Gaitskell at the 1957 Party Conference, accepting the Bomb and accepting the 'Industry and Society' statement on nationalization. Critics declared that, in his attempt to keep the party unified, he had sold himself too cheaply to Gaitskell and his 'New Thinkers'.

'Victory for Socialism' was a Labour group revived in 1958 but which dated back to 1944. Before the 1960 successes of the uni-lateralists within the party (see p. 127) it was complacently said of V.F.S. that it was ineffective because it lacked real leadership—it was Bevanism without Bevan. The aim of the revived V.F.S. was to create fresh discussion of Socialist principles. In foreign affairs it was opposed to the Bomb and to American bases in Britain, and it demanded a rapprochement with Russia. V.F.S. campaigned for cuts in defence expenditure and, at home, for more spending on social welfare, more economic planning, more social ownership. In education it attacked private schooling while in housing it demanded public ownership of all tenanted accommodation. (See note on Housing for details of Labour's modification of its 'municipalization' plans.) V.F.S. sought to achieve its ends by holding 'brains trusts' and conferences and by issuing pamphlets: the group had a national executive committee but was persuaded from forming local branches. Labour leaders said that V.F.S. caused confusion in the public mind by issuing competing policy statements. To criticism that the Labour Party was already over-organized, V.F.S. replied that it was just another Fabian Society, another organization for discussion and research: Zilliacus said that V.F.S. was, in this respect, like 'Socialist Union', a group of which Gaitskell was a member.

At the beginning of the 'fifties Cripps and Bevin died: a few years later Attlee, Morrison and Dalton had left the front ranks in Parliament. The Labour Party's conflicts of policy and personality led observers to ask if Labour was capable of offering the nation a stable alternative government. In the 1955 General Election the party made but a dismal showing: its votes declined by a million and a half and the activists and election workers were fewer and less enthusiastic than at any time since the war.

When Gaitskell assumed the leadership of the party in December 1955 he had three tasks: first, to give Labour a smooth and efficient machine; second, to secure a faction-free party; third, to frame a moderate policy which would appeal to a relatively prosperous electorate. In response to these demands there was set up the Wilson Committee, which was to report on the damage wrought upon the party machine by electoral defeat and the old age of its personnel; Bevan was weaned from Bevanism; and, in 1958, a new policy, 'The Future Labour Offers You', was put before the public. The new policy document was a symbol of party unity and in it social equality was seen to have replaced nationalization as the centrepiece of party thinking. ('National Superannuation—Labour's Policy for Security in Old Age' had been published the previous year but was not intended for general reading—even party workers found it rather weighty. See Vol. II, p. 172.) 'Victory for Socialism' was active in 1958: as the General Election drew near its opponents were angry because it threatened party unity. Certainly its pamphlets—'A Roof Over Your Head', 'Equality in Education', 'Industry Your Servant', 'Socialism or Slump' —had the flavour of solid uncompromising Socialist gospel.

At the post-election Blackpool Conference in 1959, Gaitskell made a thorough examination of the causes of Labour's defeat. The programme had been good, he said, and a re-writing of political aims ought not to be attempted for a few years. Among the factors of failure he did admit were: inadequate spending on publicity; the public vision of a divided party which spent its time dissecting rather than disseminating policies; confusion in the public mind about Socialism, possibly attributable to the party's constitution, which had been written 40 years previously; misrepresentation by Labour's enemies of the party's plans for nationalization; inadequate explanation to the electorate of the party's intentions as to the financing of their various published plans; and the tarnished image given to Labour by such activities as unofficial strikes among trade union allies.

Gaitskell went deeper in his analysis when he outlined the significant changes which had occurred in the economic and social background of British politics and suggested that the party might be losing touch with the electorate. The typical worker of the future would most likely be the skilled man in white overalls rather than the badly paid cotton operative: the proletariat, as far as Labour was concerned, was a wasting political asset and there was a revulsion from class politics on the part of the new middle class. In a cry from the heart, Gaitskell declared the need for missionary activity by party workers: 'We are a fairer cross-section of the community yet we let the Tories get away with the monstrous lie that they are the national party.'

In referring to changed living standards the Labour leader echoed the many criticisms of the party's 'politics of envy' (see 'Labour and Profits', Vol. II, p. 55). It had been said many times, and many different ways, that Labour was a party which spoke of bread-and-butter in an ice-cream age, of a society of 'have's and have-nots' when we really had a society of 'have's and have-mores'. (But see Vol. II, p. 211, 'The Questionable Assumptions of the Welfare State'.)

Labour's failure to attract the votes of women, those of the newly married on the new housing estates, and those of young people generally was admitted at Blackpool and attributed to the fact that the party had been a party of change in a society which feared the experimental approach. This leads us back to a pronouncement which is made about elections—people normally vote not *for* things but *against* them. The electorate, in 1959, must have been content.

The division in the Labour Party between the Reformists and the Fundamentalists has been examined above. The dispute over Clause Four (see Vol. II, p. 52) which began after the election showed that the division still existed. But the Clause Four dispute was only one manifestation of the difference of opinion as to Labour's position in the affluent society. Crosland, for instance, said that Labour seemed to be more of a class party, less of a national party, than the Conservatives, and that it should rid itself of its old proletarian class-consciousness— the name 'Labour' was losing its appeal. Jay, also, asked whether the name 'Labour' was not on balance a vote-loser. In his 'Forward' article (see Vol. II, p. 53) he suggested 'Labour and Radical', or 'Labour and Reform' as an alternative which might help to remove the class-image created by the Labour Party in the mind of the electorate. Further, he said, the party's writing should be purged of such phrases as 'the militant working class', and 'working-class solidarity'.

In the Clause Four controversy, and on other topics of dispute, some Fundamentalists have been content to express straight-forward antagonism for their opponents—as when, for example, Mikardo referred to 'Crosland's fraudulent prospectus'. In 1960, in the Clause

Four controversy, Wilson and Crossman were anxious to avoid fruitless argument. This is the dilemma of the Labour Party: controvery may be more than fruitless, it may be damaging. The Fundamentalists risk the danger of losing the new generation of the electorate, while the Reformists risk losing the old.

THE NEW LIBERALISM

The study of the place of the Liberal Party within our political system holds considerable interest for any student. The party has been called a political irrelevance, a 'gadfly', and its members have been called misfits with no real political aspirations. If these insults represented the truth the effort of having to write this section of the book would be unnecessary. The Conservative and Labour Parties would like to think that they are in possession of the electoral battlefield: in fact, over recent years, the Liberals have been trying hard to re-establish themselves as a truly national party and one cannot easily discount their efforts. Many of the most interesting, and most difficult, political questions of the day relate to the future of the Liberal party, to the distinctiveness and viability of its philosophy. Study of the Liberals tests one's knowledge of the whole of the British political system, talking about them involves a good deal of conjecture. What follows relates to the function and aims of the Liberal party, the type of support it can hope to attract, its alliances with and separateness from the other parties, and to Liberal policy.

The Liberals have said that their long-term aim is to reshuffle the political cards. Differences of political opinion exist in Britain but these no longer correspond to official party lines. Liberals see the real political division today as one between Liberals and Tory-Socialists: the Liberal Party seeks to attract liberals of all parties to counter a conservative enemy of Conservative and Socialist non-liberals.

The Liberal Party intends to be a home for political refugees; a voice to canalize public frustration; a voice against 'machine politics', artificial quarrels, and insincerity; and to be the agent in removing public cynicism towards politics. Until 1950, declare Liberals, the Labour Party had momentum, today it has become indistinguishable from the Conservative Party and neither giant knows where it is going.

The Liberals will be a national party, resisting the use of the State for sectional interests, rejecting the kind of rôle played by Labour as a political wing of the T.U.C. Britain is now a prosperous society and in it are men neglected by the two major parties—the educated, the skilled, professionals, scientists, the self-employed and small-business people, and the energetic. The Liberals will give expression to the aspirations of these for a less rigid, more mobile society—a society on the American or Australian model which offers a wider basis of opportunity.

Some Labour politicians have referred to the unhealthy tinge of the new Liberalism—to its irresponsible appeals to the self-interest of the lower middle-class. If a true assessment, this would be a denial of the Liberals' stated aim to be a national party, and the new Liberalism would not get far at election time. In fact, some commentators have doubted whether the Liberal Party can achieve success without capturing a large segment of the electorate as its own:

> For to succeed a political party needs more than an Idea or a Programme: it needs an Interest. This need not be an economic interest, as Marx thought, for the Anglican Church meant more to the Tory Party than landlords and the Nonconformist meant more to the Liberals than the cotton trade; but it must be something which unites a substantial body of voters. It is the lack of such an interest, far more than the lack of ideas, that is the present weakness of the Liberal Party. (*Observer*, 12th April 1959.)

And:

> The Liberal vote may lack the stability it would have if it were tied to some large distinctive class or interest-group, in the way that Labour's support has been anchored amongst trade unionists. Thus a prolonged economic depression, by sharpening class antagonism, might bring about a renewed polarization of the electorate between the two great parties, so cutting away the hard-won Liberal gains. (H. Berrington, 'Future of the Liberal Party', *The Listener*, 6th Oct. 1960.)

The Labour Party gains mass support from the workers, the Conservative Party from the middle-class, from agriculture and from business. The Liberals have regarded the lack of an Interest as an asset—emphasizing their appeal to individuals—thus demonstrating, perhaps, the lack of realism of a permanent minority party according to which no party is good if big. There are still two sides of industry, workers and management, and the bulk of Labour supporters may continue to be persuaded that they have something to gain from the redistribution of wealth, the levelling of class structure, and the expansion of educational opportunity. Thus, if it is the Labour Party Liberals' wish to replace, they will have to appeal to the workers: here they may find it very difficult even to start—the Liberals are predominantly middle-class, they have too many accountants and too few bricklayers.

The Liberal approach to politics has been intellectual—they have preferred principle to programme and have put their emphasis on the need for political leadership, on the national rather than the sectional good. (This relates directly to the question of the rightful place of public opinion in government, referred to above in the section on Conservatism, and to the 'factors of modernation' discussed in the next section.) While Liberal intellectualism may please those who deplore the politician's slavery to mass sentiment it makes more difficult the party's self-imposed task of creating a public image, of 'putting a face on Liberalism'. If the party does decide to court the electoral battalions they will have to 'devalue' their Liberalism.

How firmly wedded to the Labour Party is the working class? When the Socialists were deeply and bitterly divided in 1960 over defence and Clause Four the idea was canvassed that the Liberals might become their residuary legatees. (Lord Altrincham has written:

> I have only once felt tempted to join his [Grimond's] party. That was in 1960. My own party—the Tories—had been re-elected on a record which, in foreign affairs, was calamitous, and on a programme which was as smug as it was nebulous. The outlook for a Radical Tory seemed almost intolerably bleak. Meanwhile the Labour Party was in a state of chaos. For the first time there appeared to be a serious chance that it might destroy itself for ever as the alternative governing party, so making way for another. [*The Guardian*, 7th March 1963.])

During this period Gaitskell was aware that the Liberals were waiting in the political wings. Just after the 1959 election he said: 'If they were ever to look like becoming a serious political force again, the process might easily gain momentum. We must not allow it to start.'

Liberals have said that they wish to replace Labour as the progressive wing of British politics. Some Liberals have seen their future in terms of a Liberal-Labour alliance, in a 'healing of the radical rift'. Grimond has said that Liberals have no basic differences with radicals of the

Labour Party. The Chairman of the Liberal New Orbits Group has declared:

> Neither party can be wished out of existence by the other. A combination of the ideas of both is just what the Left needs. If this is not the time for those of like mind to get together, then when is? (*The Guardian*, 16th Sept. 1960.)

Liberal and Labour attitudes to nationalization and to the affluent society have been suggested as points of approach by those who have sought a revived 'Lib-Lab' pact. The arguments run as follows: nationalization has been advocated by Labour only as a means of securing a more equal and prosperous society, an aim common to both Labour and Liberal Parties; the parties could co-operate if Labour would put new emphasis on the *purposes* of nationalization—which could, in fact, be achieved by other means. (The Socialists had been looking away from old-fashioned nationalization and no longer loved controls for their own sake, said Liberals.) Labour and Liberal Parties could also join in opposition to the affluent society: in Britain, material rewards and private benefit, emphasized by Conservatives, were preventing the creation of a sense of common purpose. The two parties could lead public opinion away from consideration of material gain towards an idea of sacrifice—not only for the public good at home but also for the benefit of the underprivileged abroad. (Grimond suggested a new political slogan—'Service!')

In November 1961 Woodrow Wyatt, the chief Labour propagandist for an alliance with the Liberals (see 'My plan for a Lib-Lab Pact', *New Statesman*, 26th Jan. 1962), said:

> Why don't we do the obvious and consider coming to terms with the Liberals? The modern Liberal is not all that different in outlook and policy from the great majority of Labour's forces. A joint approach to the electorate by Labour and Liberals might easily sweep the country. (*The Guardian*, 20th Nov. 1961.)

At the end of 1961 and the beginning of 1962 the question of the possible Lib-Lab pact received much publicity. Mark Bonham Carter, speaking at a rally of Young Liberals in Manchester, said of a realignment of the left-wing of British politics that if it did not come before the next election it had to come and would come after a fourth successive Conservative election victory. (*The Guardian*, 23rd Nov. 1961.) A few days later, Donald Wade and Mark Bonham Carter said at a press conference that any alliance must be spontaneous, from below, and not brought about by any pact between leaders—there were signs that this was happening. (*The Guardian*, 28th Nov. 1961.) In a letter to *The Guardian* (23rd Nov. 1961) Woodrow Wyatt stated that Arthur Henderson had made a secret electoral agreement with Lloyd George in 1931 and reminded readers that Lord Samuel had pointed out that a precise understanding in advance would have made the Labour Governments of 1924 and 1929 more effective.

In a speech at Cardiff at the end of November 1961 Gaitskell rejected the idea of Lib-Lab pact: he was all in favour of Liberals running candidates because it split the Tory vote. About the same time Grimond rejected the idea of a pact. In March 1962 Woodrow Wyatt was warned by the General Secretary of the Labour Party not to pursue the matter.

As seen above, there were introspective Conservatives, Liberals, and Socialists in the early 'sixties. One can only guess to what extent Grimond was antipathetic towards a pact with Labour—his rejection may have been nothing more than an obligatory public act. If one assumes that, at this time, there was a strong undercurrent of feeling in favour of a new political party one is forced to ask whether this was because the political party had come to be regarded less as vehicle for ideology than as a part of the machinery of government thus making it possible for Liberals and Socialists to build a new political team with which to oppose Conservatives. (See 'The Political Divide, below.)

Some propagandists for a pact said that magnanimity towards the Liberals on the part of Gaitskell would bring rich rewards. Clearly, one must ask here, if Labour was in need of new areas of support among the electorate, at what speed was Labour's traditional support eroding—how quickly was the electorate changing? It would seem that the Liberals had little to offer Labour and that the latter, in the early 'sixties, would have been foolish to assist in its own suicide. On the basis of the 1959 election results one can say that Labour was not as weak and ineffectual a party as the over-all result of the election may have indicated. Labour attracted over 12,500,000 votes in 1959—in some places there was a swing of 1·1 per cent. to the party while the most unfavourable swing against it, in London, was not more than 2·3 per cent.

At the 1958 Liberal Assembly, a motion was carried which stated that the party could in no foreseeable circumstances enter into formal pacts with either Conservative or Labour parties on the national or local level. The Liberal Executive repudiated the idea of electoral pacts for several reasons: the party was too busy to play the negative rôle of seeking the exclusion of others from Parliament; nobody had the right to disenfranchise Liberal electors by agreements with other parties; the Tories and the Socialists had more in common with each other than with the Liberals. Outsiders agreed that, to be respected, the Liberals had to be unfettered: Liberal success, it was felt, came from the party having fought the Conservative and Labour machines, from the obvious need of a third party—the 'protest vote' could not be delivered to either of the giants.

While the Liberal Party officially refused to countenance electoral pacts with the major parties, individual Liberals, as seen above, toyed with the idea of an alliance with Labour. In fact, however, constituency Liberal parties were operating pacts, *with Conservatives*—the 1958 Liberal statement on pacts did not result in a clear-cut change in policy. Perhaps a blemish on the party's integrity, accommodations with the Conservatives were felt to be necessary—in Bolton East and Bolton West at least.

(The Bolton history is interesting. As a result of an unofficial pact with the Conservatives, the Liberals won Bolton West in 1951 and 1955. In February 1959 the Conservative Executive in Bolton West decided to end the pact because the Liberal M.P. for the constituency, Holt, had helped Ludovic Kennedy fight the 1958 Rochdale by-election, which had been a Conservative seat. This decision caused a squabble within the Conservative Constituency Party since it had been made when the Conservative menfolk had been away at a football match—there were cries of 'petticoat government!' Holt, it was said, declared that a straight-fight suited him. In April 1959 the Conservative Constituency Party repudiated the decision of its Executive to end the pact—possibly as a result of a visit to the town by Lord Hailsham. [It has been said that in 1950 Hailsham, as plain Quintin Hogg, defeated Churchill's desire to join the Liberals in an anti-Socialist pact. See *The Guardian*, 4th March 1959.] In May the Bolton Liberals announced that they had no agreement with the Conservatives, but they had decided not to fight Bolton East, the Conservative seat.

At the General Election a Liberal from outside the constituency threatened to form a 'No-pact Bolton (1959) Parliamentary Liberal Association', basing his action on the 1958 National Executive declaration against pacts. On nomination day, a Conservative from London was in attendance at Bolton Town Hall, ready to hand in his papers as a candidate for Bolton West if the 'No-pact' Liberal carried out his threat to fight Bolton East. In the event, there was a straight fight with Labour in each constituency.

The pacts were ended in August 1960 when the Liberals fought the by-election in Bolton East: the Conservatives held the seat narrowly, and the Liberals came third.)

In the early 'sixties, those Liberals who desired to join with Labour were opposed by others who reiterated all the old arguments relating to the maintenance of the party's integrity—for them an alliance would not only have led to a breakdown of constituency organizations (where Liberals stood down in favour of Socialists), but also have caused a loss of self respect and alienated support. A motion put to the 1962 Assembly demanded that pacts with other parties should be rejected.

Grimond has shown a certain suspicion of programmes, and a certain flippancy about them: every pamphlet produced by the Labour Party, he said in 1958, lost them a quarter of a million votes. Liberal policies at this time were being criticized as vague, amateurish, eccentric, and lacking clarity and punch. Megan Lloyd George, who was defeated as a Liberal in 1951 and came back into Parliament as a Labour Member in 1957, said that only in the Labour Party could she be true to the radical tradition—the Liberals had lost their radicalism and nine times out of ten voted with the Tories. Liberals defended themselves against the charge that they had no policy by saying that they were a party of principle, not programme. Did Keir Hardie have a detailed programme? Having produced a spate of pamphlets and statements in recent times, Liberals need not now assume this defensive attitude. On major issues Liberal thinking has been both vigorous and advanced. On the question of Britain's entry to the Common Market, trade union legislation, on the 'Non-nuclear Club' they have been stimulating—in retrospect, Lady Megan's pronouncement seems very inappropriate.

Certain disagreements on policy have attracted criticism to the Liberals. The desire to maintain individual freedom with the recognition of the need for State action in the interests of social betterment have long been twin elements in Liberal thinking. As at the beginning of the century (see above), the party has been faced with difficult choices. Angus Maude has spoken of the Liberals as being '. . . still

3

torn by conflict between the libertarian *laissez-faire* of their grand-fathers and the dirigiste radicalism of their parents'.

In respect of the Liberal Party's electoral hopes, members have said that they would be happy to become a balancing party in the Com-mons. Grimond, in his 'New Liberal Democracy' (1958), declared that such a Liberal Party in Parliament would prefer to hold a balance outside the government. Its support for the government of the day would have limits: on certain critical issues such as taxation, defence, nationalization, it would take a clear stand. (Labour leaders, in these circumstances, might be glad of the opportunity to abandon their plan to renationalize steel.) Liberals would hope to influence govern-ment policy without veto and, on all but critical issues would not seek to thwart the government of the day. Longer-term Liberal aims would be kept in cold storage. To critics who make the charge that a government kept in office by the support of a small balancing party is an unstable government the Liberals have a definite answer: if a balancing party of Liberals were to bring a degree of instability to our government, then this would be better than wrong-headed stability.

In assessing Liberal hopes we have to pay particular attention to the working of the British electoral system. David Butler has said:

> It would require no special statistical ill-luck for a national party contesting every constituency and securing on the average a full quarter of the total vote to elect no more than a handful of M.P.s. This is the Liberal dilemma.

Under our electoral system one party might win 30,000 votes and yet lose the constituency to a second party with 30,001 votes: since our electoral system is not one based on proportional representation, since the apportioning of seats does not coincide with what one might call abstract arithmetical justice, no electoral advantage falls to the party which has lost by one vote. (Since one party may win seats with huge 'wasteful' majorities, it is even possible that its opponents may win a majority of seats with a minority of votes.) One does not compare votes won with seats except to illustrate the peculiarity of the system:

1959 General Election

	Con.	Lab.	Lib.
Seats	365	258	6
Votes (in 100,000s)	137	122	16

The system exaggerates both failure and success:

1955: VOTES NEEDED TO ELECT ONE SUCCESSFUL CANDIDATE

Conservative	39,000
Labour	45,000
Liberal	120,000

In 1955 Liberals gained only 2·7 per cent. of the vote: in 1959, although their share of the vote rose to 5·9 per cent., and although they put nearly twice the number of candidates into the field, they failed to win an increased number of seats. (The improved share of the vote, nevertheless, led to the saving of a large number of deposits.) There is no likelihood that our two major parties will introduce reforms to produce a statistically fairer system.

This brings us to the question of electoral participation. At the 1960 Liberal Assembly Grimond gave the party ten years to 'get on or get out'. What has been the Liberal effort at General and By-elections, and at local elections?

The following table gives details of Liberal electoral participation at post-war General Elections:

LIBERAL PARTICIPATION AT GENERAL ELECTIONS

Year	Candidates	Total votes	Share of Total vote %	Seats won
1945	306	2,248,226	9.0	12
1950	475	2,621,548	9.1	9
1951	109	730,556	2.5	6
1955	110	722,405	2.7	6
1959	216	1,638,571	5.9	6

(In March 1962 the Liberals won Orpington from the Conservatives. They gained 21·2 per cent. of the poll in 1959, 53 per cent. in 1962; 9092 votes in 1959, 22,846 in 1962.)

In each General Election, of course, there have been more than 600 seats to contest: thus, even in 1950 when the Liberals' participation was greatest, they could not claim to be a national party in the very strictest sense.

To become a major party the Liberals need to contest most, if not all, seats at a General Election. Constituency organization must be improved for parliamentary contests. In January 1963 three hundred and nineteen prospective parliamentary candidates had been selected by the Liberals. They were to fight four Conservative-held seats for every one which Labour held: Liberal associations in the big cities, which are for the most part Labour, are very weak. The Liberals hope to field more than 400 candidates at the 1964 election.

In the long-term, to form a government Liberals would need to gain, as other victorious parties do, a huge number of votes—so that they can benefit from the peculiarity of our electoral system, which, as noted, exaggerates success. In the short term, the likelihood of big Liberal gains is small: in no election since 1945 has the swing from Labour or Conservatives been more than $3\frac{1}{2}$ per cent.—voting habits are very sluggish at General Elections. A reshuffle of parties, which may have been conceivable at the beginning of the 'sixties, is now out of the question. In the immediate future one can see for the Liberals only hard-won, limited gains.

As far as getting on in By-elections is concerned, Liberal participation has improved considerably:

LIBERAL PARTICIPATION IN BY-ELECTIONS

	1955–9	1959–63*
Contested	20	37
Not contested	29	6

(*up to the Swansea contest in March)

Figures supplied by the Liberal Party Organization show that, in the 37 By-elections contested by all three parties in the period 1959–63, the total vote for each party was:

Labour	450,723
Conservative	441,328
Liberals	337,331
Others	38,057

(The six seats not contested by the Liberals were all Labour-held seats. At Brighouse, in January 1960 resignations from the constituency party followed the headquarters decision not to fight.)

A small party, lacking a strong base in Parliament, has great difficulty in maintaining its national appeal. In recent years, the Liberals have drawn much comfort from the publicity provided by certain by-election successes—Torrington in 1958 and Orpington in 1962. They created a sense of promise in the Liberal camp. By-election optimism can be misplaced, by-election successes may be, not revival, but artificial respiration. Fewer people vote at by-elections than at General Elections, and those who do vote, knowing that they are not electing a government, become, to a degree, politically mobile. The Liberals scraped home by 219 votes at Torrington in 1958: in the following year the Conservatives took the seat with a majority of 2,265:

1958	Votes
Liberal	13,408
National Liberal Conservative	13,189
Labour	8,697
1959	
Conservative	17,283
Liberal	15,018
Labour	5,633

The really basic task is to build up its ward as well as constituency organization. Ward organization can be built in preparation for the fighting of local election contests. Gains have been made here:

COUNCILLORS ON ALL AUTHORITIES

1960	590
1961	993
1962	1613
1963	1850

(Figures: Liberal Party Organization)

Liberals can hope that success will breed success, that able candidates and able M.P.s will bring an improvement of their position and afford bright long-term prospects. The Labour Party, as already mentioned above is conscious of the fact that young voters today are inhabitants of an affluent society and that their attitudes are not those belonging to the pre-war years of economic distress: inevitably the question one must ask is whether the Liberal Party can capture the new voters by making itself the new, youthful, empirical, and forward-looking party. The results of the 1959 election seemed not to justify Liberal optimism. They enjoyed success in the old centres of traditional Liberalism— the South West, rural Scotland, the West Riding—as well as in Lancashire and the Welsh Marches. They did not enjoy successes in the prosperous, go-ahead regions and districts—the new towns, the new housing estates, London and the Home Counties, or Birmingham:

> The truth of the matter is that the Liberals, like Labour, found their greatest support in decaying areas and industries. The Liberal Party remains an alliance between Lands End and John o' Groats, South-west England and the Highlands, the Lancashire cotton district—all of these areas are declining in population and importance. Ironically, the Liberal gospel had the greatest appeal in the dying and not in the expanding trades and regions; ironically because the modern Liberals, more than either of the two major parties, lay stress on free trade and *laissez-faire*, on the virtues of competition, and in a rejection of any policy of tenderness towards hard-pressed industries. (H. Berrington, *op. cit.*)

The above was written just after the last election: will the General Election of 1964 see a change of Liberal fortunes? The increase of electoral participation we have already mentioned, and the vigour of Liberal policy. Liberals may quite legitimately operate as an opportunist party, attempting to win votes by exploiting the grievances among supporters of the other parties: the question arises as to whether votes thus gained are merely the result of temporary dissatisfactions with Conservatism and Socialism, or the beginnings of a permanent take-over by the Liberals of a new electorate. Early in 1964 there were signs that a polarization of electoral support was occurring: one Liberal declared that he would vote Labour to keep the Conservatives out— it was 'country before party'.

One of the writers in the book of Liberal essays, 'The Unservile State' (1957), declared that the Socialists were now the reactionary Right of British politics, the Conservatives the *status quo* Centre, and the Liberals the real Left. The use of the Left, Right, and Centre nomenclature can be very confusing, and very question-begging, but even if we accept this Liberal's definition we do not settle all questions. If, in the present condition of British politics, to be Left is to be radical and vigorous and forward-looking (not radical and vigorous and backward-looking) the Liberals have formidable opponents in the Socialists and the Conservatives. 'Clothes stealing' is traditional in British politics—Liberalism has long been more successful than the Liberal Party. After 'The Unservile State' was published, the Conservatives adopted the Liberals' European policy, the Socialists their defence policy.

In the immediate future the Liberals will, very probably, have to be content with their position as a minority party, *not* holding a balance in Parliament. Unless one admits that parliamentary debate is meaningless, then this position may be acknowledged to be a useful one. There is a need in Parliament for the M.P. who will make independent speeches, ask awkward questions, inject frankness into debate, and 'throw shafts of light'. Independent M.P.s can be a tonic if the Labour and Conservative giants become flabby, can strengthen radical minorities in the two major parties.

THE POLITICAL DIVIDE

The Labour Government of 1950 ended its life after only a short period and the Conservatives came to power in 1951. The early and middle 'fifties were not a period of universal political satisfaction. To many there seemed to be little to choose between the parties—the terms 'Butskellism' and 'Macrossmanism' were used to denote the bipartisan condition of politics. There seemed to be little difference between party programmes: since four-fifths of each party appeared to agree about four-fifths of the things to be done, commentators and public alike were led to ask what politics were about. David Butler ('The British General Election of 1955', p. 164) said of the 1955 election that there were no deep, dividing issues—the election was merely a census to register political allegiances. Dispassionately, some people remarked that both parties had had a creditable post-war record—the one mobilizing national effort during a difficult period of reconstruction, the other releasing national energies during the succeeding period, when peace really started—and that it was no tragedy if either were returned to power since their battle was not one between good and evil.

At the beginning of 1958 Macleod wrote:

> A popular reason advanced by some Conservatives for their recent discontent was that there was no difference between the two major Parties; that 'Butskellism', so-called, was not dead but sleeping. Is this true? On the face of it there is some supporting evidence. Many of the bitterest arguments have been resolved. Rationing is a useful taunt, but is not an issue. Controls are a minor part of the argument. Our defence policies are largely accepted, although, typically, the Socialists attack the consequence of them. There are few divisions on Commonwealth and Colonial affairs except for the long agony of Cyprus. The National Health Service, with the exception of recurring spasms about charges, is out of Party politics. True, housing is a battlefield and education may become one, while the line-up on pensions is not yet clearly seen. All the same, one by one a dozen or more issues have been hammered on the Parliamentary anvil into accepted shape. ('The Future of the Welfare State' ed. Goldman, p. 11.)

In the post-war years, said Macleod, the party-lines had been more distinct. During the Second Reading of the Industrial Injuries Bill in 1946 the opening speeches from the front benches had been followed by a stream of contributions from the Labour back-benches without a word of reply from Conservative back-benches. This could not have happened, and did not happen, after 1950: since that date, all debates on social welfare—even when on such matters as workmen's compensation, where Conservative knowledge was inevitably more theoretical than practical—had been shared by Tories, and often dominated by them. On the other hand, said Macleod, whereas before 1945 defence and Imperial affairs were the prerogative of the Conservatives in debate, after the 1945 landslide, which brought into Labour's parliamentary ranks youngish men with experience of active service and of foreign countries, this was no longer the case. Borrowing in part from Churchill, Macleod referred to those centripetal tendencies which 'threatened the symmetry of party recrimination'.

In seeking the 'factors of moderation' which brought the parties together in the 'fifties, which operated to the detriment of old-fashioned cut-and-thrust politics, one must first refer to the importance of the administration of the economy. Economics, in a sense, had replaced politics. We now had a mass society wherein there was emphasis on high living standards, a high level of consumption. We had 'Welfare' or 'People's Capitalism'—free enterprise was tempered by State control in order that full-employment and high consumption be maintained. (See Vol. II, p. 9, 'The Instruments of Economic Control'.) In our new society, an enlarged middle-class type of electorate, enjoying a greater degree of comfort than in pre-war days, was relatively apathetic towards political issues. There was no mass enthusiasm for the politically 'romantic' issues of the day such as juvenile delinquency, commercial television and advertising standards, the law on homosexuality and divorce. For the intellectuals the Welfare State, the decline of unemployment, the 'taming of the Tories', and the stalemate in international affairs, brought boredom. (See Amis, 'Socialism and the Intellectuals' 1957.) The Suez cauldron did not bubble for very long, and anyway did not inflame ordinary people.

Second, we must look to what, in the jargon of the political scientist, is called the condition of 'pluralist stagnation' or 'quasi-corporatism'. In pre-war days the campaigns against bad social and economic conditions were mass campaigns: in more recent times we have seen the development of pressure-group or interest-group politics which involves regular and automatic consultation between the leaders of the various groups on the one hand and Civil Servants and Ministers on the other. This situation places restrictions on the pre-war brand of political enthusiasm and makes unlikely major political changes:

> Perhaps in an individualist society where groups were less highly organized and less aware of their interests, mere majority support might suffice as a basis for large-scale reform. But today the extent of group power, nurtured by the Welfare State and the quasi-corporatism of the relation of government and economy, means that Britain is close to a point at which a society must move with near unanimity or not at all. (S. H. Beer, 'The Future of British Politics—an American View', *Political Quarterly*, Jan.–March 1953.)

In the 'fifties it seemed, then, that a condition of politics existed which excluded the possibility of radical and reactionary policies. Various powerful groups in society could adopt policies of non-co-operation with the Government. The Conservatives had to treat the trade unions carefully—hence the dropping the 'final settlement' of the contracting-out and compulsory unionism issues—and could not let their 'unreconstructed Tories and rugged industrial individualists' stray into anti-union policies. The Socialists, for their part, had to consider the possible flight of designers to the United States when thinking of the nationalization of the aircraft industry. Both parties had to treat farmers carefully: the National Farmers' Union was more active in the prosperous post-war years than during the pre-war depression.

The last ten years has seen much discussion of the activities of pressure groups and there is a growing literature relating to them. The conventional view of the functioning of our system of government might seem to imply that an election decides the pattern of legislation for a five-year period and that a government is responsible only to those who put it into office. A justification of pressure group activity serves to correct this over-simplified picture. While the broad pattern of legislation for the succeeding four or five years is decided at an election, on thousands of points of detailed policy there is no majority will, no 'public opinion', and the government seeks the advice of sectional publics—there is carried on continuous consultation with a conveniently limited number of expert bodies. Thus stated, the activities of pressure or interest groups, or 'the Lobby', are seen as an extension of the democratic process. One must, however, examine the proposition that pressure groups distort the democratic process.

The right of association cannot be denied to people of like interests and their right to badger the Government has to be defended. Nevertheless, vocal sectional interests may work against the public good. Finer ('Anonymous Empire') speaks of 'raids on the public purse' by those groups which provide services, have firm memberships, and can mobilize their forces quickly to apply sanctions against the general public. While steel manufacturers, doctors, teachers, and boilermakers are able to apply administrative or economic sanctions—to some the word 'blackmail' is not too strong—the general public is held to ransom.

The Government's task is to strengthen the numerical majority against the sectional interest—the consumers against the trade unions or the monopolists—or to ensure that the claims of badly organized or unorganized sections like the pensioners are not forgotten. There are significant failures: the Government has found it impossible to enforce a wages policy on the trade unions and, broadly speaking, to persuade manufacturers to concentrate on export rather than on domestic markets. Over the years, the Government has also found it impossible adequately to decontrol rents, to ensure that all landlords received money sufficient to keep their property in good repair.

In March 1962 Harold Wilson referred to the growing influence of professional public relations firms on government, and to the need for legislation requiring lobbies to register and divulge their activities. A related problem is that of electoral expenditure. This is dealt with below, p. 45.)

With an evenly divided electorate and a pluralist society one heard complaints during the 'fifties that political philosophy had become a political liability—politics had become a question, not of ideals and beliefs, but of electoral calculation. This condition of politics presented Labour, in particular, with great difficulties: by tradition a radical party, it worked best in a radical atmosphere. It had to learn to be a party of protest without the backing of one or two million unemployed. We have mentioned Macleod's reference to Conservative discontents, and, in a previous section, the history of Labour's battles in the 'fifties and the party re-building which occurred after 1955. While Gaitskell was 'putting a face on Labour' there was a feeling of malaise and frustration on the part of Labour activists—a regret for days gone by, for the soap-box, the street-meeting, and the protest-march. But, while some resented the 'chloroform sleep' of British politics, others were ready to accept it. For the time being there were no political issues worth fighting over: it was silly to try to revive old 'politics', the electorate was apathetic, and the ill-conducted disputes of the politicians had the flavour of warmed-up tea—and this was a symptom, not a cause of political apathy. (A. J. P. Taylor, *The Guardian*, 11th Feb. 1958.)

As the 'sixties approached there was a revival of British politics. In 1957 Labour produced its 'National Superannuation' plan with its concept of graduated benefits, and published 'Industry and Society' with its new thoughts on state control of industry and with its implications for developments of technique in the field of economic planning. (How deficient Labour was to permit the Conservatives to resurrect the nationalization bogey in 1959!) In 1958 came 'Plan for Progress' and 'The Future Labour Offers You'. In early 1958 the

Campaign for Nuclear Disarmament was founded. (One must mention here that the question of German rearmament was certainly a 'romantic' issue in the early 'fifties, just as the questions of Britain's possessing the Bomb and the West's using nuclear weapons have been 'romantic' issues more recently. However, then and now, the electorate at large has not been stirred—voters have viewed Labour Party disputes on defence matters from outside, as it were, and have not themselves been stimulated to controversy. The Labour Party's official attitude on defence issues for long precluded the possibility of a straight political battle in Parliament or in the country. While the weakness of the Liberals prevented their renunciation of the British deterrent from being widely appreciated, the differences between Conservative and Labour defence policies were not clearly understood —and recent reformulations of Labour policy have not helped.) The arrival of Granada Television at the Rochdale by-election in 1958 was one of the important steps towards the ending of the aridity of political broadcasting. (See below, p. 198, 'The Freeing of the Political Air'.) While the Cyprus Act 1960—which put into effect the London Agreement of February 1959—appeared to end a phase of our colonial history, the National Insurance Act of 1959 (see Vol. II, p. 170, 'Pensions for the 'Sixties'), and the European Free Trade Association Act of 1960 ended nothing—they were merely staging-posts in debate on our economic and social affairs.

Before introducing the various sections of this book it may be appropriate to quote a comment on the subject of the current political divide:

> Borderlines are always difficult to establish with precision, and political borderlines are no exception. A Frenchman living in Alsace may not be a typical Frenchman, and he may have more in common with a German living on the left bank of the Rhine than with a Breton or a Provençal. Nevertheless the frontier between Germany and France is a valid frontier, corresponding to objective realities.
>
> By the same token a Tory of my persuasion may have (indeed has) more in common with Roy Jenkins, say, than with a Tory of the John Eden type. All the same, we live on different sides of the party frontier and are therefore, in a true and inescapable sense, political opponents. The conflict between parties must be judged by the character of the two sides, seen as a whole, not by the character of those who, as it were, live near the border.

Neither of the two big parties occupies an extreme position, though both contain extremists. Their basic attitudes are subject to numerous reservations and qualifications. But the basic attitudes are distinct, and the distinction between them is all-important. (Lord Altrincham, *The Guardian*, 7th March 1963.)

THE CURRENT POLITICAL SCENE: A PREVIEW

In the preceding sections we have examined basic Conservative, Socialist, and Liberal attitudes: the political divide has also been studied. The rest of this introduction is devoted to a brief examination and preview of party differences seen in the light of practical politics in the 'sixties—issues being dealt with in the same order as in the body of the book.

The 'sickness of Parliament' is a condition which flows directly from our having a 'quasi-corporate' State: there is a great weight of government business today and much of it involves the short-circuiting of Parliament. There has been a 'monarchization' of government, but the Prime Minister shares his power with many people and many bodies. Despite Parliament's decline it is congested with work—improvement of its procedures, and its facilities, is very slow indeed. Given the fact that expenditure flows from political decisions, the Commons are incapable of controlling the total of public expenditure: further, because of the inadequacy of the parliamentary machine, the Commons are also incapable of supervising the nation's finances, whatever the total of expenditure decided politically.

No attempt has been made below to examine the central administration as such, although the machinery for the planning of the economy and the administration of the Health Service and of Education are dealt with in their places. But there is a growing interest in administration in Britain: just as business is taking interest in management training, the Government is now taking seriously the job of finding out, not what to do but how to do things. There is a lot to be done:

There has been an uphill battle to get educational administration right; much has been achieved—but we now see how immense the task is; similarly with the hospital service; similarly with nationalized industries. We seem to have fought our way through a period of administrative bewilderment in these fields; perhaps foundations have been laid, but certainly there are no glorious victories to boast. .... Much the same things are said about our football as about our military technology, about our currency as about our higher education. 'Could do better' is written all the way down our annual school reports. ... (W. J. M. Mackenzie, 'Does our Administration Need Reform?' *The Listener*, 21st and 28th Feb. 1963.)

In view of the great emphasis placed upon the need for 'active government' the effectiveness of the central governmental machine is crucial. Wilson has said that an economic plan should be drawn up in Whitehall, and *then* submitted to the National Economic Development Council: two Ministries should be concerned with economic expansion—one a new Ministry of Production. (Fabian meeting, Scarborough, 30th Sept. 1963.) Wilson has said that Labour, in power, would rely upon a smaller Cabinet than that now existing, and upon a stronger Cabinet Secretariat: on television, Wilson has rejected the idea of a Labour 'White House'—strengthening of the Cabinet Secretariat would occur from *within* the Civil Service, with one or two outsiders possibly brought in. (3rd Jan. 1964.)

Criticism of our dilettante Civil Service is not new. (See H. R. G. Greaves, 'The Civil Service in a Changing State', 1947.) The strongest demand for an end to amateurism in our government has come from Professor Brian Chapman in his 'British Government Observed', 1963. Professor Chapman urges the following immediate reforms to improve the operational efficiency of our government:

1. An Office of Administrative Reform to review present practices of central government.
2. The reallocation in a rational and coherent way of the functions of government.
3. The provision of Ministers with private offices capable of forward planning.
4. The creation of strong regional centres of government to act as links between country and Whitehall.
5. The increase of active parliamentary participation in the formulation of public policy.
6. The opening of the top, administrative, class of the Civil Service to outside recruitment.
7. The revision of laws relating to official secrets and the operation of public bodies.

(*Sunday Times*, 1st Sept. 1963.)

Liberals have been much concerned for the development of regional government: in a major political speech in Manchester at the end of February 1964, Grimond suggested the setting up of a small, high-level unit to plan regional government. Regional government would help solve economic as well as administrative problems: if one takes seriously accounts of the 'depopulation of the North' and the 'drift to the South' one will have to take seriously some regional remedy. The massive investigation of local government now proceeding will provide some mitigation of problems: the establishment by Birmingham University of an Institute of Local Government Studies is to be welcomed. The development of regional government proper is only just beginning, in the North-east.

Professor Chapman's reference to the need for a change in the law relating to official secrets opens up the question of the availability of information. It has been pointed out that no one knows the statistical background of the Government's development of the North-east. Complaints have been made that Parliament is ignorant of the facts relating to the TSR2 bomber.

At the end of 1960 there was voiced a complaint about suppression of information. The T.U.C. expressed its concern about the Government's tendency to take important decisions on the basis of confidential reports by outside advisers—for example, the Chandos Committee Report on the replacement of the *Queen Mary*, and the Stedeford Committee Report on the finance and organization of the railways—while refusing people outside the Government the opportunity of judging the wisdom of such decisions in the light of the full reports. This touches on a subject of constitutional significance.

The serious political student in Britain does not get all the political information he would like. A Government instruction in November 1959 that statements or lectures by officers bearing on major defence policies should first be cleared by the Defence Minister followed some public debate of the question as to whether Civil Servants and Service chiefs should support their views in public, and of the question as to whether conflicts between Ministries, or between a Minister and his chief advisers, should be made public. These questions raise, in a more concrete form, the issue discussed in the preceding paragraph—the degree of secrecy the Executive can rightfully claim.

Among recent criticisms of government secrecy by academic commentators have been statements that foreigners have a better acquaintance with the realities of British life than the British themselves, that the covering of disagreements within the Government is perhaps one of the worst abuses of modern British life, and that politicians and the Government treat the public as if it were half-witted.

> Democracy implies a full participation by the general public in the argument and debate about issues of policy which affect them. (Professor Devons: 'Government on the Inner Circle', *The Listener*, 27th March 1958.)
>
> The real issue of contemporary government is to ensure that (the) policies are right at the time, that the areas of agreement and disagreement are known, and that when choices are made they are made with the cards on the table and the motives clear. (Dr. Chapman: 'Lifting the Curtain of Secrecy— lessons of Conference "Prospect" ', *The Guardian*, 14th May 1958.)

These writers have regretted that the informed public gets glimpses of inner conduct of government affairs, of the arguments and forces influencing policy-makers, only on abnormal crisis occasions such as the Bank-Rate Tribunal (1957) and the Thorneycroft resignation (January 1958), and have deplored the fact that the advice given to Ministers on such issues as the Sandys Defence Policy, and the likely economic effects of the Suez Campaign has not been made public.

The Royal Air Force conference 'Prospect' in May 1958 discussed the morality and desirability of deterrents and touched on the possibility of disengagement in Europe: it raised the question as to whether a Service should sponsor what might become a highly controversial political discussion. Constitutionally, Civil Servants and Service chiefs are responsible to Ministers, and Ministers to Parliament: the rule has it that the Civil Servants and Service chiefs should not trespass on the function of Parliament, should not initiate political discussion outside Parliament, should not 'live in the public arena'. Dr. Chapman has remarked:

> It is, in fact, not possible for Parliament or public to make a sensible estimate of Government policy if Ministers have the right to prevent publication of discordant views of advisers. (*op. cit.*)

This commentator points favourably to the Swedish system in which Parliament has the right to receive reports directly from the heads of all departments concerned before taking important decisions

The issue discussed in this paragraph concerns, not so much the right of the Press to probe for facts, as the right of Parliament to information from the Executive. Members of Parliament as well as academics have complained about 'secret government'. (For example, Jo Grimond—'Too Much Secrecy', *Observer*, 22nd Feb. 1959.) Wilson spoke in March 1963 of the Executive's growing disregard for the right of Parliament and the rights of a free Press:

> On vital issues, such as defence, huge sums are voted, and Parliament is told less and less about them. We have vitally important discussions going on about N.A.T.O. and the European deterrent and the foreign press know more about what the British Foreign Secretary says than Parliament does. (*The Guardian*, 25th March 1963.)

It seems that we not only have a presidential-type of government (see 'Sickness of Parliament', p. 91) but also that we might take on its trappings. Parliament is really dying, one feels, when it is suggested that the Prime Minister should begin to hold press conferences. (See Francis Boyd, 'Telling all', *The Guardian*, 14th May 1963.

The civil wars of the Labour Party have received much attention since 1951. Wilson has seen his main task in the extroverting of his party's energies. (*Observer*, 16th June 1963.) In 1955 Wilson had the task of re-examining Labour's machine and found that it was a 'penny-farthing bicycle in a jet age': when George Brown began to retune the party's muscles in January 1962 it was with the thought that, if these had been at their maximum efficiency in 1959, Labour would have gained 50 extra seats.

The inner-workings of the Conservative Party have received most attention recently. The Profumo Affair enabled some Conservatives to question not only the leader but also the method of electing the leader —this questioning pre-dated the Macmillan resignation and the 1963 Conservative Conference. Macleod's comment on the succession of Lord Home to the premiership received much attention: whatever Macleod's motives in writing the *Spectator* article—jealousy, concern for what had happened to Butler, desire to show his mettle and to establish that he was not a 'soft centre' Conservative—his efforts earned him odium. So much so, that in February 1964 an Independent

Conservative announced his intention of standing against Macleod at the General Election.

As far as the Liberals are concerned, although the impression lingers that Grimond is carrying the party on his back, funds are increasing and organization at headquarters and in the field has improved. Liberal publications are frequent and well-produced.

Socialists have demanded to know the sources of Conservative finance, and have demanded a control of political expenditure. In July 1960 Butler refused to undertake an amendment of the law on political expenditure. In March 1961 the Commons refused leave to Robert Mellish, a Labour Member, to introduce a Bill which would have made compulsory the publication of accounts by political parties. In a speech on 5th May 1963 Wilson challenged Macmillan to name the financial and property interests who, without the authority of their shareholders, contributed in such massive style to the Conservative Party's election funds. At the end of November 1963 the allegation was made that the Fisons group of companies had made donations amounting to £2,320 to the Conservatives during 1962: Lord Netherthorpe, chairman of Fisons, admitted the charge, which had been made during the course of a by-election campaign. A shareholder should have the right to information regarding the expenditure of company money: if he objects to political spending he will, presumably, either sell his shares or refuse to re-elect directors. But information about political spending is often denied to shareholders. Complaints about this were made at the time of the Fisons episode: one correspondent to *The Guardian* alleged that the British Motor Corporation had refused all information about political contributions, and had demanded £275 for a copy of the register of shareholders. (6th Dec. 1963.)

Conservative wealth enables a general slick efficiency in the running of their party-machine—up-to-the-minute canvass checks, the certain garnering of postal votes, and so on. Socialists, if they come to power, will introduce legislation to enforce publication of the sources of party funds.

Conservatives declare that Labour's published accounts do not give a complete picture of Socialist finances—a lot of trade union political expenditure in the interests of the Labour Party does not appear in the party's national accounts (for example, that money spent on the production of union journals), and the Co-operative Retail Societies' expenditure on 'education' covers a good deal of political publicity.

It may well be, in present circumstances, that the Conservatives are not fully aware of the exact sources of their income. Funds are channelled by firms into such national organizations as British United Industrialists Ltd., which do not spend all their money with the Conservative Party—B.U.I. will not reveal where it gets its money or where it spends it. One of B.U.I.'s principal aims is,

> To promote, preserve and protect so far as legally practicable the principle of free enterprise in trade and industry and by any and every legal means to oppose or further opposition to the nationalization of any trade or industry or any development considered likely to prejudice private trading. . . .
> (Mark Arnold-Forster, 'The sources of Tory cash', *Observer*, 9th June 1963)
.

The questions of the origin of Conservative funds and that of the control of the totals of electoral expenditure are linked. Socialists were very angry about the 'cheque-book' election of 1959. The Conservative Party, they said, had obeyed the letter of the law but had killed its spirit. In the six weeks before the election the Conservative Party, it was claimed, had spent five times as much as their opponents on advertising. The advertising was done by 'front organizations' such as Aims of Industry, the Institute of Directors, the Road Hauliers, and so on (see note on Nationalization, Vol. II, p. 62), and it reached its peak just before polling-day. The same thing is happening in 1964. (Butler has declared that the Conservatives did not introduce large-scale press advertising for political purposes—credit for the innovation, he believed, should go to Herbert Morrison, who made extensive use of the medium in the 1934 London County Council elections.)

At the beginning of 1963 relations between the Conservative Party and the City were not good. City magnates were angry about Transfer Stamp Duty and the Short-term Gains Tax: the City was ignored in the New Year's Honours List—the retiring Government broker did not receive the customary knighthood, which the City took as an open and deliberate gesture of hostility. *The Guardian* report of these facts ventured the information that,

> The feud between the East and West ends of the capital has its political repercussions. Contributions to Conservative Party funds by the financial

community have already been drastically reduced, and unless there is a change of heart the Tory party will not get its usual campaign support from City adherents when the general election approaches. (12th Jan. 1963.)

Both Butler and Sir Toby Low in the 1961 debate asked the Opposition how one could define 'political expenditure': the Labour and Liberal Parties, they said, did not publish full accounts and could not do so because it was quite impossible to give a clear picture of the full activities of a political party—a change of the law would effect the expression of political opinion in plays, books, films and newspapers. How could one define a political party so as not to limit the freedom of political expression? If the Government introduced legislation allocating each party (supposing 'party' had been given a strict definition) a block sum for advertising purposes, what would happen if the party split?

A regulation of political spending in Britain is needed: the assumptions that a General Election is nothing more than the aggregate of local contests, that the limitation of individual candidates' spending is all that is needed, and that the campaign is limited to a few days before the election are absurdly out-of-date. However, while realizing that Butler, above, was speaking with his tongue in his cheek, one must admit that the regulation of electoral spending cannot be effected until we have a definition of 'political activity' sufficiently precise to be enforced.

One way of approaching the study of politics is to examine the nature of constitutional government. In this context one considers the propositions that constitutional government means limited government and that constitutional rulers exercise only limited authority. A formal study of the British Constitution would involve a review of its sources in statute, convention, judicial interpretation, and in the writings of recognized constitutional authorities: it would also involve an examination of certain constitutional features such as the rule of law, the supremacy of Parliament, and the separation of powers. No such formal study of constitutionalism is attempted in this book but examination is made of certain aspects of government which, so far as the maintenance of a proper limitation of powers is concerned, have seemed to give cause for alarm. The debate of constitutional arrangements is a useful occupation for Britons, as well as for Pakistanis, Sudanese, the French, and the Ghanaians.

The Conservative view is that a government should use the minimum amount of force necessary for the maintenance of public order, and administer justice according to a known body of public law. Socialism, they claim, is a centralizing force, which irons out with a heavy hand the untidy diversities of social and economic life. While Socialists enhance the powers of the 'gentlemen from Whitehall', Conservatives traditionally support a wide diffusion of power. To this one can merely say that there is little evidence of the diminution of State power under Conservative governments—Crichel Down and the Chalkpit belonged to the 'fifties, not the late 'forties. The Conservative Government, in October 1962, declined to adopt the recommendation of the Whyatt Committee that we should have an 'Ombudsman', a parliamentary commissioner, and its attitude to the Council on Tribunals has been churlish.

Conservatives have said that, although government powers should be at a minimum, it is vital that they should be exercised firmly:

> One of the curiosities of Socialist thought has been its unquestioning ardour for State power when used to secure economic rights, real or fancied, coupled with its nagging suspicion of State power when designed to secure, at home or in the Dependencies, the foremost of political rights and needs —public order and defence. (Goldman, 'Some Principles of Conservatism', p. 19.)

Conservatives, on the other hand, belong to the party of order. No severe criticism has been made of the Conservatives' handling of recent civil disobedience—in fact, the 1963 Aldermaston March of the nuclear disarmers, developing as it did into an 'attack' on the 'secret' Regional Seat of Government—made them seem ridiculous. The mildness of the Conservative Government towards the 'bus strikers in 1957 has also been noted. (The Conservatives retrieved themselves a little by their efficient handling of those people who, in the summer of 1963, wanted to shout rude things to the Greek royal pair.) In contrast, one should remember that Attlee invoked the Emergency Powers Act twice, in 1948 and 1949, and sent troops into the London Docks to keep food moving during a strike.

Further illustration of the Conservative Government's mildness is provided in another direction: party leaders have held in check the 'hangers and floggers' of the party. The Homicide Act of 1957 was as much a dog's dinner as an Act of Parliament could be (see p. 76 and p. 178), but Butler at the Home Office was the symbol of humanitarianism, not repression.

★   ★   ★   ★

In 1899 the United Kingdom's share of the world trade in manufactures was 33 per cent.: in 1962 it was 15 per cent. Britain no longer dominates world trade—she is often a victim of slight shifts in trade, of changes in the prices of commodities, and of speculation. (As far as commodities are concerned, world trading agreements are beginning to achieve a better balance between supply and demand.) Britain has not worked out a detailed policy for imports: she can easily overspend and upset her balance-of-trade and the trade figures are watched almost as carefully as football results. In January 1964, when trade figures were bad and there was much discussion of the dangers of excessive expansion of economic activity, there occurred a certain amount of speculative short-selling of pounds. The days of heavy currency speculation, discussed in the body of the book, are over: the central banks, working closely together, can now defeat any speculative attack on any major currency without much difficulty. Movements of confidence in currencies now depend, not on the grave weakness of any currency, but on the availability of stronger alternatives.

In October 1963 there was a world monetary conference at which the ten most industrially advanced nations agreed to organize a formal inquiry into the shortcomings of the world monetary system. In the United States the Trade Expansion Act (1962) has authorized cuts of 50 per cent. in American tariffs: negotiations for the 'Kennedy Round' of tariff reductions to ease world trade barriers started in May 1964.

With the Government's operation of economic controls, as with the monkey's performance at the piano, the wonder is not that the thing goes badly but that it goes at all. The Radcliffe Committee on the Working of the Monetary System gave its eager public no easy answers. In January 1964, during the minor trade upset referred to above, Wilson demanded a vigorous use of the tax weapon, a decisive investment allowance to enable industry to afford a speedier write-off of machinery, and new emphasis on exports and on import-saving production.

In the Political Section of this book Parliament's lack of control of the nation's finances is considered: in the Economic Section public expenditure is dealt with from the point of view of economic management. Looking ahead is becoming popular in governmental circles: Macleod thought that the study week-end, 'Britain in the 'Seventies', held at Chequers in April 1963 was largely pointless (see Vol. II, p. 20), but other exercises have been very useful. (See Vol. II, p. 20, *Variation of Government Spending*.) Plowden's estimate of the total of public expenditure of all kinds (see Vol. II, p. 17) does look frightening until one remembers that part of the figure relates to growth industries which are within the public sector. In December 1963 the Government forecast an annual increase of 4·1 per cent. in public spending for the 4 years to 1967–68: Callaghan, for the Opposition, accepted the rate of growth, incidentally remarking that the figures proved a falsity the Conservatives' claim of 1959 that Labour's plans were too expensive.

The National Incomes Commission has published several reports since the first, which came out in April 1963. The question of a national incomes policy has had more than its fair share of newspaper space since the war: an incomes policy is undoubtedly important, but it is only one element of the economic problem. When the unions squabble over differentials, as they did at Port Talbot Steelworks in 1963 they are blamed, and when they come together to make claims, as they did in the electricity supply industry in March 1964, they are blamed. The arguments as to why the trade unions should be 'responsible', and the conditions they might reasonably demand, are given in detail in the body of this work: what is so often forgotten is that wage-restraint (which is synonymous with 'incomes policy' in the minds of many people) to be effective must be operative at all levels. It is often spurned at the local level by both unions *and* employers: similar dual resistance occurs at national level—in February 1964 the Engineering Employers' Federation declined to give evidence to 'Nicky' about the effect on costs and prices of the November 1963 pay settlement in the industry. The argument that economic stability will come with the control of demand, and not incomes, appears to be sound.

In January 1964 the Journal of the Purchasing Officers' Association complained of the hasty and inflated passing on of wage increases by manufacturers—it gave a warning to buyers in industry, commerce and public undertakings. The journal said that wage increases provided the right climate for price increases. At this time the National Economic Development Council was still studying wages and prices after many months but the Chancellor's attempt to persuade the two sides of industry to pledge support for the restraint of these was seen, by February, to have failed.

The political parties have been very hesitant in dealing with monopolies and restrictive practices. In 1945 the Labour Government proposed the abolition of retail price maintenance but was held back by the trade unions, who feared that many workers in small shops might lose their jobs. After the 1955 Report of the Monopolies Commission on restrictive trade practices the Conservative Government ignored the majority report which demanded a general outlawing of a number of trade practices—it did not believe that an 'odour of criminality' should be attached to practices without investigation. The 1956 Act initiated the slow process of the examination of specific practices. Action against monopolies has been very slow since 1945: governments have been slow to arrive at a definition of the 'public interest' and have thus not had the will to take drastic action. In 1958 the Conservatives declared that an inquiry into consumer protection was unnecessary: less than a year later the Board of Trade's Molony Committee was set up. The Consumer Council, which was set up after the publication of the final report of the Molony Committee in 1962, has lacked both teeth and money.

Throughout 1963 there was considerable turmoil over trading stamps: the extension of the trading stamp systems made evident the fact that the nation's consumers were having to support a little too much advertising. Having introduced a Bill in November to tighten up the law relating to hire purchase, the Government published a White Paper, 'Monopolies, Mergers and Restrictive Practices' (Cmnd 2299), in March 1964 which outlined plans to abolish retail price maintenance, to reorganize the Monopolies Commission to enable it to work more quickly and effectively, and to give the Commission powers to deal with mergers.

The Conservatives, it seemed, had become death-bed converts to the competitive system. The publication of the Resale Prices Bill in February 1964, appearing as it did in the last months of the Government's life, was viewed either as an act of folly or an act of courage. Conservative backbenchers quickly mobilized themselves with the aim of weakening the Government's resolve to end resale price maintenance. The task of modernizing the British economy is no easy one.

We are all planners now. The Conservatives' bland *volte-face* on economic planning in 1961, had it not been inevitable, would have been breath-taking: only a few months previously sneering at 'growthsmanship', in July, they began to gear the nation to the achievement of production targets. Two years later, David Howell, a Bow-Grouper, was still not sure of his party: in the July 1963 issue of *Crossbow* he asked Conservatives to accept that the relevant debate was no longer about freedom and individualism versus planning, but about how to ensure freedom and opportunity within a framework of planning. Editor Howell complained of his party's intellectual lag, and of a distinct lack of candour and robustness in Conservative thought.

It might seem that the Liberals, opposed as they are to anything hindering the freedom of the individual, would oppose the idea of economic planning. There has been some evidence of ambiguity of attitude. In June 1960, David Boulton, assistant editor of *Liberal News*, said that although he had been a life-long Liberal he was joining the Labour Party:

> You will find virtually no reference to economic planning in Liberal literature. The Party has fallen victim of its own and Tory propaganda depicting Socialist controls as corsets and red tape. Alongside the Grimondites—who recognize the need for planning so long as it does not upset capitalism—are the hosts of Liberals at every level in the Party to whom planning is the arch villain. Thus I leave the Party that sees Capitalism as capable of reform without basic alteration. (*Daily Herald*, 13th June 1960.)

Had he waited three years, Mr. Boulton could have stayed at home. Liberals want a Ministry of Expansion and a systematic incomes policy—the Liberal Council disagreed about these proposals in May 1963 but they eventually approved them. In his pamphlet, 'Liberals and Planning', published in September 1963, Desmond Banks spoke of a five-year plan and of a Ministry of Expansion which would take charge of the Treasury, the Board of Trade, and the Ministry of Labour. Liberals accept planning, demand a 'military operation to bring the nation's roads up to date', seek the control of advertising, and are enthusiastic for town and country planning and a 'more beautiful, less noisome Britain'. Liberals are not completely liberal—the chairman of the 'New Orbits' group has rejected the law of the jungle, '*à la* Enoch Powell'—but balance individualism with collectivism.

The ideas of the parties live in association with each other, and the desire to plan for growth is part of the ethos of our age. In 'Industry and Society' (1957) Labour proposed the investigation of the activities of our 500 largest firms: in 1964 we plan 'Little Neddy's', which will supplement the work of the National Economic Development Council by investigation of particular industries. The Conservatives declare that public ownership is unnecessary for the control of major industries, but massively support the steel, aircraft, and motor vehicle industries.

The question of the efficiency of our national administration has been touched upon above. In economic development and planning we are only beginning to organize ourselves efficiently. 'Neddy' is something but the development of the 'Little Neddy's' is vital—many must have been the national campaigns brought to nothing for want of organization at local level. The Conservatives brought out their White Paper, 'The North East: A Programme for Regional Development and Growth' (Cmnd 2206) in November 1963. According to some this was planning at the wrong level: some Socialists declared that a national population and distribution of industry plan should have come first—a series of regional plans was, by itself, not adequate. In a speech at Leeds in February 1964, Wilson spoke of the need for the physical regeneration of towns and cities, a mobilization of the building industry, and a breakthrough in governmental organization. A Ministry of Town and Country Planning, such as existed between 1945 and 1951, was needed to provide the machinery for securing the land needed at reasonable prices: there should be regional offices with interdepartmental committees.

Elsewhere, Wilson has spoken of the need for regional statistical offices which could give industry a service of necessary economic information. The provision of ten large computers for this service was part of Wilson's concept of a science-based automated economy.

The parties today are commonly interested in science. In 'Science and the Future of Britain' (1961) Labour stated its belief in the need for scientific advance and demanded a crash programme for the training of scientists—science had to become part of Britain's general culture. The Liberal pamphlet, 'Partners in a New Britain' (1963) states:

> To enable our economy to seize the full benefits of modern technology, science must be given a new high place in it. There should be more scientists in the Ministry of Science and the Ministry should be made the spearhead of a new drive to foster scientific research in the universities, improve co-operation between research in industry, government, and the universities, and encourage research in industry itself. (p. 10.)

The Federation of British Industries in its 'Civil Research Policy' (1963) suggested large-scale extra spending on civil research and development and said that the Government should use its powers as a large buyer to push forward modern productive methods. The F.B.I.'s pamphlet was, in fact, put before the Trend Committee. The Report of the Trend Committee, 'Enquiry into the Organization of Civil Science' (Cmnd 2171), was published in October 1963 and said that the Minister of Science (appointed in 1959 without a Ministry) should have more direct control in his field and should have more power to play a positive part in the promotion of research.

It has been said that, within 10 years, we may be living amidst the sophisticated chaos of automation. In February 1964 the Industrial Automation Group was formed by the directors of the country's 50 or so research associations with the purpose of fostering automation. At the Labour Party's Scarborough Conference in 1963 Wilson said that the scientific revolution must come quickly, but humanely. However, if Britain really desires a rich and developing economy she will have to accept also a changing society and the mobility of labour will involve a degree of social discomfort.

The 'brain drain' is now part of popular jargon. The Commons debated emigration in February 1964 but the flight of talent from our shores is not a new topic—it certainly long pre-dated Lord Hailsham's reference to the U.S.A.'s parasitic need for our scientists. The question of individual incentives is at the heart of the planning problem.

In the economic sphere, Conservatives have often been found talking about individual freedom. The party claims to be in favour of the enjoyment of living: in so far as Conservatism is a formulated doctrine, runs the argument, it is the by-product of real living, not the fabrication of unimpeded intellect. Conservatives offer opportunity, the Socialists equality: Conservatives offer the chance to become unequal, Socialists a drab slogan or two.

During the 'decade of direction', says Charles Curran ('Politics of Envy', *Spectator*, 6th Dec. 1957), the competitive struggle was replaced by the co-operative ethic: the allocation of goods and services was by need and not by purchasing power—there was rationing, rent control, and subsidy. Differential ability was at a discount because advantages were conferred collectively from above. The industrial worker had amended the social contract and had had his own scale of values accepted by the entire community—there had to be fair shares, there was antipathy to profits and dividends. There was hostility to those who worked hard: ability, energy, and personal endowments were resented. Later, during the mid-'fifties Labour Party documents probed the prevailing hostility towards differentiation—they were not economic proposals, but essays in morbid psychology. All very good knock-about stuff, this, with more than a grain of truth in it. (See Vol. II, p. 55, 'Labour and Profits'.)

Conservatives have declared their aim to be the removal of obstacles in the path of individual self-agency, while providing the minimum requirements of a free and civilized life for all:

> Our quarrel with Socialism is that all along the line it exalts and increases State responsibility and collectivist action, whilst reducing and depreciating individual responsibility and the sphere within which that responsibility may most naturally be exercised. (Goldman, *op. cit.*, p. 14.)

As part of their lip-service to the individual, Conservatives have often used the phrase, 'a property-owning democracy'. A wide distribution of property is desirable, they say, since power goes along with property. In fact, the Liberals are the most vigorous champions of private property today, and claim to be 'outright distributors'. Although

Conservatives have shifted the emphasis of house-building from public to private spheres, the private house-purchaser is burdened with heavy interest-rates, as well as with income tax, purchase tax, petrol tax, and death duties.

Conservatives have declared that they do not believe in a State Santa Claus and yet their Governments have supported massive State spending. Caught between the building society and the tax-collector, the middle-class man has little room for 'individual self-agency'.

The Conservative Party is by no means a liberal party in the economic sense since it believes in social measures which involve heavy taxation, direct and indirect. Burn ('Law and Opinion in England in the Twentieth Century', p. 42), writes that under any government, British taxation is:

> . . . deliberately conceived in part for social rather than fiscal ends, penal in its incidence and all-embracing in its range, adding a vast burden to life and an additional terror to death.

In the United States, Senator Barry Goldwater, a leading Republican, has declared that a government should claim only an equal percentage of all incomes and that to take a disproportionate percentage from the rich is to punish success. The Conservatives promised surtax reliefs in 1961 without significantly damaging our system of progressive taxation. Labour was the radical party in 1963 as regards tax reform. It had been negative in outlook for many years—threatening to attack expense accounts, capital gains, and surtax relief—but the Socialist Callaghan now voiced his desire to see a 'pay as you own' system, a system which would impose taxes on capital, where they would not hurt so much, in order to release 'marginal effort'. (See Vol. II, p. 81.)

In their concern for the freedom of the individual, Liberals have been anxious to encourage savings by granting tax-reliefs: to this end they have advocated economies in defence expenditure, housing subsidies, and in loans to the nationalized industries. Because of their emphasis on the cutting of government expenditure Liberals have been thought irresponsible: Mikardo, commenting on their 'down with taxation!' attitude, has referred to them as 'blatant Poujadists'.

For some economists the 'dash for planning' is escapism, a flight from reality. Certainly, with or without a national economic plan,

an unfortunately large number of separate economic problems remain.
When the first railway closures under the 'Beeching Plan' were
announced, 3rd March 1964, the secretary of the Cumberland
Development Council said:

> (The) closure will make it harder to develop Cumberland economically and
> commercially. It seems silly that after we are asked to expand the area, we
> are to be deprived of a rail service.

The Government's task of estimating the balance of economic advantage is difficult. In March 1963 the Ministry of Labour established a
Manpower Research Unit to prepare studies of future needs of skilled
manpower. The Robbins Committee Report, 'Higher Education'
(Cmnd 2154, October 1963), touched on the subject of business
schools: business education is yet another of those fields wherein
special efforts are needed. In November 1963, Sir Oliver Franks
produced his report (requested by a group of industrial leaders) on
British business schools: he recommended the establishment of a special
institution on the lines of the Harvard School. Manchester University
and the Royal Aeronautical College, Cranfield, are, in fact, to run
Harvard-type courses.

Britain's entry into the European Common Market is a dead issue
for the time being. The spate of pamphlets and statements from the
'Anti-Common Market League', 'Britain in Europe', 'The Labour
Common Market Committee', and the 'Expanding Commonwealth'
group, and so on, has abated since January 1963. Political debate on
the Common Market, which had been proceeding for years, became
much more vigorous after Macmillan decided to apply for full membership in the summer of 1961. Both parties were divided.

On 14th April 1962 Gaitskell made a speech at Fulham during which
he posed what he thought were the vital questions for Britain before
she joined Europe. At the October Conference he listed five broad
conditions for entry: safeguards for the Commonwealth; freedom for
Britain to pursue her own foreign policy; fulfilment of pledges made
to our European Free Trade Association partners; the right to plan
our own economy; and, safeguards for our agriculture. Gaitskell
had said that the best thing that could happen would be that Britain

should go into Europe on good terms, but that not to go in would not be a catastrophe.

Ostensibly, Gaitskell spoke at the Conference in support of an Executive statement but the tone of his speech was hostile whereas the statement had been careful. George Brown spoke, stressing the pro-Market aspects of the Executive statement. Gaitskell, in speaking as he did, parted from many of those members of the Labour Party who had supported him in the campaign against the unilateral disarmers: he was applauded vigorously by former enemies—Mikardo, Shinwell, and Cousins. The latter offered to print 1,000,000 copies of Gaitskell's speech—which he did. Anthony Howard, political correspondent of the *New Statesman*, has said that Labour's attitude to Europe was not deliberately determined by shrewd electoral calculation: just as important in deciding the Labour Party's stance on Europe was something over which Gaitskell had absolutely no control—the inherent lack of interest in Europe of British Socialism, a lack evident for more than 40 years. (*The Listener*, 15th Nov. 1962.)

While Socialist hearts are stirred by Africa and places further afield than Europe, Conservative interest, according to one commentator, has 'contracted':

> A significant feature of thinking in the Conservative Party recently has been the evident shift away from the Commonwealth to Europe. The truth is that the modern Commonwealth, a loose, multi-racial association of independent nations, has never eaten deeply into the Conservative heart. It lacks formal power, its interests conflict, and many of the ways of the newly emergent nations, particularly in Africa, provoke distrust and dislike. For many, the Commonwealth is seen as having been a valuable instrument in allowing the peaceful transition from Empire to independence. But this, with the important exception of Central Africa, has been virtually achieved. The Commonwealth may remain, but to a growing number of Conservatives it is no longer an ideal. (Ian Waller, 'The Conservative Debate on Europe', *The Listener*, 1st Nov. 1962.)

Waller noted that, none the less, a substantial group of Conservative members were arguing forcefully for the expansion of Commonwealth opportunities.

Both Socialists and Conservatives were accused of 'playing politics' with the Common Market issue in 1962 and one cannot exclude absolutely the possibility that both party leaders were motivated by the thought that they had an election-winner in their particular lines—although the above comments by Howard and Waller warn one that the issue may not have been so simple.

There was no 'round-table' conference on the Common Market. Both parties said they wished the issue to be 'above party politics' but they never decided that the issue was of such supreme importance that they should tackle it together—the Conservatives, at least, were equivocal on the question of consultations with the Opposition.

Britain's decision to try to enter the Common Market was momentous—not because of its economic but because of its political implications. Our worries would not have been dissipated had we been offered the best of economic terms in January 1963. S. C. Leslie comments:

> Whatever one thinks of the absolute merits of the case for British membership, one must feel some gratitude that we have been shut out and given a chance to think. To anyone who cares about the reality of government by enlightened consent, the whole episode of our attempted entry into the European Economic Community must be profoundly disturbing—a blot on the history of democratic public opinion. The thing appeared as a muddle of issues of entirely different kinds—economic, political, domestic, international. Some were in the centre of attention—those were mostly the economic questions; others were by accident or design obscured. Much superior gossip could be heard to the effect that the issues were far too complex for the average man. As a natural result the public mind was in truth not nearly clear or informed enough to be ready to settle a historic issue. ('Brussels—Defeat or Deliverance?' *The Listener*, 28th Feb. 1963.)

It has been suggested that Britain's attempts to stimulate economic growth through the National Economic Development Council will help her keep in step with the European Community. It may well be that European productivity will not gallop away from our own. Critics of 'growthsmanship' are not slow to point to the failures of planning in France. (The French practise planning not in the sense of rigid control but as a co-operative venture. The 'économie concertée' allows for the co-operation of a Commissariat and its various Commissions with the civil service, the chief industries, and the unions. The result is 'indicative planning'. The state is able to offer some incentives and practise some coercion but the economic machine has not always run smoothly. In July 1961 O.E.C.D. reported that

France's industrial resources were underemployed: at other times, as in Britain, the self-financing of expansion by industry has led to excessive economic activity.) At best, they have said, the results of French planning have been marginal. Monsieur Masse, the planning chief, has said that the national rate of growth might have been 1 per cent. less per annum without the stimulus of the Four-Year Plans.

In or out of the European Economic Community, Britain has to tackle her economic problems. The economic section of this book seeks to isolate these problems.

★　　　★　　　★　　　★

It is the greatest possible mistake to regard trade unions as being frivolous, unnecessary, or arbitrarily destructive. It must be pointed out that criticisms of the trade union movement in the industrial section of the book are matched by criticism of both government and management in the economic section. Union structure, as discussed in Chapter Eight, is only one part of the iceberg of industrial troubles: demarcation and jurisdictional disputes are isolated for discussion but they are not wide or general in their impact—there are pockets of serious trouble.

The trade unions have been under strong pressure to reorganize themselves and changes of structure do not now seem as unlikely as they did only a short time ago. The Trades Union Congress, in February 1964, invited unions in seven industrial groups (railways, metal trades, iron and steel, part of cotton textiles, retail distribution, building, and the Post Office) to discuss ways to achieve better working arrangements. Exploratory letters were sent out to other industries—founding, hosiery, and the other part of cotton textiles. The reshuffling of memberships will not come easily: at the General Council meeting in February 1964 the leaders of the General and Municipal Workers and the Transport and General Workers giant unions objected to the suggestion that the forthcoming discussions might reveal a situation wherein the amalgamation of their separate unions would be sensible. In November 1963 the T.U.C.'s Organizing Committee agreed on proposals for the reform of the 1917 law governing the amalgamation of trade unions. The Minister of Labour was sympathetic.

As for the employers' side of industry, here too important changes can be expected: the Federation of British Industries, the British Employers' Confederation, and the National Association of British Manufacturers are now studying methods of ending their illogical division of competence.

If one studies industrial relations one has to study the whole field. If, for example, one confines oneself to trade union structure one can easily assume that the activities of shop stewards represent aberrations from the normal. In fact, shop steward activity represents a legitimate and normal part of the process of collective bargaining. If shop stewards are able and employers are willing, as much as possible is done 'on the shop-floor'. The national union officers negotiate for bread, the shop stewards for the jam.

As far as strikes are concerned, the public very rarely finds it necessary to impute blame to any party save the unions. Leaving aside all other causes of legitimate union anger, one must mention that a good proportion of strikes are caused when workers become tired of managerial inefficiency and the halting of the production line.

Industrial democracy has long been an aspiration rather than a reality—often has it been said that the trade unions are not interested in anything but the straightforward wages issues. The Fawley Productivity Agreements signed by the Esso Company and the unions in July 1960 were an unusual and promising 'package deal' involving a usefully well-publicized recognition of industrial partnership. The Marlow Declaration, published in April 1963, was part of a plan to improve the system of human relations in Britain, particularly in industry: it was signed by church people, members of the educational world, by employers and trade unionists.

One can criticize the Conservatives for their long neglect of the problem of the improvement of the worker's status in industry. Their 1947 'Industrial Charter' was for long ignored: only in recent times have they sought to begin to implement its proposals—by the enforcement of better contracts of employment. However, Conservative Ministers of Labour have been very active in recent years and one should give them credit—particularly in respect of their efforts to improve industrial relations in the motor vehicle industry. In early

1964 the Government was studying the possibility of a royal commission on, or an inquiry into, trade unions.

★   ★   ★   ★

In the social section of this book we examine the State's gradual assumption of responsibility for the individual's welfare; the rôle of the social services in our 'affluent' society; the future of the Welfare State; and the administration of services and the training of social workers. In the last few years there has been much debate as to whether we should humanize, nourish, modify, or dismantle the Welfare State.

Butler has summed up Conservative acceptance of the Welfare State by saying that his destiny was in the field of social reform. The Tory, as opposed to the Conservative, is not frightened of controls to protect those who may suffer from poor social or economic conditions. Just as Macmillan tried to educate his party in the inter-war years, so Macleod—the 'essential post-war Tory', the 'Welfare State Tory', the 'Tory New-Dealer'—tried to educate the Conservative Party in the early 'fifties when he helped to found the 'One Nation' group.

Conservatives do not neglect to claim a share in the building of the Welfare State. According to some, its foundations were laid down long ago:

> The nineteenth century gulf between the Two Nations, rich and poor, capital and labour, which Disraeli exposed in his novel 'Sybil', has been progressively bridged; and Conservatives have helped to bridge it. Shaftesbury's crusade for better conditions in factory and mine, Disraeli's own measures to give the working man the vote and complete the legalizing of trade unions, Baldwin's search in troubled times for 'peace in industry' and, in our own day, the Industrial Charter with its stress on full employment and the status of the worker—all are in the same tradition. (Goldman, 'Some Principles of Conservatism', p. 11.)

The Labour Party's claim, say Conservatives, to be the sole author of the Welfare State is a piece of preposterous impudence. Socialists, seeking to keep the notion of the 'Two Nations' alive, pretend to forget Conservative efforts in public health administration, in bringing about contributory pensions, slum clearance, the milk-in-schools scheme, family allowances, and educational reform.

Official Conservative doctrine stresses the steady development of welfare services and the avoidance of unwise crash programmes. But 'Expansion!' is the slogan of the 'sixties. Some Conservative Party members have entertained misgivings about the 'affluent society' and have expressed concern about the 'areas of hidden hardship' of our society: Socialists have been among those who have expressed the fiercest sense of outrage over our depressed minorities. Speaking of social services for the generality of the population, demands for expansion of educational provision has been very strong: examination of the missed opportunities in this field reveals a catalogue of stark tragedies. In 1963, at a late stage, the Conservative Government was converted to an acceptance of large-scale expansion. In income maintenance the Socialists introduced their plan for wage-related pensions in 1957: wage-relation was to defeat, not primary poverty, but comparative poverty—the poverty of those who, having earned relatively high incomes, had to retire on low basic pensions. The Conservatives adopted Labour's idea: a very modest element of wage-relation appeared in the National Insurance Act (1959) scheme. Liberals have adopted wage-relation but stress the need to develop private benefit schemes. Continentals spend more money than we do on welfare: expansion of our welfare services and improvement of welfare standards is intimately linked with the improvement of our economic position. Some of the most vociferous Socialist expansionists have regretted that increased productivity is so much emphasized in the welfare context: speaking on the issue of 'equality' versus 'economic expansion', Wilson has said that too sharp a distinction ought not to be drawn between the two—they were not incompatible, there could be 'fairer shares in expanding prosperity'.

Socially, the Liberals have interesting and courageous things to say about the ending of the victimization of non-trade unionists in industry, and about the laws relating to licensing, divorce, homosexuality—the party condemned the action of the Conservative Government on the 1957 Wolfenden Report on Homosexuality and Prostitution, condemned the conversion of a humane report into a single, petty and futile repressive measure (the Street Offences Act 1959) against the advice of the Church and of Law. As a minority party in Parliament, the Liberals have had time to think about important issues sometimes neglected by the two political giants. (In respect of the topics mentioned above, how odd it is to read of Liberals wishing to 'throw out the nonconformist conscience'!).

The Liberal Party's 1962 Report carries the following declaration:

> The Liberal Party exists to build a Liberal Commonwealth, in which every citizen shall possess liberty, property, and security, and none shall be enslaved by poverty, ignorance or unemployment. Its chief care is for the rights and opportunities of the individual, and in all spheres it sets freedom first. (p.3.)

Liberalism has been most powerful when people have been restricted—liberalism has gained support from nonconformist resentment, manufacturer resentment, and from the resentment of those without the vote and without an adequate standard of living. In the 'sixties the party has declared itself to be dedicated to the task of removing shackles from the citizen, of ending illiberal restrictions and controls. The party is against silly purchase-tax regulations, old age pensions earnings limits, restrictive practices in industry: Grimond has deplored the exploitation of fellow-citizens by those wishing to take excess profits, wages or pensions, and by those evading taxation. For long, Liberals have adhered to the Beveridge principle of subsistence benefits: the most significant thing to be said about the party today is that it has countenanced some departure from Beveridge. (See Vol. II, p. 232, 'Liberal Welfare in the 'sixties: Security in a New Society'.)

If it is admitted that Socialists seem most often to express a 'sense of social outrage', can one correct the balance by saying that Conservatives are administrators rather than reformers, that they consolidate rather than pioneer? Improvements in the administration of education, health, and housing have been very slow and little has been done as regards basic social research. Timothy Raison, once of the Bow Group of Conservatives, admitted not long ago that:

> From the Webbs to Professor Titmuss the most intensive social researchers have sprung from the Left, and though recently Conservatives such as Sir Keith Joseph have started to emulate them, the party is only just beginning to scratch the surface. ('A New Toryism', *Observer*, 1st Nov. 1959.)

Raison suggested that a Social Research Council might be set up. (One of the first matters it might investigate, he said, could be the fact that, although the National Health Service cost over five hundred millions a year, only three millions went on medical research—'Little wonder that there is a flight of good medical researchers to the United States.') Social research is relatively cheap: investigation of such things as crime and punishment has been held up, not from lack of money, but from lack of effort—we have been very slow. People of all political persuasions deplore the lack of research into social problems. Timuss has written of the difficulties of the social reformer and has deplored the lack of social investigation. Seldon, a free-booting liberal, has argued the case for a Permanent Commission on the Social Services to discover those in real need. ('Crossbow', Autumn 1961.)

When one has done one's research one can tackle social evils either by increasing spending or by altering the flows of existing spending. It may well be that the radical approach to the improvement of social services in the 'sixties involves the better spending of public money rather than its increase. It is an interesting exercise to try to approximate the ideas of the parties on this issue. The Labour Party has called for an expansion of the welfare services to end the 'double standard' now existing in Britain: Titmuss, while dealing with poverty and declaring that too many have recourse to National Assistance Board benefits, has said that richer people regard state benefits merely as useful supplements. Wilson, while asserting that the Welfare State has brought the different social classes together, has repeated the common statement that the middle-classes have gained most from the introduction of the National Health Service. Do these statements justify the demand by Seldon and others that ways should be found of returning welfare to private enterprise? Some Conservatives have wished to see the switching of state expenditure from free drugs and free doctoring to hospital building and the cleaning of rivers. There has been some support from official quarters for this Conservative innovation: subsidies have been removed from house building in general to that needed to further slum-clearance; the Rent Act was an attempt to increase national spending on housing; general food subsidies were first reduced then abolished altogether; and charges were put on prescriptions and health foods. There seemed to be little likelihood that the Conservative Government would 'go the whole hog' in order to gratify its Enoch Powells until the 1963 Conservative

Conference when Macleod gave a hint of a move in official thinking towards the need for the reallocation of welfare spending. Liberal empiricists and Conservative innovators have spoken of a massive simplification of welfare services, of the concentration of state aid on a single object—the maintenance of a national minimum income. The Socialist Titmuss has pointed to the complexity of present services. The great difficulty for party-leaders, of course, is the removal of existing benefits and the ending of existing systems; one feels that there will be no quick end to the 'Newcastle card party', to the massive administrative game of stamps and cards.

The maintenance of income is important and it is given much space in the body of the book. In 1908 there began the redistribution of income on a national scale (redistribution at local level was, of course, centuries old) and about this time Sidney and Beatrice Webb, the Socialists, were referring to the need for a 'guaranteed minimum' of the requisites for efficient parenthood and citizenship. In the 1950's the Labour Party was criticized by some of its supporters for having 'declared a truce on inequality'—its emphasis on production and its neglect of the redistribution of incomes was deplored. The Labour Party has since elaborated proposals to end 'the poverty that exists in the midst of plenty' and has declared itself to be determined to get what Beveridge never got—subsistence for all with the National Assistance Board reduced to its originally intended rôle, that of rescuing the few unfortunates. Under the Conservatives national benefits had been kept to a low level, thus necessitating wholesale applications to the N.A.B.—exceptions had been made the rule quite deliberately. And yet the National Assistance Board was not an accurate instrument—perhaps three-quarters of a million needy people did not apply for help.

What is a 'national minimum' in the 1960's, should it involve a departure from mere subsistence standards? Or is it that the 'minimum' should be strictly interpreted, compulsory insurance being kept to a very modest level? What burden should be placed on contributions or on taxation in the financing of benefit schemes? In the discussions on social and private insurance there is much emphasis on the need for individual responsibility to exercise itself—the State has the right to encourage private pensions schemes, for example, because these schemes give the individual, who can save to whatever limit desired, the feeling of private possession. Self-help is very worthy. In the past a parallel line of argument has been that private insurance is worthwhile because the State must needs measure out benefits because it has not got a 'bottomless purse': compulsory state insurance is good for the poorer sections of the community but the insurance fund must not be unbalanced because this would cut at the roots of the citizen's self-respect, his 'citizen freedom'.

'Equality' in social welfare used to entail equal calls on all citizens in return for equal benefits: today, on the grounds that the nation is richer, we have graduated pensions and may have graduated sickness and unemployment benefits. We must have 'half-pay on retirement' because there must be no class division in old age, no catastrophic fall of earnings. Does this graduation of benefits meet a genuine social need, do the needs of old age vary from person to person, or will the extension of graduation (and the need to pay higher contributions) increase the scramble for more pay among workers, and saddle posterity with an enormously great bill? Do graduated schemes reflect the Webbs' 'enforced minimum of civilized life' or ar they an extension of Austen Chamberlain's 'intolerable bureaucratic tyranny'?

Grimond, shortly after the 1959 General Election, wrote that the election had been fought on the cost-of-living, pensions, and the social services—issues which did not really divide the nation. As far as pensions were concerned, the two major parties were 'a single dog with two barks'. The Conservative pensions scheme which came from the 1959 Act was, in fact, a very modest one compared with what Labour's would have been. The Conservatives were very anxious to limit the cost to the Exchequer: Labour was ready to take more risks, banking on the fruits of state investment producing a significant national economic expansion. When publishing its latest insurance programme, 'New Frontiers for Social Security', the Labour Party gave a warning that people would have to be prepared to pay for the scheme. Less ambitious than the schemes of a number of European countries, Labour did offer to all workers benefits similar to those offered by the better occupational and private schemes. Labour will have to concern itself with the levelling of wages if it is to avoid the charge that its 'half-pay' schemes will perpetuate inequality in sickness, unemployment, and retirement.

On the one hand, Liberals have called for a great reduction of state spending on welfare, on the other for a development of private provision. Their new scheme, 'Security in a New Society', justifies high expenditure—contributions are high, although a reduction is envisaged for those now earning less than £16 per week—but the State contracts out of this.

The public is showing an increasing awareness of education and demand is growing—'What the best and wisest parent wants for his children the community must want for all its children'. Comparing their own state educational system with those abroad people are far from content. The British (or European) system of education is an élite system which involves selection, segregation, and ascent: the American (or Russian) system is an 'open door' system; education is for consumption. The publicity of the 1963 Campaign for Education and the Crowther Social Surveys have made nonsense of the 'more means worse' argument: there is privilege and waste involved in the superiority of provision in the south as compared with the north, in the facilities afforded to middle-class as compared with working-class children, in the opportunities available to girls as against boys. Sir Edward Boyle has said that the task of the schools should be to compensate for social inequalities in other spheres: it is a fact that the working-class child suffers from a poorer physical, cultural, and domestic environment—from what Professor D. V. Glass has called 'an interlocking network of inequalities'.

One can speak of education either in terms of spending or of organization. The Conservatives have made advances in their period of power since 1951: expenditure has tripled; there has been a slow reduction in class sizes; the capacity of the training colleges has doubled, and a three-year course has been introduced; we are in sight of the ending of all-age schools; late-stayers at school above the legal minimum leaving-age, one in ten in 1951, were one in six in 1962; many schools have been built; and Colleges of Advanced Technology have been founded and technical education given a boost. But the expansion of the last twelve or thirteen years has not been dramatic and latest

expansion plans represent no more than a keeping pace with demand
—they are not a breakthrough. In announcing, at the end of January
1964, that the school leaving-age would be raised to sixteen in the
year 1970–1 the Conservative Government were making an unim-
pressive award to the nation—an award delayed since the promise of
the 1944 Education Act.

In the 'Years of Crisis' (March 1963) pamphlet the Labour Party
elaborated an extensive programme for higher education. The Taylor
Committee recommendations contained in the pamphlet anticipated
the Government's Robbins Committee findings and demanded a
massive expansion with forty-five new universities. The Robbins
Committee Report on 'Higher Education' (Cmnd 2154) published on
the 23rd October 1963 contained one basic assumption and three
targets. The assumption was that there should be places available in
establishments of higher education for all those qualified: the targets
were—328,000 full-time students by 1967–8, 390,000 by 1973–4,
560,000 by 1980–1. (In 1963-4 there are upwards of 230,000 students.)
The Government accepted the first two targets, thus committing the
nation to an annual expenditure on education twice that of the year
1962–3: eighteen months previously the Government had denied the
nation a much more modest expansion. Crossman, speaking of
Labour's welcome to the Robbins Report, had reservations: he
said that the expansion of higher education should not overshadow
the needs of the less gifted children (see Newsham Report, 'Half
Our Future' [October 1963]) or the needs of further and adult
education.

British educational facilities are deficient not only in size but also in
shape—there are significant failures due to adherence to traditional
rigidities. Part of the rigidity is due to pure tradition, part to shortages
and the need to ration. The tripartite system of secondary education—
grammar, secondary modern, technical—comes from a haphazard
system of selection and results in a fortuitous division into sheep and
goats. By no stretch of the imagination can it be said that the system
results in our children being educated to the limits of their capacity—
the introduction of G.C.E. courses, and now the Certificate of Secondary Education, into the secondary modern school are but patches on a
very poor pair of trousers. Distortion starts from the top: there is a

shortage of university places and a high degree of specialization and concentration in university courses; specialization has to occur early at grammar school because of competition for and preparation for university places; there has to be selection (however faulty) of children who can benefit from the grammar school régime; and, there has to be primary school cramming so that the 'Eleven-plus' sheep are neatly penned.

Lord Altrincham, now John Grigg, while suggesting the abolition of fee-paying preparatory-schools, the democratization of the public schools, and the breaking down of the 'Iron Curtain' between modern and grammar schools, has advised the Conservative Government to give British education a 'seismic boost': these measures would open the doors of opportunity, help rid the nation of the bogey of class, and build a genuine élite for the country—the objection of some Socialists to an élite of any kind was ethically and practically wrong. (Nevertheless, perhaps our ultimate problem is that of the 'Meritocracy'—the efficient sorting-out of people according to educational ability and the equation of worthiness with intellectual attainment.)

The social programme of the Labour Party, in its educational sector, shows a desire not merely to rescue unfortunates but also to alter the shape of society. In the interests of equality, in order to destroy the existing class structure of British society, and to facilitate both social mobility and the full use of talent, the party wishes to extend comprehensive secondary education. In respect of the 'iron curtain' between the modern and the grammar schools, the idea of comprehensive education as a means of creating a society of equals is dear to the hearts of some Socialists. The extension of comprehensive education has been slow—much local experiment on less ambitious lines has occurred—and it may well be that significant changes in our system of education will come from straightforward expansion rather than from basic re-organization. Wilson has said that the grammar school would be abolished 'over his dead body'. In a speech in May 1963 he said that each local authority would be left to devise its own version of the comprehensive system.

Whether there should be a private à la carte as well as a state table d'hôte side to education has remained as a question of debate. In April 1961 it was reported that the Labour Party planned to assimilate public schools into the state system—some would become county colleges or grammar schools, others universities or training colleges, according to the needs of the locality. These arrangements, which would go forward at the same time as improvement of the state system, were confirmed in 'Signposts for the 'Sixties' (1961) and the proposal, once supported by Gaitskell, that the (greatly democratized) public schools should be allowed to continue their existence, was dropped.

The public schools have been attacked on various grounds: they distort the choice of people for top jobs; they damage national efficiency; they offend the sense of justice; and, they create an irrational social cleavage. It has been said that they ensure that an important sector of the nation's educational resources are sequestered for the exclusive use of a financially endowed minority. The public schools, and the private sector of education generally, have been defended on the ground that a man should be able to spend his money as he wishes— in their drive for democracy and equality, opponents of private spending on education left liberty and fraternity out in the cold. The public schools existed because they were wanted: education was not merely an acquiring of knowledge, but also a spiritual training, and it was a violation of fundamental rights if a citizen were not allowed to buy it, often at great sacrifice, for his children. Further arguments in favour of the maintenance of a private sector in education have been that, when talent is in demand, the 'old school tie' does not matter; and, whatever the school attended, leader-type parents will produce leader-type children (!). Socialist arguments against the private sector, say its champions, are socio-political rather than educational: pre-occupation with the end-product of social planning does not make for good education.

In his May 1963 speech on education, referred to above, Wilson said that Labour in power would replace inadequate maintenance grants for students with something better. The Anderson Committee's Report ('Grants for Students', Cmnd 1051) was published in May 1960 and recommended, among other things, that a student who secured a place at university for a degree course should automatically receive an award from public funds. In July the Minister accepted the proposal. Some would argue that the change should have been in the opposite direction, with awards replaced by loans. The question of putting education on a 'hire purchase' footing is superficially attractive, the argument that gifts to the bright penalize the less clever seems very persuasive, as does the further suggestion that money regained from graduates could then be ploughed back into education. In practice, the task of disentangling the webb of social indebtedness is an impossible one.

One political battle-line in the debate on education is not yet clearly seen—that relating to a possible further diminution of local democracy. There is talk of the need of a 'genuine' Ministry of Education (just as there is talk of the need of a 'genuine' Ministry of Health) to deal with teachers' pay, building programmes, teacher training, and school curricula. An extension of state power over the local authorities would be a major act of re-organization. There have been certain interesting developments within the Ministry: in October 1961 the Minister announced the setting up of a research fund for education, also that he had set up a research and intelligence branch for the improvement of communications between the Ministry and outside foundations. (The Labour Party applauded the spending of £130,000 on research for the Robbins Committee—a Beeching-type operation—but deplored the fact that the Newsham Report cost only £13,000, two-thirds of which went on printing.)

For many people, the National Health Service *is* the Welfare State (see 'Family Needs and the Social Services', P.E.P./Allen and Unwin, 1961). The real effect of the N.H.S. has not been to cause a large increase in expenditure, but to transfer the burden of paying from the sick to the fit. (The fraction of the national income devoted to health has not been much larger during the last decade than it was twenty years ago, although the national income itself has risen, and so consequently has the absolute amount of resources devoted to medical care. The fraction of the national income we devote to health is not strikingly different from that of other advanced Western countries. Enoch Powell: Conservative Conference 1961.)

In seeking to limit the cost of the 'free' Health Service, British governments have shifted the burden of payment, to a degree, from the taxpayer back onto the consumer. In 1949 the Labour Government took power to impose prescription charges, in 1951 it imposed charges for dentures and spectacles: in 1956 the Conservative Government imposed a prescription charge of one shilling per item, in 1961 it doubled this to two shillings. These measures may have allowed welfare developments outside the Health Service, they may have removed the need for cuts in the Health Service itself, but they were strongly resented as attack on a 'free' service and gave rise to furious political debate. Flat-rate contributions and charges weigh most heavily on those with low incomes: increases in contributions and charges have a more than proportionate impact on them. Mrs. Braddock declared that there had been a twelve-and-a-half per cent. drop in the number of prescriptions issued in the three months following the last rise in prescription charges: the take-up of welfare foods (orange juice, cod liver oil, and vitamin tablets) appeared to fall more than 50 per cent. in the six months following the imposition of a charge on 1st June 1961 (*The Guardian*, 27th Dec. 1961). Did the imposition of the above charges cause hardship, or did they merely cut out waste and kill off hypochondriacs? Did people go without medicines, or did they just buy items—aspirins, cotton-wool, and so on—over the counter as a cheaper method of obtaining them?

Labour has said that it would abolish prescription charges and make the Health Service again free at the point of access. The party has also demanded the improvement of hospitals, the cutting-down of the general practitioner's list, and the development of local authority domiciliary and preventive services. Apart from seeking general expansion in the Health Service, the Labour Party has broken new ground in publicizing the need for an occupational health service.

The question of private health provision has not caused nearly so much debate as the imposition of health service charges but it involves a clearer issue of principle. It is argued (see Vol. II, p. 190) that the development of a greatly enlarged private sector in the provision of medical services would lead to 'better' medicine, would maximize consumer satisfaction by widening the possibility of choice and the taking of responsibility, and would enlarge professional freedom. Opponents have said that, as far as medical facilities are concerned, we should not run the risk of creating a double standard of health.

Facilities of the highest standard should be available to all, so choice should be irrelevant: if the best is not available to all it should not be rationed by price. (One should note here that private insurance does not cover the biggest risks, anyway.) Choice in medical care—now existing under the N.H.S. as far as selection of one's general practitioner is concerned—should, on the ground of quality, be an illusion. As for private enterprise calling forth greater professional effort, Professor Titmuss has said that the conflict between the 'professional' and the 'economic' man should be reduced to a minimum—the question was not whether health services should be organized by the State but how they should be organized.

Professionals working in the field of State medicine have criticized the existence of restrictive regulations: others have deplored the lack of central direction within the Health Service. Certainly many difficulties of co-ordination and co-operation stem from the tripartite division of the Service. (Why there should be so many administrative weaknesses—in health, education, local government, and central government—in so small an island as our own is difficult to see.) In October 1962 the Minister of Health announced the setting up of a research fund for investigations into the working of the National Health Service. The general practitioner's plight is worthy of study: one doctor has told the story of his month-end sorting out of dispensing chits; fees are paid to him on the calculated average of a number of chits; he thus cannot afford to submit a random sample of (possibly low-cost) chits but has to make a true sample—taking the better part of one Sunday over the job. The quality of service offered to people is also a useful subject of study: Professor Morris, of the University of London, remarked in 1961 that having a baby in hospital was sometimes like holding a marriage service in a crematorium.

The Mental Health Act 1959 introduced a new informality into the obtaining of treatment. No longer was it necessary for a patient to sign a form expressing willingness to obtain treatment or to give seventy-two hours' notice of intention to depart (Mental Treatment Act 1930). The class of 'voluntary patients' disappeared because the legal formality of a request was removed. (There will always be cases where compulsion has to be applied: the Royal Commission Report of 1957 recommended much simpler procedures and under the 1959 Act certification was abolished—instead a recommendation for treatment was to be signed by two doctors, one a psychiatrist.)

The changes envisaged by the framers of the 1959 Act are a challenge to the public conscience. Increased expenditure will be needed to develop local authority services: there have been some doubts as to whether these services can be developed quickly enough to cater for the outflow of patients from mental institutions. Professional opinion is divided on the possibility of a drastic reduction in the number of occupied beds envisaged as part of the post-1959 reorganization. In Mental Health services, as elsewhere, there is a need for the tightening up of the administrative machine.

When the Conservative Government initiated a measure of decontrol of rents in 1958, as a result of the 1957 Rent Act, the point of the exercise was to try to make people move from under-occupied houses, to secure a more sensible use of property, and to secure greater expenditure on repairs to property. The limitation put on the decontrol of rents—the 'expedient pledge'—raised the ire of the housing 'free-marketeers' who believed that a free market in housing would produce results parallel to those achieved by free enterprise in the field of consumer durables. It may well be that we should spend more on housing, in either a free or a controlled market, since the proportion of our incomes going in this direction has been small and we may have been 'wasting' our money on less important things. If the Government found it politically impossible to carry decontrol of rents very far—the Conservatives' caution was an apt illustration of modern governments' enslavement to public opinion—local authorities have also found it difficult to introduce differential rents schemes.

In the 1961 Housing Act the local authorities were given new powers to deal with houses in multi-occupation: the effect of the 1961 Act was slow. The White Paper, 'Housing' (Cmnd 2050) of May 1963 considered the question of compulsory powers being given to local authorities to secure the improvement, maintenance, and repair of houses. A Bill was introduced into the Commons in November 1963 broadly to give effect to the White Paper: the 1961 Act was to be stiffened, the local authorities given power to enter a badly-managed house and to act as landlord for five years.

Labour's housing policy includes repeal of the Rent Act; low interest-rate loans to the local authorities; the reintroduction of general subsidies; the more efficient exploitation of town space; and, the quicker planning of new towns. These measures, say the Socialists, will help obviate the many family tragedies now stemming from bad housing—including unnecessary admissions to hospitals. (Audrey Harvey, 'Casualties of the Welfare State', 1960, is very concerned with welfare as it relates to housing. Housing and welfare should be joined under the local authority so that the housing department, would not, for instance, evict a family and thus create a whole bundle of problems for the welfare department. Eviction does often begin a train of disasters. Mrs. Harvey favours the widespread introduction of differential rent schemes so that those who can afford other accommodation will be discouraged from occupying council property.) Labour has said that it intends to treat housing as a social service, it being too important to be run by the gamble of profit and loss. Labour has recently played down its earlier plans for municipalization of rented property, and now emphasizes the need to step up slum clearance, the need to assure the local authorities of a steady building programme free of wasteful and inefficient variation, and the need to keep the various sides of a national building programme—houses, factories, schools, and hospitals —in proper balance. Labour blames the Conservatives for cutting building standards, making the local authorities dependent on dear money, and for allowing a free market in land—the party has said it will establish a Land Commission to purchase the freehold of land on which building or rebuilding is scheduled.

The housing problem has to be seen in a wide context. A Housing Minister should be aware of economic issues such as the control of land values, town and country planning, transport, and the distribution of employment; social issues such as the variation of housing needs of families at different stages of growth and contraction, and the provision of social amenities; and, technical issues such as prefabrication in the building industry. There is much ignorance of need: the last big official inquiry into housing was the Royal Commission on the Housing of Working Classes, 1885. The overall problem involves the decaying centres of large cities; the decline of industries in some areas and the creation of work in others; the growth of population and earlier marriage; and, the creation of an efficient administrative machine. The housing problem is vast and is only part of a wide range of economic and social problems.

Our prisons present us with a major challenge: there is need for much rebuilding. Spending on prisons must be accompanied by spending on the furthering of criminological studies—crime and the criminal are things we understand little. We have no true definition of crime. The Home Office has begun to produce very useful reports— that on 'Murder' in 1961 (see also pp. 178–179), and that on the 'Persistent Criminal' in 1963. The report first named provided much ammunition for use against that section of our population which seems to have a compulsive urge to punish. It stated clearly that most killings are domestic, most of them not planned but done under great stress of emotion: among murderers the incidence of mental disturbance is high—many commit suicide. Lord Chief Justice Parker has said that the situation created by the 1957 Homicide Act is a 'hopeless muddle'. Sir Ernest Gowers, Chairman of the Royal Commission on Capital Punishment 1949–53 has commented: a man who shoots his wife must hang; if he misses and finishes her off with a coal-hammer, a less severe penalty will do.

Some space is given below to the problems of social administration as they relate to the training and remuneration of social workers. The deployment of social workers is a question also noted. A matter which cannot be neglected here is that of information services. Audrey Harvey (op. cit.) is concerned for the poor in education, living space, opportunity, and status—those who are unaware of rights and obligations, who cannot find information and do not understand it when they get it, who have neither the bright trained minds nor the stamina to find and interpret advice. With the existence of many specialized welfare agencies, the poor sections of the community are often unaware of the facilities open to them. One means of advance here would be to develop the Citizen's Advice Bureaux, the existing officially recognized centres for the co-ordination of information.

The C.A.B.s could be far better places for the prevention of disasters than the many specialized agencies which today sweep up pieces after the family crash.

*   *   *   *

The Cuba crisis of 1962 seemed to bring the world to the brink of war. The United States had never imagined that Russia would place missiles in exposed Cuba—Russia surely thought Castro too unreliable an ally, she surely knew that the United States would react against such an initiative. America miscalculated, and Russia miscalculated in thinking that America would accept a *fait accompli*. The question remains as to whether other Cuba-type crises will occur—if not in the West, then in the East where the Chinese giant is stirring—when the miscalculation of one of two or three men could lead to world war. The 'balance of terror' depends on the judgement of a few men, on their understanding of each other's thinking. (The 'balance of terror' does not ensure that complete peace will be maintained: nuclear weapons did not prevent the Berlin Blockade, June 1948 to May 1949; the Korean War, June 1950 to July 1953; nor the Hungarian or Suez operations of 1956.) Peace also depends on the limitation of the spread of nuclear weapons, on the restraint of the minor powers tempted to acquire their 'international status symbols'. This book ends with a discussion of defence problems, neglecting these broader issues of international relations.

On the one hand, foreign affairs and defence issues may appear to present to the electorate large and complicated problems. The issues, bound up with strong traditions and permanent necessities, and involving the crucial question of the nation's security and important long-term advantages, may seem difficult and distant. On the other hand, external problems may be seen with excessive simplicity, may seem as immediate as domestic issues.

Although foreign affairs are usually less immediate to the electorate than domestic affairs, politicians and statesmen have, during the past, looked for public support for their foreign policies and public interest has been encouraged. Foreign Secretary Canning, in the 1820's, declared that foreign policy should be both intelligible and popular: realizing the necessity of national unity in matters of foreign policy he made frank speeches and published dispatches as means of forming electoral opinion. (Maurice Bruce, 'British Foreign Policy', p. 85). Gladstone's anti-imperialist agitation against the Afghan War led, at the end of 1879, to his Midlothian Campaign: Gladstone's journeying to Edinburgh and Glasgow was historic—before this it had never been the etiquette for leading British statesmen to 'stump the country'. (R. C. K. Ensor, 'England 1870–1914', p. 63.)

If some philosophers regret the importance of public opinion in government today their regret is most strong in relation to the formation of foreign policy. In no other political activity, they say, is the 'doctor's mandate', the expert knowledge, judgement and guidance of statesmen, so needed. In no other sphere is the ordinary citizen likely to be so ill-informed and prejudiced, since his interest is only intermittent, responding to scares and crises. The electorate's interest in foreign affairs shows a high degree of inconsistency:

> Prepare for war in time of peace? No. It is bad to raise taxes, to unbalance the budget, to take men away from their schools or their jobs, to provoke the enemy. Intervene in a developing conflict? No. Avoid the risk of war. Withdraw from the area of the conflict? No. The adversary must not be appeased. Reduce your claims on the area? No. Righteousness cannot be compromised. Negotiate a compromise peace as the opportunity presents itself? No. The aggressor must be punished. Remain armed to enforce the dictated settlement? No. The war is over. (Walter Lippman, 'The Public Philosophy', p. 25.)

Public influence on foreign affairs issues may not make for peace and understanding: the electorate may well swing from belligerence and nationalism to pacificism and appeasement. In the Boer War jingoism, in the 'Hang the Kaiser!' mood of the first war, in the punitive peace settlement of 1919, in the appeasement of the inter-war years, we see what may be taken for the evil of popular extremism. It is permissible to argue, however, that this extremism stems not from the electorate itself but from the exploitation by the politicians of the electorate's interest or lack of interest in external issues—at one juncture the politicians stimulate the nation with such slogans as 'Unconditional surrender!' and such concepts as 'massive retaliation', at another they fail to provide the leadership involving calls to duty.

A democrat must assert that the electorate cannot trust its leaders implicitly. Further, he should insist that his government take pains to explain the main features of its foreign policy since the electorate may react violently to surprises—the Hoare-Laval agreement of 1935, involving the suggestion that Italy should be granted territory and concessions in Abyssinia, led to reaction in Parliament and in the country. Sir Samuel Hoare was sacrificed by the Government. As regards the more recent Suez episode (and quite apart from the merits or demerits of the operation) one might ask whether it was wise for the British Government to start hostilities without the assurance that a large majority of British citizens was certain to give its support.

(Whichever party be in power there can be no argument but that Britain's status in world politics has declined in the last twenty years: she is no longer a giant, she is an important member of an alliance. Given this fact, the action of the Conservative Government in initiating the Suez War of 1956 came as a great shock to world opinion. Defended as a police action against aggressive Arab nationalism, against the flouting of international agreements and the disregarding of commercial treaties, it was condemned as a breach of international peace by men who had been firmly committed to the principle of the peaceful settlement of disputes. The episode divided the nation deeply, but not strictly along party lines. The Archbishop of Canterbury condemned the Government, the Archbishop of York did not. Two hundred and forty Cambridge scholars and three hundred and fifty Oxford scholars protested at the Government's action: another group of Oxford scholars, headed by Gilbert Murray, declared its support for the Government. *The Guardian*, the *Observer*, and the *Economist* called for Eden's resignation. The division of the country went deep, but the episode receded from the public mind remarkably quickly.)

The most recent example of the Conservative Government's neglect to keep the electorate informed concerned the European Economic Community. Macmillan failed to explain adequately the political implications of Britain's entry—he merely dangled the promise of economic gains before the nation.

In the chapter of this book relating to political information (pp. 180–203) will be seen references to demands for more open discussion of, inter alia, Government foreign policy. Space is also devoted (Vol. II, pps. 276–282) to the activities of one group of people, the Campaign for Nuclear Disarmament, and to certain associated groups, who have acted just beyond the fringes of legal action in order to make their views known and, they say, to open the eyes of the people.

British parties each express the desire to see an easing of tension between Russia and the West and each expresses allegiance to the United Nations Organization, the North Atlantic Treaty Organization, and the Anglo-American partnership. (A vocal section of the Labour Party has had doubts about N.A.T.O. and the Anglo-American alliance. Senior Conservatives have expressed doubts about U.N.O., which the Western powers no longer dominate.) British parties have disputed over nuclear tests, foreign bases on our territory, the control of British-based missiles, and the recruiting of an adequate number of non-conscripted soldiers, but, in defence, the Bomb has been the supreme issue.

At the end of 1962 Dean Acheson made his famous West Point speech on which occasion he declared that Great Britain and lost an empire and had not yet found a rôle. While trying to maintain the position of a first-class power the burden of defence costs on Britain's shoulder has been great:

> . . . (after 1950) we still felt bound in our military planning to play the game of frog and bull, whereas the other second-rate powers had been compulsorily deflated. (W. J. M. Mackenzie, *The Listener*, 21st Jan. 1963.)

The story of the British Deterrent is one which stirs much emotion: as in other sections of the book, the defence sections below seek to be objective even though the use of the phrase 'dependent independence' may seem to indicate otherwise.

The Liberals were in the forefront in demanding the rationalization of the Western defence programmes: Liberals were for long the sole advocates of the abandonment of a separate British deterrent, long stressing the need for international co-operation and reliance on joint Western nuclear power—an arms race between West and East was bad enough, an arms race between West and West made nonsense.

Like Labour, the Liberals have not been wholly united on the question of nuclear arms—some Liberals have been members of the Campaign for Nuclear Disarmament. At the 1960 Liberal Assembly a unilateralist amendment, urging the renunciation of the use of nuclear weapons by Britain and by N.A.T.O., sought to modify official policy. It was defeated by 607 votes to 78, but there was an unknown number of abstentions. In 1962 there was strong opposition to bomb-tests.

The unilateral renunciation of defence by nuclear weapons—either British weapons, or American weapons used on Britain's behalf—is a demand which has sustained the activities of the Campaign for Nuclear Disarmament and which has caused civil war within the Labour Party. Until 1960 one could have said that C.N.D. had not succeeded to any significant extent in mobilizing conscience or pricking public apathy. Witnesses of the Campaign marches may have been stirred but the majority of the British people either refused to think of the problems associated with the possession of nuclear weapons, or trusted their leaders. But in 1960 the Bomb Issue was dominant in trade union conferences: a situation of tragicomedy existed—in a kind of Alice-in-Wonderland world trade unionists were voting both for and against possession of the Bomb and a nuclear defence policy.

In early 1964 there seemed to be a possibility that C.N.D.'s position might shift significantly. John Gittings and Richard Gott submitted a pamphlet—designed, it was said, to help anti-nuclear Labour Party members—to the Campaign's literature committee. It suggested that C.N.D. might accept the idea of N.A.T.O. (which it had always opposed) and even a 'minimum deterrent'. So far, the movement's objectives had been sufficiently diffuse to attract a widely-based following motivated by emotion but the time had now come for C.N.D. to clarify its objectives in a changing situation. Withdrawal from N.A.T.O. need not be advocated if N.A.T.O. could move in a satisfactory way, that is if it could negotiate with the Warsaw Pact Powers for a minimum deterrent and a nuclear-free zone in Europe. The pamphlet's authors eventually complained that their views had been oversimplified: they intended disengagement in Europe and the minimum deterrent only as a first step towards the total dissolution of N.A.T.O. and the Warsaw Pact—they did not accept N.A.T.O., they wanted to end it. The views of Gittings and Gott, unofficial though they were, confirm the belief that one should never imagine that the shape and pattern of British political opinions is static.

The defence policy of the Labour Party has been ambiguous during the last five years: when Wilson stood against Gaitskell for the leadership of the party at the end of 1960 he said that the left of the party wanted an assurance that Labour would not hanker after the Bomb, after a British deterrent, if the means of obtaining one again became available. In November 1963 the Prime Minister declared that the new unity the Socialists had found on defence was so fragile, artificial, and thin that they had not dared run the risk of an open debate at their annual conference.

Labour rejected the idea of a British deterrent in 1960: after the Conservatives had negotiated the 'Polaris' agreement with the Americans in December 1962 students of defence affairs wanted to know what Labour would do with the agreement if the party came to power. Further questions related to Labour's attitude towards the mixed-manned N.A.T.O. nuclear force and the more general issue of the control of western nuclear weapons. At Oxford in May 1963, Patrick Gordon-Walker, Labour's chief spokesman on foreign affairs said that Britain could not be a super-power but she could make herself an indispensable power by possessing adequate forces properly equipped with conventional weapons. A Labour Government would negotiate with the Americans to create a unified N.A.T.O. to which Britain might commit her remaining nuclear weapons—Britain would demand a real and effective share in the whole nuclear policy of the West. Labour regarded this policy as being far more sensible, realistic, and farsighted than proposals for a European or N.A.T.O. multilateral deterrent.

When, in the February 1964 defence debate, the Minister of Defence announced that the Government had decided to build five 'Polaris' submarines he also challenged the Opposition to say whether it would scrap them if it came to power. Dennis Healey, for the Opposition, disclaimed the 'independent Polaris'. In Washington in March 1964 Wilson made it clear that if his party came to power he would seek early discussions with the United States: these were urgent because of Labour's firm opposition to the multilateral force and to any further attempt or pretence at maintaining an independent British nuclear deterrent.

Within the Labour Party there remain three elements—those who reject all nuclear weapons, those who accept a western deterrent in either America's or N.A.T.O.'s hands, and those who still want a British deterrent. The latter, in fact, have not been silenced by the latest official Labour pronouncements quoted above. In a series of articles, 'Labour's Hidden Icebergs', in the *New Statesman* magazine, Paul Johnson asks—'Will Wilson Keep the Bomb?' (13th Dec. 1963). Speaking of the need to defend our economic interests in the East he declares:

> In short, in these areas, Labour may face a straight choice between liquidating its responsibilities—and so winding up the Sterling Area—and retaining tactical nuclear weapons. There seems little doubt that it will choose the second.

and of the strategic deterrent he says:

> . . . the Labour leaders may conclude, when and if they take office, that the independent deterrent is not quite so derisory an instrument as they have so often maintained.

Aubrey Jones, a former Conservative Minister of Supply, has been a lone voice in the Conservative Party arguing against the insistence that Britain must retain ultimate control over her own nuclear arms. The British Council of Churches' working report on 'The British Nuclear Deterrent', published by the S.C.M. Press in December 1963, said that the differences between Conservative and Labour on the independent nuclear deterrent were not nearly so wide as they were made to seem, also that there was no case for independent nuclear action by Britain in any part of the world. Sir Tufton Beamish, chairman of the Conservative Parliamentary Foreign Affairs Committee, was among the working party members.

In the 1964 Defence White Paper the Conservatives confirmed that Britain had agreed to take part in an experiment to test the feasibility of a multilateral, mixed-manned force of surface ships. (The White Paper, 'Central Organization for Defence' (Cmnd 2097), was published in July 1963 and outlined plans for a unified Ministry of Defence: the new reconstructed Ministry became operational on 1st April 1964.)

Having first said that Britain's deterrent would be an election issue Sir Alec Home then advocated a bi-partisan approach to defence (at a meeting with the Parliamentary Press Gallery on 2nd December 1963).

In January 1964 Harold Wilson took up the theme of a bipartisan appraisal of defence: he spoke of this in the context of a possible build-up of Britain's conventional capacity to deal with 'brush-fire' emergencies around the world.

It is fitting here to say a few words on colonial matters. In the last few years Britain has been greatly preoccupied with the problems of the welfare and the self-government of colonial areas—Cyprus, Kenya, Nyasaland, Central Africa, Guiana, and Malta. Enlightened politicians of all parties have wanted to turn the attention of the British electorate from marginally important material improvements at home to more urgent needs abroad. In fact, given the social and economic conditions existing in the colonies, some have asked whether Britons deserve their domestic well-being. Appointed by Butler in March 1963, a Conservative Committee on Voluntary Service Overseas published its report in the following December: in January 1964 Harold Wilson spoke of the need for a Ministry of Overseas Development.

With all parties committed to the granting of colonial self-government, disputes between them have often hung on the question of competence. Remembering the Hola Camp deaths in Kenya and the handling of the Nyasaland state of emergency in 1959, Socialists have accused the Conservatives of being wedded to strong-arm methods of colonial government. The long Cyprus emergency, they have declared, was a Tory-created artificial problem—a policy maintained by the Government for years was finally abandoned with arguments for settlement precisely those previously rejected. Liberals, too, deplored the illiberality shown by Britain in Cyprus, Nyasaland, and at the time of Suez, as well as her insensitiveness to changes going forward in Africa and Asia.

Conservatives, for their part, have claimed that the Labour Party has been irresponsible in its attitude to difficult colonial problems, given to scoring party points.

In their consideration of certain colonies, both parties have had to grapple with the problem of the mixed society, the society wherein white and coloured people are living together. While some Conservatives have admitted that a kind of Stalinist system has existed in these areas—settlers and officials exercising what seemed to be permanent minority rule—some Socialists have recognized the difficulty of introducing a greater degree of democracy into governments and have cast doubt on their leaders' ability to impose a Socialist solution on settler minorities. The Conservatives have had trouble within their party over African policies. Just as they were divided in the 'thirties over India, in recent times they have differed sharply over the question of the proper rate of constitutional advance in the multiracial states of Africa—in Kenya and in Northern Rhodesia in particular. Lord Salisbury and others have been concerned to safeguard the position of the Europeans in these territories. Lord Salisbury has said that a large proportion of colonial peoples prefer to be governed rather than govern themselves—this was true even of British people at home today(!) Ian Macleod has rejected Lord Salisbury's views and defended his policy while at the Colonial Office between 1959–61: the emerging countries were not fully ready for independence—India had not been either—but bloodshed would have been the alternative to freedom. 'Men marching towards freedom could be guided but not halted.' (*Spectator*, 31st Jan. 1964.)

In the summer of 1963 Butler was strongly commended for the smooth and efficient manner in which he presided over the winding-up of the ten-year-old Central Africa Federation at Victoria Falls. The coloured peoples of Northern Rhodesia and Nyasaland, like those of the East African territories, go their own way: the future of Southern Rhodesia is less sure.

*　　　*　　　*　　　*

It seems fitting to end this introduction with a short estimate of the parties in the immediate pre-election period. Just prior to the 1959 Election responsible newspapers expressed no strong predilection for either party: the *Observer* said that it could see no great issues of social or economic policy compelling it to abandon its neutrality, neutrality maintained since the paper became non-party in 1942; the *Spectator* was 'reluctantly for Labour', while the *Manchester Guardian* was for Labour, with a strengthening of the Liberals. How do the parties stand today?

The Macmillan era ended only a few months ago. The Profumo Affair of 1963 revealed what may be taken to be a casual, amateurish approach to security matters: the Soblen deportation order of August

1962 and the return of Enahoro to Nigeria in April 1963 seemed to some to be illiberal. In the sphere of economics, the Macmillan Government came round to planning after many years of tinkering with the problem of inflation; the Government took its courage in its hands and applied for membership of the European Common Market, only to be rejected; Macmillan's 'never had it so good' speech of 1957 seemed to be out-of-keeping in a country where there existed areas of high and persistent unemployment. In foreign affairs Macmillan earned some praise for his salvage operation after the Suez débacle and for his re-establishing of the American connection: his 'wind of change' speech to the South African Parliament in Capetown in February 1960 was courageous; his Government's action in winding-up the Central Africa Federation was wise. The Moscow Test Ban Treaty caused President Kennedy to pay Macmillan a handsome compliment.

The refusal of Ian Macleod and Enoch Powell to serve under Home was, possibly, more damaging than any Opposition attack could have been. For at least one right-wing commentator, Home's election to the party-leadership was a turning-aside from progress: in fact, in office, he seemed intent on modernizing Britain regardless of expense —making a lurch to the left which, possibly, would not have been acceptable under Butler. A spate of official reports were published at the time of Home's succession—on education, scientific training and organization, roads, and regional development: a spate of Bills rolled off the Government press—concerned with housing, industrial training, the police, ports, horticulture, shipbuilding, hire purchase. If the Conservatives win the 1964 Election, Home has said, there will be a great leap forward from prepared positions. Cynics talk of 'death-bed repentance': if it took thirteen years to build the launching-pad, how long will it take to make the rocket?

Gaitskell's achievements have been noted above. He has been described as a 'passionate moderate'—in principle a man of reason, a man of unusual lucidity of thought, in practice he was strongly emotional. The essential criticism which has been made of him is that he did not possess the 'feel' or 'touch' of a politician—he was too much of an administrator or academic. His management of the Labour Party—for example, over the Clause Four issue—was less than perfect:

his appeal to the Conservative back-benchers to turn out their leader at the time of Suez was a tactical error. Gaitskell dragged his feet over the Common Market issue.

In the Wilson Era the titles of those post-1959 books and pamphlets— 'Must Labour Lose?', 'Can Labour Win?', 'Where?'—seem strangely out of date. Wilson, the *New Statesman* has said, is free from the besetting sin of Labour leaders—he does not lie low, seeking to avoid mistakes. His vigour has taken him to Moscow and to Washington: at home his skill in using people has been exploited to the full—Wilson does not have 'friends' he has 'contacts'. The 1945 Labour Government was strongly criticized for not having had blueprints: in 1963 the Labour research department was busy preparing plans for incoming Ministers—plans for training in industry, for hospitals and hospital beds; for air transport; for building and contracting; for economic planning and the machinery of government; for regional planning; for fuel; and, for science and industry. Wilson seems to have built well on Gaitskell's foundations.

It seems unrealistic to expect great Liberal gains in 1964. The following quotation sums up one's feelings admirably: 'The party appeals because it appears as an honest party of new men, middle-class and moderate, not tied up with the big interests—because, indeed, it is the party least like a party'. (David Butler, *Listener*, 27th Sept. 1962.)

We are not here concerned with the parties' electoral chances so much as with the many difficult problems they deal with: what follows is an attempt to present a picture of British Political Issues in the round. The task is one of some complexity:

> Even as late as the 'thirties, issues were clear cut—like unemployment, the means test, Spain, appeasement. Political questions are more complicated and technical than they were. A good politician has to be less of a prophet and more of a technician. The same basic things need to be put right. . . . But the issues are more complicated to express—graduated pension schemes, differential capital investment write-offs, world liquidity, multinational versus multilateral deterrents. (Harold Wilson, *Observer*, 16th June 1963.)

ONE

POLITICAL

ONE

POLITICAL

I. GOVERNMENT AND PARTIES

1. *Parliament*

(i) *The Sickness of Parliament.* That Parliament is sick has been a common assertion for many years. The reference here is to the decrease of power, over the last sixty years of the House of Commons as a whole in relation to the Executive or Cabinet, and of the individual Member in relation to his or her political party. The shift of power has been associated with the growth of governmental business and the consequent shortage of parliamentary time, and with the arrival, gradually since 1832, of universal suffrage—factors which have led to the need for disciplined party organization both inside and outside Parliament. Westminster was the best club in London but has become an overworked legislative factory. The growth of governmental business during the two world wars, the increased responsibility assumed by the State in the process of building the social services, have led to a vast growth in the powers of the Executive which controls and initiates legislation. We no longer have parliamentary government—Parliament has lost pride of place to the Executive and the centre of gravity in government has moved from the floor of the House of Commons to Whitehall. There is no evidence that the powers of the Executive will decline, no evidence of a possible 'withering away of the State'.

The concentration of power in British government has gone even further than the above paragraph suggests. In January 1958 Thorneycroft resigned as Chancellor and his two Treasury colleagues went with him (see Vol. II, p. 19). Macmillan described this event as 'a little local difficulty'. In 1962 Macmillan decided on, and carried through, a massive reshuffle of his Cabinet. These examples are adequate proof of the Prime Minister's great personal power today. (The 1962 reshuffle may have been caused by pressure from within the Cabinet.) There has been a 'monarchization' of government in Britain—the Premier has become very much like an elected sovereign. Crossman, in his introduction to the new edition of Walter Bagehot's 'English Constitution' (Fontana, 1963), declares that the Cabinet, like the Monarchy, the Lords and Commons, has become part of the 'dignified façade' of our government, the essential of which is now Prime Ministerial rule.

The inadequacies of parliamentary control over the Executive stem from the scope, variety, and extent of current legislation: these are such that the individual M.P. may have little grasp of the greater part of the business coming before the House—he is the amateur, civil servants the professionals. In certain major fields—the control of the nation's finances (see p. 105, and Vol. II, p. 17), the control of the nationalized industries (see Vol. II, p. 63)—the Member has very little power. Because of the scope of Government activity today, Parliament has had to delegate much authority to Ministers and to Departments. Civil servants frame legislation, parliamentary lawyers draft Bills, and Parliament passes skeleton legislation—the blanks to be filled in by Ministers and civil servants. Although this procedure ensures that the Government's will is speedily carried out, there is a danger of inadequate parliamentary scrutiny. (In 1944 there was set up a Select Committee to examine legislation involving the delegation of powers and to report on features of this legislation that were suspect—where, for example, sections of Bills seemed to involve a retrospective effect, to exclude the possibility of challenge in the courts, or were simply obscure in phraseology. The Committee's task is not easy: over 1,000 Instruments, by which a Minister fills out skeleton legislation, are submitted to Parliament each year.)

Parliament, it is complained, has become a rubber-stamp for the

Government, a mere ratifying body, and the Member has been reduced to the contemptible status of a lobby-walking robot. The majority and minority parties in Parliament enforce automatic support for decisions made outside the Chamber: debates are dead since votes are predetermined and have little chance of affecting policy. (After the 1950 Election, when Labour was returned with only a tiny majority, the parties went to extreme lengths to bring to the division lobbies M.P.s dragged from hospitals and nursing homes who, apart from the mechanical act of voting, were otherwise too ill to take any intelligent part in proceedings.) The Press, Television and Radio, and the party conferences now vie with Parliament as forums of debate (see pp. 180–203, and particularly the question of the Fourteen-day Rule, p. 198): the House of Commons is an inferior kind of workshop, its purpose to support a government. The electorate prefers a strong Executive to a strong Parliament: political theorists declare that disciplined voting in the House of Commons means fixed responsibility—more free votes, involving shifting parliamentary majorities, would make it difficult for the electorate to judge its rulers. However, one can feel only disquiet over certain aspects of our strong, responsible government. On 2nd April 1963 a strongly-worded motion was tabled in the Commons deploring Ministers' evasion of open statements to the House and the planting of 'stooge' Questions.

Amery, a Conservative writing during the bustle of the 1945 Labour Government, declared that, although government majorities helped dispatch business, legislation should not be merely the will of majority-government. Ultimately, government was either by discussion or by force. Parliament was a device for goverment by discussion: the Government, facing a continuous verbal challenge, ought to convince and persuade. Parliamentary government meant the maximizing of consent and the minimizing of coercion. (L. S. Amery, 'Thoughts on the Constitution', p. 46.) The Socialist Laski, more content in this post-war period, was not concerned over the shortness of parliamentary time. He asserted that when a Bill was debated in the Commons—a Bill relating to nationalization or to the raising of the school-leaving age, for instance—its principle was well known, having been the subject of debate in the country, possibly for many years. Since parliamentary debate did not involve the discussion of a subject from scratch, such debate was not as vital as it might otherwise have been. (H. J. Laski, 'Reflections on the Constitution', p. 31.)

Adequate parliamentary opposition is important in the British system since there are few formal restraints on a government, restraints which, elsewhere, are sometimes contained in a written constitution. K. C. Wheare has said (*The Listener*, 12th March 1959) that he would be surprised if the time available to the Opposition for the choosing of subjects in which to criticize the Government were less than thirty per cent. of the sitting time of the House—and criticism was not confined to these periods. However, adequate parliamentary opposition is not simply a matter of the supply to minority parties of opportunities for criticism, but also of the minority parties' political will. The Labour Party, defeated in three successive general elections, and disturbed by internal disputes, lost some cohesion in its opposition to the Conservatives in the late 'fifties and early 'sixties. In November 1959, a few days after the opening of the new Parliament, debate finished early on a day devoted to foreign affairs—the Whips, it was reported, had found difficulty in getting speakers.

The situation described above caused a renewal of interest in the question of effective opposition in Parliament after 1959. (See B. Crick, 'Public Law', Spring 1960.) The Conservatives had won three successive electoral victories with increased majorities and reference was made to the 'myth' of the inevitability of alternating party-government. In theory the Opposition held itself ready to take office in order to remedy abuses or introduce new policies. Students of politics now viewed what they imagined to be a permanently weakened Opposition and asked if the Conservatives, using Keynesian techniques of economic management (see Vol. II, p. 9) to create short-term booms, and also high-pressure public relations techniques, could not remain in office for ever. Demands were made that Britain should introduce formal constitutional safeguards against a government's perpetuating itself in office by the above techniques—for example, the fixed-term election, which is a major feature of the American political system. (See N. Hunt, 'Interested Parties', *The Listener*, 20th July, 1961.)

In the middle of 1963 one saw a Conservative Party in some disarray, divided on the question of its leadership. The Labour

Opposition, despite the loss of Gaitskell, was in full vigour and thirsting for office. 'On most of the current features at Westminster it is Mr. Wilson who is deploying the initiative and dictating the pace and direction of events, ranging in the space of a few days from science and higher education to rents and property.' (James Margach, *Sunday Times*, 21st July 1963.) Parliament and Her Majesty's Opposition were not dead.

Professor A. H. Birch has recently examined the nature of our government in his book 'Representative and Responsible Government' (1964). In the nineteenth century government was responsible to the House of Commons: the Commons made and unmade governments, controlled legislation and expenditure. Today the Commons never destroys a government and hardly ever drives a minister from office. The electorate out of doors is now the important control on government. However, the 'liberal' theory of the nineteenth century still supplies the vocabulary and much of the content of political thought and discussion today although the reality has gone. Enoch Powell writes:

> In the political crises of 1963 it was this sense of power being out of their hands, of the battle going over their heads, which imparted a tang of bitterness to the feelings of Conservative M.P.s. In the Profumo affair was Mr. Macmillan trying to appeal from the party in the House to the party in the country? At his resignation was he trying to shift the choice of the new leader, *their* leader, the Parliamentary leader, from the Cabinet and M.P.s to the Conference and the National Union? Never mind if the questions were justified; that they could arise was significant. (*Sunday Times*, 12th Jan. 1964.)

(ii) *The Backbencher.* An *Observer* survey published 17th March 1963 showed that Members of Parliament were highly dissatisfied with pay and conditions of work. For many, there is considerable financial strain attached to being a Member of Parliament. In 1911 M.P.s secured a 'salary' for the first time: in 1937 their £400 per annum was raised to £600; in 1946 to £1000; in 1957 to £1750. In the latter year Labour Members in particular were finding it difficult to subsist on their parliamentary salaries and there was said to be smouldering discontent—there was even a report (which was denied) that the Labour Whip was finding difficulty in securing an adequate number of Labour Members to man parliamentary committees. (In November 1956 Macmillan, as Chancellor, had announced that only two M.P.s were not drawing their parliamentary salaries—one of these was a director of forty companies.) A committee of inquiry will report on the pay of M.P.s, Ministers, and Peers after the 1964 General Election.

While the financial position of M.P.s is not happy, their working conditions in congested Westminster are also very poor. In February 1960 one Member pointed out that the standard of accommodation in the Palace of Westminster was lower than that laid down in the Offices Bill, then before Parliament. M.P.s do not even have enough telephones at their disposal. In July 1963 the Holford Plan for the extension of the Palace of Westminster was published by the Minister of Public Building and Works. Minor improvement work began in 1963.

Complaints have been made of the dearth of commanding intellects in the Commons today. On the other hand it has been claimed that Members now show a greater all-round competence than in former days and that, when legislation is initiated in such volume, the possession of M.P.s of all-round competence is more important to the Commons than that of a number of 'intellects'. M.P.s certainly work hard: whether they have to work too hard is debatable. Nigel Nicolson has said that M.P.s are not overworked providing they concentrate on two or three special subjects—resignations of Members occur, not from overwork, but from enforced idleness, from having to hang about Westminster unnecessarily. Members of Parliament, says Nicolson, should regard the House of Commons as peers regard the House of Lords—as a place for frequent visits and occasional demonstrations, not as a place of residence (*New Statesman*, 21st March 1959). Procedural changes (see pp. 102–104) might help the Member, but more essential to the alleviation of his position is a change of attitude concerning attendance requirements.

The backbencher is important in Parliament when passions have been aroused—for example, during the Crichel Down and Waters cases (see p. 166) or at the time of Suez (see p. 115). As far as legislation is concerned, the initiative of the private Member is restricted—he has influence and not power, he is brakes and accelerator but not the steering-wheel. Recent Private Members' Bills have dealt with Divorce

Law Reform, Sunday laws, Betting, Licensing, the Colour Bar, Consumer Protection, the Press and the Local Authorities, and Compensation for Victims of Violence. These Bills have occasionally been bipartisan—for example, the Obscene Publications Bill, which led to the 1959 Act, was sponsored by Roy Jenkins and Lord Lambton—but, whether bipartisan or not, they have enabled Members to feel the satisfaction of expressing themselves as individuals. Often, M.P.s feel themselves to be prisoners of party discipline.

The personality and quality of a candidate are not essential factors during an election—generally speaking, electoral support goes to the party rather than to the candidate. Without party support it is virtually impossible to be elected: the party candidate must accept, and be prepared to defend, his party's programme. Having been elected, he is controlled by the Whips, by party Standing Orders, or by some unwritten understanding as to his conduct. The benefits of this party control are that political programmes are prepared and made known nationally, and that the legislative chamber is organized for business in a way which would not be possible if its members were a mere collection of individuals. With unified party control of Commons business the public can easily apportion praise and blame, and the individual M.P. is sheltered from the importunate demands of pressure groups. (See p. 36.)

The disadvantages of party control in the Commons are, briefly, a tendency to overrigidity and excess in discipline. Bitter complaints have been made about this discipline, particularly by Labour members, and demands made for a less sensitive attitude on the part of both Front Benches towards disagreements and minority suggestions of amendments to legislation. In 1955 Crossman declared that the forum of decision in parliamentary affairs was not the floor of the House of Commons but the party caucus (see also Local Government, p. 153): Cabinet government was a name for alternating party oligarchy, democracy was the iron rule of majorities. (*New Statesman*, 2nd April 1955.) The Labour Party, said Crossman, confused service to the party with implicit obedience to it. There was systematic abuse of majority rule: in parliamentary votes on important issues the divisions were made questions of confidence in the party leadership; party leaders used the powerful machinery of the Whips Office to unite support for the party-line, yet forbade others who wished to modify this line any form of group activity or organization. It all amounted to the exploitation of Members' loyalty to majority decisions—the system was little less ruthless than the Democratic Centralism of Leninist theory.

The essence of the party discipline problem is contained in the question as to whether the Member's right to vote in a private meeting 'upstairs' should exhaust his moral right to disagree with his fellow party-members, specifically on the floor of the House, and in the further question as to how far the idea of collective responsibility extends in the parliamentary context. A Cabinet must hang together and members of the majority party will normally support the Cabinet: one would expect members of the Shadow Cabinet to observe a common line—it was said in criticism of Bevan that he wanted to combine the advantages of being a Shadow Minister with those of being a backbencher—but not, perhaps, the Opposition as a whole. It has been argued that to expect Opposition M.P.s always to toe the party-line in the Commons is a mistaken application of the concept of collective responsibility. The Parliamentary Labour Party has its Standing Orders for the purpose of securing concerted action in the House. These Standing Orders were not in force during the years 1945–52, this freedom being ended by the Bevanite turmoil. The Standing Orders were again lifted in 1959 but the change was probably one of letter rather than spirit: the Standing Orders were replaced by a 'Chairman's Statement' which mentioned the possibility of withdrawal of Whips from Members, the need for Members to observe party decisions in order to ensure that the Party was an effective political force, and made the request that Members should consult Party officers before tabling any motion or amendment in the Chamber.

There has been a conflict between the natural rebelliousness of the Labour Party and its tight parliamentary discipline. The public has obtained the impression that the Parliamentary Labour Party is more disunited than the Conservatives since it draws more attention to itself by attacking rebels more fiercely. Crossman has said that Conservatives in Parliament have a comparatively easy time since the party is openly oligarchic and its sanctions unobtrusive—Conservative methods of discipline are unlike those of Labour but have the same results. To a significant extent Conservative discipline is exercised through the Constituency Associations, rather than through the Whips Office, and the parliamentary leaders are able to affect a certain detachment from its brutalities (see Suez, p. 117). Roy Jenkins, writing of discipline as exercised in the Conservative Party, has remarked on this 'trap-door' approach to politics but has made other interesting comments:

> ... the Conservatives, with a theory of tolerance, have been moving surreptitiously but steadily towards a tighter control, while the Labour Party, with a theory of iron unity, has been moving at least equally rapidly towards a freedom bordering on disarray ... Conservative discipline is always more effective than it looks, while Labour discipline is more notable for the terrible curses with which it is launched than for the casualties which it inflicts. (*Spectator*, 8th April 1960.)

(The internal cohesion of the parliamentary parties varies of course. In March 1964 the Parliamentary Labour Party appeared confident and united: the Conservatives, by contrast, were quarrelling over Resale Price Maintenance. Messrs Finer, Berrington, and Bartholomew —'Backbench Opinion in the House of Commons 1955–1959' (1961)— made a novel examination of the parliamentary parties as organizers of ideas. Because of the strengthening of party discipline at Westminster, the authors said, it was impossible to tell from the division lists the exact state of party feeling on any particular issue: an examination of Early Day Motions was made—these motions, not intended for debate, could be read as 'spontaneous un-whipped back-bench manifestos'. The conclusion of the study was that, while in the Labour Party there was a tendency for ideas to live in association with each other so that a revolt on one issue tended to become a revolt on a broad front, in the Conservative Party revolts were usually *ad hoc* affairs involving no total attitude, no total rejection of leadership.)

Note (a). Reform of Parliament

(i) *Institutional Reform.* In September 1960 a pamphlet by Christopher Hollis ('Has Parliament a Future?') suggested that the formal and technical discussions of Parliament, in which it was not possible for the ordinary Member to have many opinions, should be ended.

The House of Commons reduced to a maximum of a hundred M.P.s should discuss matters of general policy.

Suggestions relating to the radical reform of political institutions in Britain have been more common in conception than in execution. Developments do occur. Taking into account the importance of economic factors in modern politics, suggestions for a forum to give a voice to functional representation have been made from time to time: the National Industrial Conference (1919) recommended a National Industrial Council, Churchill a 'House of Industry'. We now have such a body, in a very rudimentary form, in our National Economic Development Council.

Churchill's suggestion of a 'Heptarchy' was but one demand for regional government in Britain. Following success in Northern Ireland, suggestions have been made that there should be a further effective devolution of powers upon Scotland and Wales. In 1964 the topic of regional government is very much alive, not simply involving discussion of the improvement of the machinery of government, the better control of traffic, or the improvement of employment prospects, but also embracing a regard for the development of community and environment. In November 1963 the Government published its White Paper, 'The North East: A Programme for Regional Development and Growth' (Cmnd 2206). One of the things flowing from this will be the greater co-ordination of the work of government departments in the area. In December 1963 the Minister of Public Building and Works announced a transfer of work to the provinces—a large transfer but one falling short of the dispersal of scarce skills.

(ii) *The Lords.* Reform of the House of Lords has been frequently discussed during this century. Debate has encompassed two main questions, composition and powers. (It has also, of course, encompassed the suggestion of abolition—see, for example, 'The Privy Council as a Second Chamber': A. Wedgwood Benn, 1957.)

The Life Peerages Act of 1958 made way for the revitalizing of the Lords by allowing for the creation of non-hereditary peerages, and for the admission of women on a non-hereditary basis. The 1958 Act has had some useful results: life peers have enlivened debate, which has encouraged other peers to attend, and a general increase in the activity of the Lords has been shown by the fact that Monday sittings are now more common than they were.

The 1958 attempt to make better use of the Lords did not withdraw their lordships from the reformer's gaze—the question of the House's composition remained a political issue. The Conservatives have been reluctant to abandon the hereditary element: in January 1961, for example, the Government appointed six life peers and one hereditary peer. Even if the Government followed the, to some, 'logical' course of allowing hereditary titles to die out a problem might remain—it has been noted that people of sufficient weight to merit inclusion in an enlarged body of life peers are often too busy elsewhere to accept peerages. In February 1961 the Parliamentary Labour Party rejected a proposal that Gaitskell should cease to make nominations to life peerages. After 1958 the exclusion of Liberals from those offered life peerages was a cause of some criticism.

The Wedgwood Benn–Lord Stansgate case caused a considerable stir in 1961. Wedgwood Benn succeeded to the peerage in November 1960 when his father, Viscount Stansgate, died: he was thus automatically disqualified from sitting in the Commons. His disqualification was upheld by the Committee of Privileges in March 1961. In the following month the Government announced that a joint Select Committee would be set up to consider the composition of the Lords, the surrendering of peerages, and the remuneration of peers—the committee was not asked to consider the powers of the Lords. The Peerage Act 1963 was the result: it enabled a peer to renounce his title, for himself but not for this descendants.

The Lords can delay legislation for a year. The second chamber, however, devotes its time largely to revision—here the Government, having had second thoughts, can introduce amendments to legislation. The Lords is also used as an initiating chamber for the introduction of technical and non-party Bills. It is doubtful whether the Lords, by initiating or amending legislation, saves a great deal of precious parliamentary time. The advantages it offers in these directions may be largely imaginary. A Bill has to go through both Houses and one going from the Lords to the Commons can spend as much time there as in the Lords itself. Amendments inserted in the Lords have to come back to the Commons for debate.

In 1961 Gaitskell said that a review of the Upper House's composition should be accompanied by discussion of possible further curtailment of its formal powers. (Even though a constitutional matter, Labour had not been consulted on the committee's terms of reference.) Labour, whose attitude towards reform of the Lords since the war has been largely negative, is frightened of a strengthening of the Upper House. Individual Socialists have long differed in their attitudes to the Lords: Bevan thought it the 'last refuge of ignorant reaction' while Morrison has said that, provided political passion is not aroused, the Lords is good at revision.

(iii) *Procedural Reform*. On the 12th June 1958 Shinwell asked the Leader of the House if it would be to the advantage of the House and democracy if Members used the House more as a sounding board to illuminate the mind of the public on important topics than for the discussion of cosmetics, babies' dusting powder, and ladies' unmentionables. The complaint came during a week spent on the Finance Bill after what Shinwell thought was an excessive period of discussion on the incidence of purchase tax on a wide range of goods. Along with criticism of the excessive debate of minor matters there often goes that relating to Parliament's wastage of time taken in Divisions —frequent votes occur, the results of which can be easily guessed.

There have been frequent investigations of parliamentary procedure. The most recent detailed investigation was initiated in January 1958. The Report of the Select Committee on Procedure was published in March 1959. It favoured attempts to cut down unnecessary attendance at the House, at inconvenient hours, but held that Members should not expect too much from reform—M.P.s should rightly be 'about the House' for informal discussion, for the maintenance of the corporate spirit of the Commons, which had been built up over centuries. The Report came out against the printing of undelivered speeches in Hansard; Wednesday morning sittings, mechanical voting, and voting by proxy: the Report did favour a longer period for the questioning of the Prime Minister on Tuesdays and Thursdays; a one hour period to be set aside during major debates when only short speeches would be allowed; the limitation of the precedence allowed to Privy Counsellors (who had the traditional right of being heard when they wished), and the giving to the Speaker of more freedom in accepting for Debate on the Adjournment matters of definite urgency. The Report recommended the abolition of the rule that prevented the putting of emergency motions which anticipated other motions, questions or proceedings—the House should judge 'public importance', not the Speaker.

The Hansard Society has said that the core of any large-scale procedural reform lies in the use the Commons makes of committees. Perhaps the most encouraging aspect of the Select Committee's findings was the favour it showed for the reduction of the number of Committee Stages of Bills taken on the floor of the House, for the clearing from the floor of specialist business. The removal of the Committee Stage of the Finance Bill would be the biggest single saving that could come from procedural reform: the Select Committee approved R. A. Butler's memorandum which showed how part of the Finance Bill could be taken from the floor of the Commons. The setting-up of specialized committees (to encourage the formation of informed opinion among M.P.s, and to allow them to take part in active business instead of sitting about the House) has long been a demand of reformers: the Report of the Select Committee did not favour this particular reform.

In June 1958 Butler had spoken of the need for parliamentary procedure to 'Chime with the spirit of the times'. When the Report of the Select Committee on Procedure was debated in July 1959 the Government had, apparently, not made up its mind on the findings but it was evident that there would be no severe overhauling of procedure. The Government was against the House having a 'beehive atmosphere' and it offered no strong lead to reformers. Despite the assertion of one M.P. that, to his knowledge, the division lobbies had killed three Members, mechanical voting was rejected, as were specialized committees and morning sittings. Butler agreed that there ought to be more time available for Members to question the Prime Minister, that Front-benchers should shorten their speeches, that there ought to be introduced the suggested 'short speech hour' (referred to by one M.P. as 'Parliamentary Children's Hour'). The Government favoured the removal of business from the floor of the House, although the acute shortage of accommodation would stand in the way of the setting up of additional committees: as far as the removal 'upstairs' of part of the Finance Bill was concerned, there might be experiment by the Government.

In a further debate on procedure in February 1960 it became evident that the Government had decided to make even less use of the Select Committee's suggestions than had seemed probable in the first debate. The suggestion that part of the Finance Bill might be removed from the floor of the House had been forgotten while, on the subject of the detailed business carried out in the Chamber, Butler declared that Parliament was a legislating body, not a platform for entertaining debates on general topics. In the July debate Butler had reported the Prime Minister as being content to meet as far as he could the wishes of the House on the matter of Questions addressed to himself. The reform in this direction was disappointing: Questions to the Prime Minister, it was promised, would now begin at Number 40, instead of at Number 45.

On 15th March 1963 the Commons debated a motion put down by the Opposition:

> That this House resolves to maintain Parliament as the paramount forum of the nation and to bring its practices and procedures into harmony with this end and in accord with the needs of 1963.

Said *The Guardian* on the morrow:

> In yesterday's debate in the Commons, the Leader of the House, Mr. Macleod, backed away from the impatience of the critics with a series of soft answers. There are to be talks on the salaries of M.P.s at a 'very early date'. Experiments in streamlining Finance Bill procedure may be tried this year. There is a case for television reports of Parliament 'in due course'. This helps a little, but it does not take us very far. And when it comes to the reform of parliamentary procedure, Mr. Macleod is inclined to fade away like the Cheshire Cat, leaving nothing but a solicitous smile. So when he says, as he did yesterday, that forms of procedure have not changed swiftly enough, and when he acknowledges that an enormous backlog of Bills has built up over the years, one recalls that he was saying much the same sort of thing in a debate on procedure on 24th November 1961, and that nothing much has been done about it in the interval.

The proposal that some parts of the Finance Bill might be debated in a standing committee 'upstairs' was rejected by the Select Committee on Procedure in April 1963.

(iv) *Reform of Financial Control.* The reform of parliamentary procedure—like the improvement of M.P.'s working-conditions—has scarcely begun despite frequent complaints and investigations. The lack of adequate parliamentary control over the nation's finances is a distinct problem worthy of special attention. The control of government spending is one of the traditional tasks of Parliament and complaints of inadequacies of this control are far more serious than complaints about Parliament's procedure as a whole. The issue here is not that relating to political decisions on government spending (see Vol. II, p. 17) but that relating to detailed control.

In theory, control over government spending is exercised at several levels. Each Minister is responsible for keeping expenditure reasonable and he has a civil servant, a Departmental Finance Officer, to give particular help with this task. The Chancellor of the Exchequer curbs government spending as a whole—when the Cabinet considers matters which involve spending no proposal is circulated until the sanction of the Chancellor has been obtained. The Chancellor co-ordinates the spending of various government departments through the Treasury, which keeps a watch on Departmental Finance Officers. Traditionally, the Treasury's job has been to 'save candle ends' and it has done this by keeping a general oversight of the whole civil service— it scrutinizes departmental estimates, sanctions expenditure of voted money, and has to approve the diversion of voted funds from one head to another.

Much House of Commons' time is spent, in debate and in committee, in considering finance: the Commons considers Estimates and makes Votes on Resolutions of Supply; it authorizes spending by Resolutions of Appropriation; in debating the Finance Bill it considers whether it will authorize the raising of revenue. The Select Committee on Estimates and the Public Accounts Committee are watchdogs working on behalf of the Commons as a whole. The S.C.E. performs a kind of pre-audit—it examines a selection of Annual Estimates to see if economies can be achieved, scrutinizing the activities of the various departments. The P.A.C. examines a selection of the Appropriation Accounts prepared by departments to satisfy itself that money has been spent as directed by the Appropriation Act—it compares expenditure with amounts voted and sees that the departments' books are properly maintained. It has a discretionary power to see that no waste has occurred, and to see that contracts have been made in the correct manner. The Comptroller and Auditor-General, a Parliamentary official and not a civil servant, watches receipts of revenue, gives covering authority for the issue of money from the Consolidated Fund, audits the accounts of government departments and reports to the Public Accounts Committee.

So much for the system in theory. Serious defects have been alleged at several of these points of financial control. Reporting on the work of the Treasury in August 1958, the Select Committee on Estimates said that it was an abuse of language to speak of a 'system' of Treasury Control. Treasury effort was not always applied in the right direction and, while new expenditure received careful attention, old recurring expenditure was insufficiently regarded. The Treasury, said the S.C.E., often made inadequate assessments of eventual commitments and had sometimes gone very much awry in its estimates. Expenditure on new weapons development was one field of error: other errors included one associated with the refitting of an aircraft-carrier— instead of costing less than ten millions over four or five years, it had cost twenty millions over eight years. The Treasury had made a poor estimate of the increase of service pay to be met after the abolition of conscription. The S.C.E. Report accorded praise to the Treasury and the Ministry of Defence for their development of control of defence expenditure, by 'forward looks' at expenditure for three year periods, but regretted that no forward looks were made on the civil side. In the field of hospital building, for example, scrutiny came at the wrong end—there was tight Treasury control of capital projects once approved, but inadequate Treasury control in the actual drawing up of the list of capital projects. The origin of the Treasury's present short-comings is probably in the fact that it is today much concerned with spending, less concerned than in former days with economy.

In October 1960 the Select Committee on Estimates noted that the Central Office of Information had needed supplementary estimates— extra funds, that is—four times in six years. Some of the C.O.I.'s publications were unduly lavish and expensive and the fact that not all British representatives abroad knew of the C.O.I.'s functions did not make for economical working. The S.C.E. can make important criticisms like those just quoted but it is hampered by not having adequate staff. Its task is difficult: dealing as it does with large figures, searching analysis is impossible—particularly in view of the speed with which it must work if its efforts are to help the Commons at all. Further, by the nature of its work, it tends to interfere in the running of a department by its responsible head. Estimates are, for the most part, drawn up by the responsible head on the basis of the Government's predetermined policy and it is difficult to criticise them without criticizing the Government's financial policy. This the S.C.E. cannot do. The demand has been made that there should be an entirely new committee to supervise national expenditure.

In March 1958 the Public Accounts Committee commented on the number of boots bought by the Army since 1955 in excess of requirements. The Army's Central Clothing Depôt had a declared surplus of 1,250,000 pairs of boots. In March 1960 the Comptroller and Auditor-General described how the Treasury had given permission to the Ministry of Supply to test a new navigational system for 150 flying-hours at a cost of £40,000: by an oversight flying-time had reached 615 hours and the cost had mounted to £300,000. The chief criticism attaching to the work of the P.A.C. is concerned with the delay which occurs before it uncovers inefficiency, when remedies are no longer possible. The amount of work the P.A.C. can do is limited and it has to confine itself to particular areas of government spending.

The Committee of Supply, which means the House of Commons as a body, deals with the Estimates as a whole. The floor of the House is no place to discuss detailed figures—although, as seen above, serious criticism is made of excessive attention to minutiae—and the task of checking the figures here would be too big. In March 1963 the Treasury began a new system of presenting Estimates—they were simplified and their lay-out was changed. By abandoning the form of estimates established in 1866, it was hoped that Parliament and public would obtain a much more vivid picture of the general effects of the year's expenditure. However, it remains true that, during Supply Days, time is insufficient to debate all the estimates and large blocks of these go uncriticized, voting proceeding according to a strict timetable.

There are several other factors which diminish the power of the House to come near to controlling finance. Government spending is large—spending on defence, the social services, and so on—and government borrowing has increased. The nationalized industries have been virtually autonomous, allowed to run as private businesses yet drawing deeply on public funds (but see Vol. II, p. 21). Finally, politicians and governments are more intent on spending than on saving.

The last fact leads us to the central issue. Parliament today approves large expenditure because parties are elected to power on ambitious programmes which carry with them inescapable financial implications. Money matters are a government concern: the Government's financial proposals are questions of confidence. The convention has grown that the Estimates should be treated formally. The House regulates expenditure, not by dealing with actual figures, but by discussing policy—debate takes place on the principles of policy rather than on the pounds, shillings, and pence.

2. *Party Politics: the Conservatives*

(i) *Leadership and Constituent Elements of the Party.* In this and the following sections the party machines are discussed. Our two major parties differ significantly in their organizations but they serve the same purpose—they mobilize and expound political opinion and periodically offer themselves for office. It has been normal, when speaking of the Labour Party, to emphasize democracy, and when speaking of the Conservative Party to stress leadership. In 1964 the emphasis is the other way: Conservatives are examining the processes of leadership and democracy within their party, and Socialists are united in an attempt to build up Wilson as a national leader. (There is another partial reversal: Conservatives have traditionally emphasized men, Socialists measures; the distinction is not now so great.)

The powers of the Conservative leader are extensive: he has the choice of his own ministers or shadow-ministers, he appoints party whips and controls the party machine outside Parliament. Further, he has the sole ultimate responsibility for the formulation of his party's programme. The Conservative Party's Maxwell-Fyfe Report, the result of a stocktaking after the post-war defeat, stated:

> Endorsements and pronouncements on party policy are the prerogative and responsibility of the leader, who is served by the various policy committees. These in their turn are influenced by the views of the party as revealed in the various resolutions of the party conference.

Unkind commentators have described the Conservative Party as an autocracy flavoured by advice, as a party democratic except at the top: apologists have described the position within their party as one of 'leadership by consent'.

While it is true to say that the Conservative Party is oligarchic rather than dictatorial in its leadership it is also true that the parliamentary leaders, an oligarchy though they be, need the support of the mass party in the country. Power in the party is divided, not only between the parliamentary leaders and Conservative M.P.s, but also between the parliamentary party and the party-members at large. The Selwyn Lloyd Enquiry into Party Organization of 1963, like the Maxwell Fyfe Report of 1949, showed that party leaders were concerned that the various elements of the party should work together. In discussing the powers of the Conservative parliamentary leaders on the one hand, and those of the party outside Parliament on the other, the essential question to be asked relates to the limits of democracy in the mass party organization when responsible parliamentary government has to be maintained—responsibility being acknowledged to the House of Commons and the nation, and not merely to the body of party-members. In discussing the Conservative Party, as in discussing the Labour Party, one has to ask what are the limits of extra-parliamentary control of the party in Parliament.

In the early post-war years the Conservative Party made several organizational changes with the aim of giving the party-membership a feeling of increased participation in decision-making. In November 1945 there was set up the Advisory Committee on Policy and Political Education. Under Butler, this committee, which had had its origins in the Post-war Problems Committee of October 1941, produced a series of 'Charters'. The Advisory Committee on Policy—Political Education has been hived off—cannot be claimed as the creature of the National Union of Conservative and Unionist Associations, the party outside Parliament. The chairman and deputy chairman of the committee are appointed by the party leader and although the National Union appoints half the remaining committee-members it has chosen, to a great extent, to be represented by M.P.s. In 1946, the Conservative Political Centre, which has published a large amount of educational material for the party, inaugurated the 'Two-way Movement of Ideas'.

In 1945 the Conservatives launched the Young Conservative movement, and the trade union and women's groups of local associations. The Young Conservatives were to replace the Junior Imperial League, and twelve full-time area organizers were appointed. The venture was not taken very seriously until Eden became Prime Minister: both Eden and Macmillan have encouraged the movement. The Young Conservatives are represented at all levels in the party—on divisional executives, area councils, central committees and constituency committees. While this is democratic (Selwyn Lloyd wants the Y.C.s further brought into the work of senior branches), it has been pointed out that Conservative youth has little room left for revolution. The concern of the Y.C.s for social rather than political activities has been a stock political joke for years: a Bow Group survey of 1959 commented on the imbalance of social and political activities and to the fact that Y.C. branches were apt to draw their strength from one geographical and social area in the constituency—Young Conservatism does appeal to social snobs and, in this respect, Y.C.s often seem more conservative than the senior members of the Party. In 1960 at a Manchester meeting Butler spoke of Conservative approaches to the young as being the best means of getting across to the nation the idea of an expanding society: he planned to organize leadership courses for Y.C.s, and Y.C. policy groups at all levels of the party. In 1961 the Young Conservatives held their first conference.

The Bow Group is a research society of younger Conservatives which was founded in 1951. There is no Bow Group 'line' on any particular policy, no collective policy: publications contain facts and opinions which '. . . merit consideration by the Conservative Party, and by a wider audience'. The Socialist *New Statesman* has paid the Group the compliment of saying that all its publications are serious and thoughtful.

The Central Council of the Conservative National Union provides Conservatives at large with an opportunity to subject the parliamentary leaders to pressure. At the March 1960 meeting, for example, a resolution was passed with a large majority regretting the failure of the Government to provide private patients with free drugs—promised by party leaders before 1950.

The Annual Conference of the National Union receives more publicity than does the Central Council. It was at the Conference that demands were made after the war for some Conservative response to the social revolution inaugurated by the Socialists—demands which led to the writing of the 'Industrial Charter'. In 1949, Conference demanded a house-building programme of 300,000 houses a year— Conference 'educated the platform'. Commenting on the latter event the *Observer* reporter said: 'One feels after this week that the Annual Conference will never again relapse into its old passivity.'

In fact, the Conservative Annual Conference is too big for serious discussion to take place, and time is short. (Selwyn Lloyd rejected the idea of changing the size.) Since 1949 the placid unanimity, the reluctance to show open opposition to party leaders, have been subjects of annual comment. Of the 1956 Conference the *Observer* said: '. . . despite the grumbling and discontent, despite the fiery resolutions on the agenda, this conference will go down as one of the quietest on record.' 'One or two ding-dong battles such as those Socialists indulged in a week earlier might have helped,' said the *Daily Telegraph* of the 1957 Conference. In the following year *The Manchester Guardian* noted in a leading article (8th Oct. 1958) that 4000 Conservative delegates had assembled for what was in danger of becoming an orgy of hero-worship: 'The Tories in conference are rarely an appealing spectacle, least of all when their party is riding the crest of the wave. A Labour conference at least gives the impression of genuine debate, fumbling and ill-informed though it may often be; the Conservatives are apt to appear as little more than a cheer-leader's chorus.'

There was no Conference in the election year of 1959 but the critics were again active in 1960. The *Observer* noted (16th Oct. 1960) that expectations of a quiet week at Scarborough had not been disappointed: the Conference had taken the well-ordered course of a session of the Supreme Soviet in Moscow. For those who had seen the Labour

Party's splendid catastrophe (see p. 127) the previous week the contrast had been overwhelming. 'When is a conference not a conference?' asked the *Observer*: when debates were not debates; when the resolutions were carefully teed up for Ministers to swipe down the fairway; when the delegates—called representatives—rushed for the doors before the vote was put, like an uncouth cinema audience before 'The Queen'; and when the motions did not bind anyone to anything anyway. *The Guardian* remarked (15th Oct. 1960) that the oddity of the Conference was shown when the Colonial Secretary, Macleod, wound up the debate on the Commonwealth and Colonies: no amendments were selected for debate, and ten motions were not put to the Conference—Macleod said blandly that he would have accepted the amendments and all the motions. The Conservatives have all the year to disagree among themselves: their public gathering is an occasion to demonstrate solidarity.

Butler, when he became Chairman of Party Organization in October 1959, declared his concern not just for the organizational efficiency of the party but also for the flow of ideas within its ranks: in his period as chairman he would deliberately try to combine the practical task of organization with the reception of ideas, he said. In the period from 1945 to 1950 policy had been made on high and carried down to the faithful on tablets of stone but now the party would reverse the process. Policy-making should be disseminated and should more often find its roots in the rank and file. (*Daily Telegraph*, 7th March 1960.) Butler expressed some mild criticism of the 1960 Conference when he noted that resistance (presumably of the representatives to the platform) was sometimes the flint on which the spark of oratory was kindled—although the loyalty and warmth of support of a great party were a good foundation on which to build for the years ahead. Butler said that he thought some of the conference debates had been too brief and he was to discuss with the officers of the National Union how the party could remedy this another time and give more room and time to the floor.

Conservative Constituency Associations conduct propaganda for the party and raise funds with a view to securing the election of Conservatives to public bodies. The model rules which summarize the objects of the Associations contain no reference whatever to the discussion of policy: there is no suggestion that the Associations should formulate their views on national and international issues for forwarding to the National Union. (See Robert McKenzie, 'British Political Parties', p. 244.) In practice the views of the local party associations on policy are expressed at Conference (however inadequately), at the meetings of the Central Council, and by pressure on M.P.s. Occasionally, the Constituency Associations become national news.

Under the headline '840 Tory Rebels', *The Manchester Guardian* reported in June 1958 that the Barnoldswick Conservatives had withdrawn all support from the Government and would withhold it until such a time as the parliamentary leaders changed their attitude towards the textile industry—the fate of 500,000 workers was at stake and the Government was sacrificing their livelihood in the interests of Hong Kong, a place of no commercial or strategic use to the nation.

In 1959 Montgomery Hyde was rejected as prospective parliamentary candidate by Belfast Conservatives because of his views on capital punishment, on that part of the 1958 Wolfenden Report dealing with homosexuality, and because of his advocacy of the return of the Lane Pictures to Dublin.

A vote of no confidence in Donald Johnson, M.P., was passed by the Carlisle Conservative Party in October 1963 after his criticism of Macmillan. In January 1964 he resigned from the association saying: 'I must state plainly my opinion that no M.P. can be subjected to such difficulties and humiliation as I was getting without Parliament itself falling into humiliation and disrepute.' (*The Guardian*, 17th Jan., 1964.)

Events in Ipswich in May 1959 offered a more unusual example of Conservative discord. The Ipswich Conservative Action Committee, a breakaway from the Constituency Association, disputed the nomination of John Cobbald, a nephew of the Prime Minister, as prospective parliamentary candidate—he had been defeated in 1955 and in 1957. The Action Committee protested at the nomination procedure: wealth and family connections were the determining factors here and thinking Conservatives of the middle and working classes were being disenfranchised. (Eighteen months after the defeat of the Conservative Party at the 1945 Election, Cyril Osborne declared to the party Conference that there ought to be working people on the party's Central Council. In 1963 Selwyn Lloyd recommended: 'Constituencies [should] ensure that among prospective candidates attending for final interview one of the women applicants and one of the Trade Unionist applicants are included.')

The subject of candidates leads naturally to mention of the relations between the party leadership and the body of Conservative M.P.s. In Macmillan's offering to Lord Home the Foreign Secretaryship, and in his 'unflappability' at the time of Thorneycroft's resignation together with Enoch Powell and Nigel Birch, one saw a high degree of self-confidence on the part of the Prime Minister in the security of his position. Macmillan's position was less secure in 1963 (see below) and he had less cause for confidence. Conservative premiers are not invulnerable to parliamentary attack from their own side. Nine months after taking office, Eden issued an official denial of a report that he was about to resign—the denial was a direct answer to Conservative criticism expressed through the *Daily Telegraph*.

Like his Labour opposite-number, the Conservative leader has to keep in touch with his parliamentary following. The counterpart of the Parliamentary Labour Party is the 1922 (Conservative and Unionist Members') Committee: it differs from the P.L.P. in being essentially a back-benchers' organization—the Conservative Chief Whip attends meetings and conveys to the party leaders the views expressed there, and party leaders attend meetings by invitation. Even when the party is in opposition the 1922 Committee makes no claim to decide policy. Work is done through a system of sub-committees: in July 1955 Gerald Nabarro, the Member for Kidderminister, resigned from the post of Joint Secretary of the Fuel and Power Sub-committee and issued to the Press a letter in which he said that the Minister of Fuel and Power had largely disregarded the advice offered by the sub-committee—Nabarro would no longer give tacit support to the policy of the Minister.

In February 1961, during the Central Africa Federation talks crisis, Macleod was so concerned to have the support and understanding of Conservative Members that he spoke to the Commonwealth Sub-committee twice in one week. (See also Introduction, p. 85.) Edward Heath was similarly active in March 1964 in face of strong opposition to his Resale Prices Bill.

Labour Party squabbles are much more of a public matter than those of their chief opponents, possibly because our national newspapers are largely right-wing, but also because Conservatives like to make as little fuss as possible about their divisions. In July 1958 seven rebellious Tories abstained from voting when Labour forced a division at the end of the cotton debate: coming from constituencies with cotton interests, they demanded that the Government should take action to protect the industry. In June 1960 Geoffrey Hirst, Conservative Member for Shipley, issued a statement to the newspapers in which he said of Amory, the Chancellor of the Exchequer: 'There can be no question but that the Chancellor's reputation has been so lowered by a chain of circumstances that his opinion now is of relatively little count.' On several occasions during 1961 the 'Katanga Lobby' of Conservative Members—numbered variously at between fifty and a hundred— sought to put pressure on the Government: they resented United Nations action in the Congo, and deplored the Government's decision to supply bombs to the U.N. forces. The Congo, however, had less of an impact on the Conservative Party than did Suez.

(ii) *Suez and Cyprus.* At the end of October 1956 the British Government delivered an ultimatum to the Egyptian Ambassador and the Israeli Chargé d'Affaires in London: it announced the intention of the British and French Governments to occupy key positions in the Suez Canal Zone unless Egypt and Israel stopped all warlike action by land, sea, and air forthwith. There was begun the most agitated period in our recent political history. The dates involved are important for our purposes:

26th July:	Canal Company nationalized.
30th October:	Ultimatum.
31st October:	Campaign begins and lasts until midnight 6th November.
23rd November:	Eden, sick, leaves for West Indies.
24th November:	General Assembly United Nations calls for British withdrawal from Egypt.
3rd December:	Selwyn Lloyd announces withdrawal in Commons.
May 1957:	Announced that British ships will be advised to start using the Suez Canal again.

The country was split over the Ultimatum and events which ensued but the turmoil occurred among the intellectuals rather than among the population at large. However, we are not here concerned with the rights or wrongs of the Suez Operation or with the divisions in the country, but with the impact of the operation on the Conservative Party.

As far as the Cabinet was concerned, reports frequently named Butler, Monckton, Macleod and Heathcoat Amory as being against the delivering of the Ultimatum: Monckton, in fact, made a speech in his constituency referring to objections to the Government's policy but there is no proof as to the line taken by the others. Reports said that Selwyn Lloyd, Sandys, Lennox-Boyd, Head, and Macmillan supported the Ultimatum. Salisbury was frightened of endangering the Anglo-American alliance. Two junior Ministers submitted their resignations—Sir Edward Boyle, Financial Secretary to the Treasury, and Anthony Nutting, Minister of State for Foreign Affairs. Nutting resigned as Minister of State on the 31st October, the day after the Ultimatum was delivered, and gave up his seat in the Commons on the 15th November. Boyle deeply deplored the Government's action: Nutting declared that he could not defend the Government in Parliament or the United Nations. Nutting did intend to put his case to his constituency party but then felt that this would split the party: out of loyalty to Eden, who had promoted him, he retired quietly to take up writing. (In January 1962 Nutting was adopted as prospective parliamentary candidate for the marginal Oldham East constituency.)

In Parliament the Ultimatum took moderate Conservative M.P.s by surprise—they sat back and watched. The Ultimatum was, perhaps, not so much a triumph for the right-wing of the party as an utter failure of the moderates. Butler and Macmillan addressed the 1922 Committee: Conservative Members gave support to the Government, this support stemming in part from the fear that, with Eden sick, the party might be split by a contest for leadership between Butler and Macmillan. The internationalist M.P.s, the 'Rule of Law Group'— Boothby, Nutting, Boyle, Medlicott, Banks, Osborne, Yates, and Nicolson—abstained in the vote of confidence but about fifty other Conservative Members 'thought better of it' when the moment for voting came. Osborne spoke in defence of the idea of United Nations collective security. Banks resigned the Whip. Medlicott, in a letter to the Prime Minister on 16th November, regretted that the Government was not working through the United Nations Organization—subsequently he announced his decision not to contest his seat again. With the declaration that 'Suez permitted Hungary!', Houston, a Conservative Research Department worker, resigned from the party and from his job. (There was a clear anti-Soviet revolt in Hungary on 25th October during the period of Anglo-French military preparations. Soviet troops entered the country on 30th October and attacked their objectives on 4th November. Ten days of intensive fighting followed —sporadic fighting went on until early December.)

Macmillan was one of the first in the Cabinet to see that the Suez Operation had misfired. With the rumours that the Government planned a withdrawal from Suez the 'strong men' in Parliament— Sir Ian Horabin, Martin Lindsay, Lord Hinchinbrooke, Angus Maude, and so on—began to raise their voices. Two days before the declaration by the U.N. General Assembly, Angus Maude said that, if Britain were humiliated while Nasser triumphed, then there would be no place for him or for scores of his colleagues in the Conservative Party under a leadership that had brought the nation to such an abject defeat. The 'strong men' feared a withdrawal being effected without guarantees that the Canal would be cleared and put into free operation.

When, in May 1957, the Government announced that British ships would be advised to start using the Suez Canal again, Lord Russell of Liverpool, who had rejoined the Conservatives from the Liberals at the time of the invasion of the Suez Canal Zone, decided to refuse the Conservative Whip and to sit in the Lords as an Independent Conservative. Lord Lambton resigned as Parliamentary Private Secretary to Selwyn Lloyd in protest at the Government's policy of appeasement. Lord Lambton continued to receive the Conservative Whip but other M.P.s rejected it. Angus Maude, Sir Victor Raikes, and Captain Waterhouse were among those Conservatives who went to live abroad. (Maude succeeded in his second attempt to re-enter the Commons at the Stratford-on-Avon By-election in August 1963.)

In the Conservative Party there is less pressure on an M.P. from above than from below. Particularly in respect of what might be called 'left-wing deviations', there is much pressure from the constituency parties. For the non-conformist M.P. 'the party battle, half a pretence in Parliament, is a grim reality outside'. Boyle was interviewed by his Executive which, though disagreeing with him, acknowledged his right to act on his conscience. Other Conservative M.P.s were less fortunate. The Executive Committee of Medlicott's constituency party disassociated itself from him and would not hear his case. The Nicolson Case was the most publicized of all the constituency disputes arising from Suez.

Nigel Nicolson, a member of the United Nations Association General Council, said that the Suez Campaign was wrong in principle and unlikely to succeed in practice. He would follow the Government in everything save Suez. Nicolson was ostracized by his Executive, forbidden to address constituency meetings, his subscription was returned to him, and a new candidate was adopted for the constituency. The situation in Bournemouth East and Christchurch became so involved that Conservative Central Office, rather tardily, its hand forced by the Press, asked Lord Hailsham to go down to clear things up. A 'primary' was arranged—constituency party members were given the choice of Nicolson and the new candidate—and Nicolson lost by a short head. The Conservative M.P. may find much tolerance in the House but he may face a lynching in the constituency if he does not conform. (At the time of the Nicolson episode, one commentator remarked that the working of Conservative constituency parties sometimes resembled those of the Electrical Trades Union.)

Turning from Suez, the Cyprus troubles are mentioned here only because of the resignation of Lord Salisbury from his position as Lord President of the Council in March 1959. Salisbury was one of the 'grand old men' of the party—one of those who, traditionally, have held great power in deciding party leadership. Salisbury had much to do with Macmillan's succession to Eden—he believed that Macmillan could unite the party and form a 'government of consolidation'. (In the post-Suez salvage operation some Conservatives thought that consolidation was important. As noted elsewhere, Thorneycroft was shortly to resign, on an economic issue. He was among those who thought that Macmillan was pointing to the right while steering to the left.) The cause of Salisbury's resignation was the fact that Archbishop

Makarios was released from captivity before he had made an unconditional appeal to EOKA, the Cypriot underground, to end its campaign —Makarios had promised to make such an appeal if the state of emergency in Cyprus was ended.

(iii) *1963: A Desire for Democracy?* The Selwyn Lloyd Enquiry into Conservative Party Organization (1963) resulted from a resolution approved by a National Union committee in August 1962:

> . . . (that) there must be much closer liaison between Members of the Party in Parliament, the National Union and the Central Office, and to this end we recommend that a committee on the lines of the Maxwell Fyfe Committee (now 14 years old) in due course be appointed to review this problem.

Selwyn Lloyd said that the Prime Minister's speaking *before* Conference proceedings rather than after might be considered. (The report made no revolutionary suggestion to the effect that the Premier might speak *during* Conference.) Trade unionists were very much in Lloyd's mind in writing his report, as were the need for improved political education in the party, and the need to improve the collection of funds. (See p. 44 and p. 131.) Selwyn Lloyd's findings were not revolutionary: they followed a routine re-examination of party machinery—a periodic need of all parties.

In the aftermath of the Profumo Affair the Conservative Party re-examined itself in a way Selwyn Lloyd did not contemplate. (In early June 1963 John Profumo, Secretary of State for War, admitted an *affaire* with a girl who was known to have associated with a member of the Russian embassy. Macmillan had to answer charges that he had been lax in maintaining the nation's security.) Macmillan retained his position as Prime Minister because he was favoured by certain facts: no senior colleague challenged him; there were no 'grand old men' to advise the Queen; there was no eminently suitable successor waiting in the wings; and, the general election could not be far removed and a resignation, too closely associated with the Profumo scandal, could have brought permanent damage to the Conservative Party.

It was said that an understanding had been reached among Conservatives in Parliament that Macmillan would resign before the election, but the situation was ambiguous.

Crossman has written (*The Guardian*, 5th July 1963) of Macmillan 'doing a Gaitskell in reverse';

> Fighting for his political life in 1963, Harold Macmillan is playing one part of the Tory Party off against another, in much the same way as Hugh Gaitskell exploited the Labour Party's divisions in his fight to retain the leadership. But whereas Hugh Gaitskell defeated the Party outside Westminster, thanks to the solid support of the Labour M.P.s, Harold Macmillan must beat back his own backbenchers with the help of the Party outside.

The relevant issue to be discussed here is the impact the Profumo affair may have had on the Conservatives' system of electing a leader. Humphrey Berkeley, Conservative Member for Lancaster, suggested that the leader should be elected by a secret ballot of Tory M.P.s. Lord Poole, joint chairman of the party, has implied that the existing method of choosing a leader is unsatisfactory:

> We have got to find a method by which we can bring the Conservative Party into tune with the second half of the twentieth century without just slavishly following the constitutional organization of the Labour Party, which suits them but does not suit us.
> I am absolutely certain that if the Prime Minister at any time, either before or after an election, should decide that change is necessary, the Conservative Party, provided we did not do it in a rush and panic, can resolve the leadership of the party in a way that is perfectly satisfactory. I do not say it will be done in exactly the same way that it was done before.
> I would certainly be against some who wish that great decisions should be taken in the middle of the great concern and emotion that is seething at Westminster during the Profumo affair. I believe it would be taken better not today or tomorrow but after some weeks or months or years of careful thought. (*The Guardian*, 10th July 1963.)

Poole did not think that the Parliamentary Conservative Party should have the sole say in the choice of a new leader.

In the October 1963 issue of *Crossbow*, Humphrey Berkeley recommended that the Conservative leader should be elected by a secret ballot of M.P.s, prospective M.P.s, representatives of the National Union, and some peers. He was critical of Lord Poole. The Joint Chairman was not entitled to pronounce upon the Prime Minister's future or the choice of an eventual successor because he was not a member of the Cabinet, did not hold any elected position in the party, he was not responsible to the Crown or to the electorate—his had been a purely personal appointment by the party leader.

In October the Conservative 'Monday Club', a group operating under the patronage of Lord Salisbury and Lord Boyd, the former Colonial Secretary Lennox-Boyd, issued a 'manifesto of beliefs' to all Conservative M.P.s. The group declared that the Prime Minister had lost the nation's confidence and that the country would not recover until there was a new leader with the energy to dispel existing lethargy.

(iv) *1963: the War of Succession.* In January 1957, after the resignation of Eden and the elevation of Macmillan to the premiership, there were grumbles in the Conservative Party about the succession. Correspondence in the *Daily Telegraph* revealed that, although soundings of opinion by Salisbury and Churchill had occurred, these may have been conducted with such subtlety that many M.P.s were entirely unaware that they were taking place.

Early in October 1963 Macmillan was ready to go to the annual conference of his party and, it was reported, intended to say that he was willing to lead the party into the general election. Macmillan fell sick. This was the one week of the year when a leadership crisis could not go underground and students of politics were provided with a highly dramatic spectacle. There were various key events and key participants: Butler was chosen to address the end-of-conference rally and thereby gained some eminence; on Tuesday, 10th October, the second day of the conference, Lord Home announced that Macmillan intended to resign, whereupon Lord Hailsham announced that he intended to give up his peerage. At conference the National Union, the party organization in the country, was of course at its most active: M.P.s were at first scattered around the country—there was a quickening of interest as they rallied after the announcement of Macmillan's resignation.

The second act of the drama began after the end of the conference. In London events were somewhat obscure and confused, although journalists were perhaps more active and more searching than they had ever been on such an occasion. From his hospital bed, Macmillan sent a memorandum to Butler relating to the question of soundings among the various elements of the party. The Cabinet accepted the terms of the document and inquiries were made among M.P.s, active peers, cabinet members, and members of the party in the country. The result was that Macmillan advised the Queen to send for Lord Home.

In 1957 the Conservative Party still appeared to be a 'gentlemanly party'. In 1963, it was said, the Conservatives ceased to be gentlemen without becoming democrats. Discussion of, and disputes over, the succession of Lord Home to the premiership increased and revived as the result of the publication in January 1964 of Randolph Churchill's book, 'The Fight for the Tory Leadership', and of Ian Macleod's reply in the *Spectator*, issue of 10th January. Several distinct areas were discernible where speculation seemed to be worth while.

Soundings within the party occurred, as noted above, on an apparently systematic basis and the results were given to Macmillan by reporters who delivered their findings separately, but then together, in Macmillan's hospital room. The full story of the inquiries is not yet known but it may be that canvassing, rather than mere sounding, occurred—that the pollsters were less than objective in their work. Macleod said that the reported results of the Cabinet soundings were absurd. It was alleged that Lord Dilhorne, the Lord Chancellor, had canvassed for Home at Blackpool, saying that Macmillan, when fit, would be willing to serve under him. But chief interest centred on the activities of Martin Redmayne: Macleod stated that the Chief Whip had worked hard to secure the maximum support for Home. Other comment on Redmayne's part in the carrying out of soundings among M.P.s put emphasis on a possibly more oblique rôle. Redmayne's activities—involving questions about first, second, and third choices, and about those not wanted 'at any price'—may have involved some 'guidance from above', some unwarranted weighting of opinion, some unconscious distortion whereby casual and incidental praise for Home was translated into positive 'first-choice' support.

Humphrey Berkeley (*The Guardian*, 19th Oct., 1963) has said that Home would not have been elected by any method of direct election. To similarly critical observers the soundings which took place were undemocratic, inefficient, and furtive—there was contradiction, misrepresentation, and suppression of facts. In assessing the *intensity* of feeling, Redmayne thereby rendered some Conservatives 'more equal then others'. (Redmayne has admitted that weighting occurred, and has defended it. See *Listener*, 19th Dec. 1963.)

Defenders of the October 1963 decision pointed to the fact that the Conservative system of selecting leaders took into account the intensity of feeling both for and against runners; it was thus acceptable that a man with the 'first choices' should not necessarily be elected. Redmayne has said that Home, in fact, had a narrow margin of 'first choices'.

A further distinct criticism brought echoes of 1957. The soundings, it was said, were not taken seriously: an alternative vote system, opposed by the Conservatives for the country as a whole, was used as an expedient—rough and ready, hastily concocted, and insufficiently explained. No one was sure who was running and who not: the final victor was for long not even regarded as a starter in the race. Macleod has declared that, twenty-four hours before Home was called to the Palace, he had no idea of what was happening. (There is some doubt as to whether Macleod could really have been so innocent after the events of Blackpool, when Home's popularity was manifest.)

Did Macmillan impose his own man on the party? Macmillan may have had Hailsham in his mind as the most acceptable leader for the party until very late in proceedings: it is alleged that, at the end of September, he encouraged Hailsham; it may only have been, however, that he stated a view that Hailsham's peerage should not debar him from the premiership. On the other hand, Macmillan may have always had his old friend Home in mind—one report has it that, of several approaches to Home by Macmillan, one was as early as the middle of 1963, during the Profumo scandal.

If Macmillan was unable to influence the soundings, did he nevertheless decide the issue by his dominance over the timing of events? Criticism was made of the speed with which he sent his views to the Palace, as cabinet opinion was seen to be rallying round Butler. (A separate issue concerns the speed with which the Queen sent for Home, without the usual twenty-four-hour delay after the resignation of the outgoing premier. The Queen did not immediately offer Home the job, he was given time to think about it. In any case, it can be argued that it was no part of the Queen's task, by delay, to help liberalize the Conservative Party.)

Even if adverse criticism of Macmillan is wholly valid it seems evident that he cannot be held fully responsible for the outcome of the Conservative leadership contest. The Conservative leadership, collectively, were very late in coming together to support Butler. The rivals for the leadership were inept: enemies were seen in the wrong places; no time was left for the support of the majority's last hard choice.

Much dubious mythology surrounds the history of the 'emergence' of Conservative leaders. Rarely has succession been entirely smooth—all elements of the party have been involved at one time or another in violent differences of opinion. The 1963 succession was an awkward mixture of the old 'customary processes' and new democratic polling, which offended many people.

Butler's personality and record were issues in the succession. His sly, intellectual jokes were disliked, his lack of political aggression (his lack of 'soldierly virtues') deplored, his stand on Suez, corporal punishment, and Central Africa regretted. His positive assistance to the party in helping to build the Welfare State and improve party organization was apparently forgotten.

One can still ask whether the Conservative Party would have rallied to Butler as it rallied to Home, and wonder whether Butler had enough 'first choices' after all. After Home had been called to the Palace Butler was in a difficult position—his agreement to serve under Home does not necessarily show that 'Macmillan's choice' was right for the party. Should Home have withdrawn from the contest when support for Butler became solidly evident, instead of 'walking backwards into the ring'?

In January 1964 Sir Alec Home let it be known that he would accept an inquiry into the processes of election to leadership of the Conservative Party: there were two conditions—that the inquiry would occur after the general election, and that it would not be held in circumstances which indicated lack of confidence in his own leadership.

3. Party Politics: Labour

(i) *Constituent Elements*. The Labour Party is composed of about 600 constituency parties, nearly ninety nationally affiliated trade unions, four Socialist societies (the Fabians being the best known), and one co-operative society. It is usual to say that the Trade Union Congress, as such, has no formal link with the Labour Party, although the important trade union members of the one are also members of the other. It is often suggested that the T.U.C. has a largely industrial task and has to treat with Conservative as well as with Labour governments. In fact, the T.U.C. has an organic link with the Labour Party and the Co-operative Union through the National Council of Labour—once a co-ordinating body for joint action and common policy on all matters affecting workers but now obsolete except for purposes of liaison. More important, the T.U.C. General Council and the Labour Party have representative meetings when the occasion demands—the 1961 reformulation of defence policy being an example. (See Vol. II, p. 271.) For many years the T.U.C. and the Labour Party occupied the same building.

(ii) *Centres of Power: Opportunities for Dissension.* Just as there are several elements which go to make up the Labour Party so there are also several centres of decision-making—in the Parliamentary Party, the National Executive Committee, and the Annual Conference. (It is convenient at this point to say that the Parliamentary Labour Party, composed of Labour M.P.s, is a body separate from the party outside Parliament, although, as we shall see, this statement calls for some discussion.) The unions hold predominant power at the Annual Conference, the party's ruling body, and on the National Executive Committee, which carries out conference decisions and interprets policy between conferences, and administers the party headquarters, Transport House.

As far as policy decisions and policy disputes are concerned, Martin Harrison ('The Trade Unions and the Labour Party since 1945', 1960) has warned us not to regard the trade unions as a homogeneous group:

> . . . the stereotyped image of the unions as a sort of orthodox lump of suet pudding clogging the party's progress is a potentially dangerous over-simplification.

The occasions when a clear-cut trade union versus constituency party split had occurred were limited—there had been perhaps a half a dozen such splits since the war, on issues of varying importance. There was no definite split between right-wing trade unions and left-wing constituency parties. When Ernest Bevin, leader of the giant Transport and General Workers' Union, dominated the conference he gained support from the constituency parties as well as from the unions.

Bevin died in 1950 and his successor as leader of the Transport Workers, Arthur Deakin, ruled until 1955. Right-wing political and right-wing industrial elements of the Labour Party during this time enjoyed an 'age of stability'. The support of the unions for the right-wing political leaders did cause some resentment among left-wing politicians. So wide did the split between union and political elements seem at Margate in 1953 that Deakin threatened that the trade unions might break with the party. In 1954 the Labour Party was split on the issues of German rearmament and the South East Asia Treaty Organization: the Bevanites rallied the majority of the constituencies but were defeated by the trade union steamroller. In 1956 the National Executive censured Ian Mikardo for an attack in the Socialist *Tribune* directed against the T.U.C.—*Tribune* had previously made several attacks on trade union leaders and had earned the censure of the National Executive.

After the reconciliation of Bevan and Gaitskell in 1957 (see Introduction, p. 19) left-wing attacks on the party leadership increased, supported by some left-wing unions. The position of the right-wing parliamentary leaders was precarious:

> . . . uncertainty is created by sudden changes in top union personnel. The Transport Workers swing from Right to Left with the transition from Deakin to Cousins. The Engineers' vote might switch completely if five more Communists were elected to its National Committee. The Miners may suddenly move Left if, as many observers expect, they shortly elect a Communist president. Such erratic changes make a strong and consistent political leadership extremely difficult. (A. Crosland, *Spectator*, 17th June 1960.)

After 1959, in some disarray after three election defeats, the Labour Party was split over defence, nationalization, and the nature of the Socialist challenge to the 'affluent society'. The left-wing, right-wing split of the party continued: the crucial change was that the left-wing politicians were now supported by an immensely powerful trade union leader—Frank Cousins of the Transport Workers. (Deakin was succeeded in 1955 by Tiffin who himself died within a few months. Cousins succeeded Tiffin.) Whereas in previous years the right-wing Labour leadership had been able to rely on the backing of trade union votes at the Annual Conference, in 1960, when the 'official' defence policy was rejected, (see p. 127), the block vote 'turned traitor'. (Normally trade unions, constituency parties, and socialist societies cast their votes in a single unit: this practice is known as 'block voting'.)

While complaints against the unions had usually come from the left of the party, the result of 1960 was that a right-wing bid for freedom from union control was contemplated. There was begun much rethinking of Labour's constitutional theory and demands for constitutional reform were made.

(iii) *The 1960 Dilemma.* After the 1960 defence split and the defeat of the platform at the party conference there was revived the debate as to whether conference decisions were mandatory on the Parliamentary Labour Party.

In July 1960 the National Executive had approved a document, 'Constitution of the Labour Party', which sought to clarify the situation. The document quoted a motion carried at the Annual Conference of 1907 which declared:

> . . . resolutions instructing the Parliamentary Party as to their action in the House of Commons [should] be taken as the opinions of the Conference, on the understanding that the time and method of giving effect to these instructions be left to the Party in the House in conjunction with the National Executive.

This declaration, stated the 1960 document, still remained the definitive statement of the relationship between the Parliamentary Labour Party and the Party as a whole. While the Parliamentary Labour Party could not for long remain at loggerheads with Conference without disrupting the Party:

> . . . the Parliamentary Party could not maintain its position in the country if it could be demonstrated that it was at any time or in any way subject to dictation from an outside body which, however representative of the Party, could not be regarded as representative of the country.

The document ended by stating:

> The Election Manifesto, which the National Executive Committee and the Parliamentary Committee are empowered to draw up on the eve of a General Election, is based on policy decision made by Annual Conference, but it may include matters which Conference has not had the opportunity to discuss. This Manifesto, on which its members are elected, is the one thing to which, under the constitution, the Parliamentary Party is bound.

'Labour in the Sixties', a report published by the National Executive in July 1960, stated (pages 19–20) that since Labour was a democratic party there were several centres of decision-making within the movement and, therefore, it was not possible (for any one centre) to lay down policy—it had to be agreed. The party urgently needed new machinery for consultation that would bring into regular contact the different decision-making centres of the party: regular consultation at, say, three-monthly intervals might take place between leaders of the affiliated unions, the Parliamentary Party and the National Executive Committee. The meetings would constitute a forum, not a new policy-making body.

The National Executive Committee, at its pre-conference meeting on the 2nd October 1960, showed some disunity on the question of the policy-making authority of the Annual Conference. It passed for discussion at Conference the following resolution:

> This conference reaffirms that the policy of the Labour Party, to be pursued nationally and in Parliament on questions of principle, shall be determined by Annual Conference. While acknowledging that the day-to-day tactics in Parliament must be the job of the Parliamentary Labour Party, this conference declares that Labour policy is decided by party conference which is the final authority.

The resolution, passed by only twelve votes to eleven in the Executive, was accepted by Conference by a large majority.

When the 1960 Labour Party Conference rejected the National Executive Committee policy on defence and accepted Frank Cousins's unilateralist motion a situation was created which posed special problems for the party. It became totally inadequate, in seeking to heal this new Labour rift, to repeat the old formula that Conference decided principles and the Parliamentary Party tactics. It was also inadequate to suggest that yet another forum for the discussion of

Labour policy was required. Conference was unilateralist and the Parliamentary Party (largely but not wholly) multilateralist, that is to say the latter accepted, for the time being, the need for a Western nuclear deterrent. The dispute was not over the tactics to be followed in regard to a principle accepted by all party elements: the dispute was over the principle itself. Either the Parliamentary Party accepted Conference's decision on unilateralism and reversed overnight its policy in Parliament or else it maintained its acceptance of the Western nuclear deterrent and flouted the wishes of Conference.

In the defence debate of December 1960 nearly seventy unilateralist M.P.s abstained from voting on their party's motion, which criticized the Government but continued to show an acceptance of the collective use of nuclear weapons. After the 1961 spring conferences of some important trade unions and the reversal of their unilateralist policies of the previous year, it appeared that Gaitskell would once again secure a majority at the Labour Conference. Although, as seen elsewhere (Vol. II, p. 272), the Crossman compromise defence policy was rejected by the National Executive and Cousins found it necessary to reassert his unilateralism, a highly dangerous period in Labour Party history had ended.

(iv) *Constitutional Reform.* Consequent on the events described above suggestions were made that changes in the decision-making machinery of the Labour Party should take place—so that greater authority should be vested in the parliamentary leaders, and that there might be no recurrence of those dangers inherent in the situation following the 1960 Conference. One writer suggested a Labour 'Royal Commission' under Attlee or Morrison: other, more specific, recommendations were made. The chief of these related to Labour's Conference and its National Executive.

At the Labour Party Annual Conference unions enjoy predominant voting-power: the five biggest unions command about half the votes and one union, the Transport and General Workers, has as many votes as all the constituency parties put together. The system of 'block-voting' is generally, but not invariably, used—unions cast their total vote either for or against a motion. Before the defeat of the platform on the defence issue in 1960, complaints against the block-vote commonly came from the left of the party: it was argued that the block-vote disheartened small organizations within the party, discouraged responsible voting, aggravated the possibility of union-made majorities, and imposed artificial unity—as far as German rearmament was concerned, for example, suppression of opposition minorities in one or two of the large unions, it was alleged, had made all the difference in the outcome of the debate within the party.

Subsequent to the 1960 Labour Conference, complaints against the block-vote came from the right of the party. At the Conference itself, just before the vote on defence, Gaitskell said:

> In a few minutes the Conference will make its decision. Most of the votes, I know, are predetermined and we have been told what is likely to happen. We know how it comes about. I sometimes think, frankly, that the system we have, by which great unions decide their policy before even their conferences can consider the (Labour) Executive recommendations is not really a very wise one or a good one. Perhaps in a calmer moment this situation could be looked at. (Conference Report, p. 201.)

This invitation was an interesting one since it raised again the question as to how, in the unions affiliated to the Labour Party, political decisions were reached. Gaitskell was not the first to complain that the trade unions made their political decisions before the Labour Party Conference debate was heard. Jay has even suggested that the Labour Conference should be held in May instead of October: this, he has said, would remove the impression given to the public that the Labour Conference merely endorsed trade union conference decisions. The Labour Party would make the decisions and the unions and the T.U.C. would hold their conferences in later months to discuss them.

However interesting the question as to how trade unions reach their political decisions we must confine ourselves here to the reality of their conference voting-power. The most important factor to be considered in estimating resistance to possible constitutional changes in the Labour Party, it has been held, is a financial one. The trade unions are said to be the paymasters of the party. But are they?

It has been claimed that the unions are over-represented at Labour Conference on the ground that trade union financial aid to the party at national level, which seems to give the unions the right to a predominant voice, distorts the true picture of Labour finance as a whole.

There is much expenditure at the local constituency level but, since information about this is not collated, the proportions of national and local party spending cannot be compared. Mikardo, a left-wing Socialist, has said that unions finance, not five-sixths of Labour expenditure, but only one-third: Harrison ('Trade Unions and the Labour Party since 1945'), puts the figure at seven-tenths.

The Political Funds of the trade unions are the result of the collection of a political levy on members, taken as part of their union subscriptions. The money raised for political purposes is used to make affiliations to the Labour Party, for subscriptions to the party's Election Fund, and, locally, for subsidies to constituencies—either as affiliation fees or as grants to sponsored candidates or Members. One hundred and nineteen unions engaged in political activities in 1959 and the average political contribution was 2s. 2d. per member. (1959 Report of the Chief Registrar of Friendly Societies, Part Four, p. 1.) In this year only eighty-seven unions were affiliated to the Labour Party.

Of over seven-and-a-half million members in the 119 unions mentioned above, 11·9 per cent. 'contracted out'. Objection is often taken to the system whereby a union member has to contract out if he wishes not to pay a political levy. Some Conservatives maintain that a union member should have to exercise his initiative to 'contract in', as during the years between 1927 and 1946, more firmly to show his political interest. Ray Mawby, M.P., a Conservative and a member of the Electrical Trades Union, has declared that the 1959 General Election showed that over 3,000,000 trade unionists had voted Conservative, whereas only 1,000,000 had taken the trouble to contract out from paying political dues to the Labour Party.

The Conservative Party, by common consent, receives large funds from business and industry—it does not publish accounts. (Labour believes that the Conservatives spent £2,000,000 before the last election.) The money, presumably, is part of the price paid by the general public for goods and services, being a cost on the public and not on business profits. Opponents of people like Ray Mawby ask how the 14,000,000 workers who voted against his party in 1959 can contract out of this particular political levy.

It is when one examines trade union contributions both in normal years and at the time of general elections that one realizes how important the trade unions are. In 1959, contributions to the party were made up as follows:

> *General Fund*
> From the Trade Unions   £214,000 approx.
> From the Constituency Parties   £39,000 approx.
>
> *Election Fund*
> From the Trade Unions   £221,000 approx.
> From the Constituency Parties   £3,000 approx.

(1960 Labour Party Report, p. 48.)

These figures show clearly the importance of union support to the Labour Party—in a very real sense, the unions *are* the Labour Party at the national level.

In 1959 the Election Fund reached £325,000. In the spring of 1963 Labour's leaders were seeking the support of the unions for the coming election. On 15th March Wilson and other leaders discussed their plans for organizing and financing a major propaganda drive with about a hundred trade union chiefs. Before this particular appeal the Labour Party had £300,000 in its Election Fund: various reports put the final target figure at £500,000, £800,000, and £1,000,000. With much optimism existing in the party the ambitious million mark may be reached: the biggest of the unions, the Transport Workers, contributed £35,000 to the Election Fund in 1959, but £75,000 in March 1963.

Taking into account contributions made to the Election Fund one has to modify one's feeling that the unions, calculating on a cost-per-vote basis, secure a good bargain at Labour Conference. Martin Harrison comments that the union contributions to Labour are so low that Transport House is starved of vital services. This may be so but then the trade unions have their own financial worries (see Vol. II, p. 127).

Coming to the point as it concerns us here, reformers would like to scale-down union voting-power at Labour Conference, at the same time increasing constituency party votes. In 1956 Victory for Socialism suggested that trade unions should affiliate to the party at the local level only and enjoy no national voting power.

To turn to representation of the National Executive. The nationally affiliated unions elect twelve of the twenty-eight member Executive and have the chief voice, at Conference, in electing the five women representatives and the party treasurer. The parliamentary leader and his deputy sit on the Executive *ex officio*, and other politicians, as opposed to trade unionists, sit with them. However, although a substantial number of the National Executive Committee members are influential members of the Parliamentary Party, and although their greater political experience (especially in foreign affairs) tends to take initiative and leadership in policy-making away from the trade union members, some discontent has been felt at the method of election of these people.

In addition to the above, the claim has been made that the five women's seats on the Executive are an anachronism—the party has always been dedicated to the equality of the sexes, but this has been achieved and there is no justification for separate women's representatives.

The Parliamentary Party members who are elected to the National Executive go as representatives of the constituency parties. These candidates, it has been claimed, take part in elections which are nothing but political auctions—M.P.s outdo each other in professions of Socialist virtue.

The radical suggestion has been made that the constitution of the party should be changed so as to give the Parliamentary Labour Party direct representation on the Executive. The P.L.P. is elected by the mass of voters and owes its existence to them: if the suggested change were made Labour voters, and not just active party minorities, would be represented on the Executive and the full freedom of the P.L.P. would be more evident to the public.

Further, say the reformers, the five women's seats should be abolished and the five seats given to the politicians. If this were done then there would be almost an exact balance of trade unionists and others on the Executive, and the Executive would be 'fairer' since it would have ceased to be elected by a few constituency activists and a handful of trade union leaders. (It is generally assumed that the largest unions have an informal agreement as to representation on the Executive.)

Strong vested interests stand in the way of a change in the balance of the National Executive in favour of the Parliamentary Party. Politicians like Barbara Castle and Tom Driberg, who have in the past been elected to the N.E.C. by the constituency parties, might have less chance of election from the P.L.P. itself, or from constituency parties to which unions were more directly affiliated. The chief objections to change, however, would come not from individuals but from the trade unions—these are very suspicious of any idea of the reallocation of power within the party.

Already, in the decline of the number of trade union M.P.s, the unions have important cause for complaint. About a hundred Labour M.P.s are 'sponsored', each having been nominated by a trade union and accepted by a constituency party; they are then said to be 'trade union Members' since they continue to receive financial help from their nominating unions. The payment of election expenses and allowances to M.P.s by trade union originated in the days when M.P.s were not paid and could not support themselves. In the early days of the Labour Party almost all its M.P.s were sponsored—in 1918 forty-nine out of fifty-seven. In 1955 only 96 of 277 were sponsored: in 1959 only 93 of 258.

Among the reasons for the decline of the number of sponsored trade union M.P.s is the fact that the unions have had the custom of 'retiring' old officials to the House—the seat being a reward for past services—while keeping able youngsters for union work. In 1957 Richard Crossman caused an 'incident' by commenting adversely on the quality of trade union Members: of over ninety, he said, only four suggested themselves for key party jobs. Trade unions may not play a continuous part in constituency activities, so even the first-class union nominee may be resented by the local party. A further suggested cause of resentment is that unions are willing to sponsor candidates only for winnable seats. (In 1959 there were 93 successful union candidates from a total of 129.)

The unions have not accepted the decline of their fortunes without complaint. When the late Morgan Phillips, Secretary of the party, attempted to secure the candidacy of North East Derbyshire his move was welcomed by one journal as an attempt to take over one of the trade union 'rotten boroughs', 'age-old icebergs which threaten the Labour Party's voyage in modern politics'. The National Union of Miners put an end to the hopes of the aspiring candidate. Sir Tom Williamson, formerly General Secretary of the General and Municipal Workers, speaking as Chairman of the T.U.C. in 1957, said that the decline of trade union M.P.s was 'just not good enough': his union had once had fifteen, now they had only three.

While one must record union complaints against Labour candidates as being too often 'soft-spoken middle-class nominees', against middle-class domination of the party, one must not forget complaints made by union M.P.s against their sponsors. Trade union Members have increasingly felt that they have been by-passed by their own unions who have preferred direct contact with government departments to indirect contacts through the House of Commons.

The unions are making moves to improve their position in the Labour ranks in Parliament. Frank Cousins spoke of his union's list of candidates for parliamentary elections in the following terms:

> What we are doing now is bringing the list up to date. We feel we can find new capable candidates for submission among the younger members of our movement, and that is why I made the particular appeal to the young people to come forward and help us. (*The Guardian*, 2nd April 1962.)

The amalgamated Engineering Union have run week-long residential courses for their potential parliamentary candidates.

(v) *The McKenzie Thesis.* As far as its constitutional arrangements are concerned the Labour Party has long suffered from a split mind—on the one hand proudly declaring the democratic nature of the mass-control of the party, on the other asserting the independence from external control of the Parliamentary Party, which has responsibilities not only to its party apparatus outside Parliament but also to the electorate at large.

Unlike the Labour Party, the Conservative Party was first formed inside Parliament. This is one of the reasons why in the Conservative Party there is emphasis on leadership and the concentration of power in the hands of the leader, whereas in the Labour Party the emphasis is on 'the movement', and on the dispersal of power. In his comprehensive review of the distribution of power within our two main parties, 'British Political Parties' (1955), Robert McKenzie laid great

stress on the fact that the party leaders were potential Prime Ministers.
As Prime Ministers they interited a post of great power and independence—this fact, and not the internal constitutional mechanism
of the parties was the governing factor determining the rôle each leader
was able to play in party politics. In acknowledging freely his leadership, the Conservative Party was merely protecting the leader against
the day when he became Prime Minister. Despite their insistence on
democratic decision-making procedures, the members of the Labour
Party had also to accept the authority of its parliamentary leader.
Although the Labour Party had long been reluctant to do this, as
far as authority was balanced with democracy in both major British
parties there was little to choose between the independence of Labour
and Conservative leaders. As far as democratic machinery was concerned the Conservative organization was a transparent sham, the
Labour Party an opaque one.

Robert McKenzie's near-equation of Labour and Conservative
democratic machinery caused a series of battles, or skirmishes. Study
of the 'McKenzie thesis' will help us get to the heart of the political
parties and enable us to make a summary of the sections which have
preceded. To begin with, some elaboration of the thesis should be
allowed:

> My central argument with respect to the Labour Party . . . was this: because
> the party accepts the conventions of parliamentary and Cabinet government,
> final authority in the determination of policy must rest, whatever the party
> constitution may appear to imply, with the parliamentary party and its
> leaders. Of course the few hundred thousand activists in the party, repre-
> sented at annual conference, exert an influence in determining the party's
> policy (as, on rarer occasions, their opposite numbers do in the Conservative
> Party). But they cannot direct the Parliamentary Party to adopt policies to
> which it is opposed. (*New Statesman*, 30th June 1961.)

And, a year earlier:

> The Labour leader in opposition is admittedly in a far more exposed position.
> But his position is not necessarily more insecure than that of the Conservative
> leader *so long as he retains the co-operation of a reasonably united team of parlia-
> mentarians, and so long as they in turn can rely on a working alliance with a group
> of leading trade unionists who understand the need to protect the parliamentary party
> and its leaders against attempts to reduce them to the status of mouthpieces of the
> party conference.* [My italics.] (*New Statesman*, 18th June 1960.)

And, in the same place:

> I never for a moment was foolish enough to suggest that *machinery* by which the ascendancy of Labour's parliamentary leaders was normally secured [while in opposition] was identical to that of the Conservative Party.

The reservations contained in the last two quotations are crucial: McKenzie appears to give much of his case away.

McKenzie's chief antagonist has been Richard Crossman. The latter has said:

> Like the U.S., the Labour Party has been endowed with a completely unworkable constitution; and the test of a Socialist leader, as of an American President, is whether he can make it work satisfactorily. If he fails and resorts to constitutional reform in order to make good the defects of his leadership, he gets nowhere. (*New Statesman*, 6th August 1960.)

And:

> Sovereignty in the Labour Party is divided between the parliamentary and the extra-parliamentary party, with the latter the final authority on policy issues. If either side tries to subject the other to its orders, the result is a deadlock, which must at all costs be resolved at the next conference. (*New Statesman*, 7th July 1961.)

In 1960 and 1961 the disputes within the Labour Party amounted virtually to a civil war—they indicated that Gaitskell, as a potential Prime Minister, did not find it easy to enforce his will on the party as a whole. Gaitskell's election to the leadership had been challenged and he continued to be unacceptable to a substantial minority of the party—in November 1960 Wilson stood against him in the Parliamentary Labour Party elections, the first such formal revolt in the history of the party.

While it would not be true to say that the Conservative Party is a homogeneous group of like-minded people (a common assumption), it would be true to say that the Labour Party is much more a federation of shades of political opinion. Professor Finer and his colleagues have shown that revolts in the Labour Party coalesce into a broad-front opposition. (See reference to 'Backbench Opinion in the House of Commons 1955–1959', p. 99.) McKenzie shows a chink in his defences when, in the second (1963) edition of his book he admits:

> One phrase in the preface to the first edition, to the effect that this book was 'not concerned with party ideologies or programmes', undoubtedly proved

> misleading . . . of course, this book is deeply concerned with the ideo-
> logical issues and policy disputes which have racked the parties, and the
> ways in which they have debated and resolved these controversies. (p. ix.)

Dissidents, in rebelling, are able to take advantage of the ample
opportunities afforded by Labour's democratic mechanism for party
decision-making and dissident opinions seem to be altogether more
serious for Labour than for the Conservative Party—the latter can
command a high degree of unity because of its ingrained belief in
loyalty to the leader.

If one equates the Conservative and Labour democracy as McKenzie
has done, and then proceeds to argue that Labour must change itself
to remove 'complications' then this would seem to constitute a significant dilution of the original statement or argument. McKenzie has
said:

> . . . the Labour Party increasingly resembles some primeval beast, huge and
> still immensely powerful, which has manifestly failed to come to terms with
> its environment.
> And now, in the current struggle over its new defence policy, the party is
> demonstrating the *disastrous consequences* [my italics] of its failure to revise the
> policy-making provisions of its archaic constitution. The basic problem is
> that 'inner-party democracy', as conceived in the Labour Party constitution,
> is incompatible with our system of Parliamentary government.
> . . . the events since last October show on how precarious a foundation the
> system rests. It depends, above all else, on the presence on Labour's front
> bench of a reasonably united team of Parliamentary leaders. . . . In addition,
> if Labour's machinery is to work smoothly, it must be able to rely on a work-
> ing alliance between the Parliamentary leaders and a sufficient number of
> leading trade unionists. . . .
> Since last October, this machinery has broken down more completely than
> ever before.
> . . . what will happen to this doctrine (of the autonomous nature of the
> Parliamentary Party) if the annual conference 'directs' the Parliamentary
> Party to adopt defence and foreign policies which would, in effect, commit
> the party to neutralism? Then, at last, the Labour Party would have to
> clear its mind on 'inner-party democracy' and undertake a wholesale re-
> vision of the party constitution. (*Observer*, 12th June 1960.)

And:

> My only quarrel with Mr. (Martin) Harrison is that, like Mr. Crossman, he
> appears to feel that the party constitution must be treated as sacrosanct. Is it

really true that the 'party of progress and planning' is incapable of rationally re-examining its own structure? (*New Statesman*, 18th June 1960.)

After all this the question which comes to one's mind is: if the Parliamentary leadership in the Labour Party approximates in independence to that of the Conservative, why bother to reform the party? To avoid inconvenience? Or, seeing that a 'wholesale revision of the party constitution' is contemplated, is it to avoid the horrible death of a primeval beast? Mr. McKenzie says:

> . . . Labour should appoint a party 'Royal Commission' to re-examine its own decision-making processes and to study the procedures used by Socialist parties elsewhere to avoid some of the internal complications which have plagued the Labour Party and hampered its effectiveness. (*New Statesman*, 28th July 1961.)

Mr. Wyatt's speech on 10th June 1960, when he described Frank Cousins as 'the bully with the block vote', showed fear of, or awareness of, the possible need to act:

> If Mr. Cousins persists in this disloyal course he will force the Labour Party into creating a completely different relationship with the trade unions under which Mr. Cousin's power to damage the party he says he supports will be reduced to zero. (*The Guardian*, 11th June 1960.)

As far as long-term constitutional tensions are concerned, both parties can put their democracy to the test by destroying themselves as cohesive bodies. In 1960 there arose a situation where the Labour Party had the opportunity to prove its democratic nature and its rejection of Conservative-type authoritarianism by such revolutionary destruction. In 1960 Gaitskell was defeated at Conference (see also Vol. II, p. 270) but retrieved his position by success at Conference in 1961. The two major contestants in the dispute we have been following took diametrically opposed views of these events. The Crossman view was that Gaitskell had had to fight to have his defence policy accepted: his effort to gain a reversal at Conference proved that the Parliamentary Party and the Conference could not *direct* each other. Conference's position was vindicated. The McKenzie case was that Gaitskell did not alter his defence policy and . . . 'after a little hard work by the multilateralists, enough unions [were] won round to reverse the

Scarborough decision'. (*New Statesman*, 14th July 1961.) Gaitskell's, or rather the Parliamentary Party's, authority was vindicated.

The Guardian view of affairs was that the McKenzie thesis was correct. The real significance of Gaitskell's victory had been that it had enormously increased the power of the parliamentary leadership and made the conference less important than it had ever been. Whatever may have been the case in the past, the parliamentary leader in the future would have less need to fear the consequences of defying the party outside Parliament. Gaitskell's victory had made formal amendment of the party constitution unnecessary. (13th July 1961.)

Crossman, about this time, referred to what he imagined would be McKenzie's 'knock-out question': what would be the position in the Labour Party if conference rejected the Parliamentary Party two years running. His answer would be—the party would tear itself to pieces. Henry Pelling, the Labour historian, supported Crossman in the above disputation. He alleged that McKenzie had never got the Labour Party quite right. The absence of effective treatment of the rôle of the trade unions, and especially the trade union leadership, could only be regarded as a serious defect, which tended to vitiate the general conclusions about the power-structure of the Labour Party. (*New Statesman*, 7th July 1961.) Subsequently, Pelling again made a comment which can be related to that made by Crossman and reported above. McKenzie's agreement on the importance of trade union leadership stood in sharp contrast to his minimal view of the powers of conference. Did McKenzie maintain that the Parliamentary Labour Party could survive indefinitely because it had reversed one particular defeat? (*New Statesman*, 21st July 1961.)

One's own conclusions on the debate on the 'McKenzie thesis' might be as follows. 'British Political Parties' drew a rough similarity between our two major parties but the author overplayed his hand. His reservations, his admissions, detract so much from the original statement that it might have been wiser for him to have 'started at the other end'—to have concentrated not on the similarity between the parties but on the differences. Perhaps the falsity of the thesis arises from a non-recognition of the place of ideology in the Labour Party: the essential criticism of McKenzie seems to be, however, that he himself has acknowledged the fact that the Labour Party was, in 1960 and

1961, in danger of committing suicide. Yet the last word must be with McKenzie: he quotes ('British Political Parties', second edition, p. 641) Crossman with what at first sight seems devastating effect. Crossman, in his introduction to the 1963 edition of Bagehot's 'The English Constitution', says:

> (Hence) the concession in principle of sovereign powers to the delegates at the Annual Conference, and the removal in practice of most of this sovereignty through the trade union block vote on the one hand, and the complete independence of the Parliamentary Labour Party on the other.

(See also p. 92.)

(vi) *Survival of the Labour Alliance*. Consequent on recent troubles within the Labour Party political commentators have examined the possibility not only of a changed power-structure affecting Labour's Annual Conference and National Executive but also that of an ending of the alliance of political and industrial party elements. There have been signs of discontent among rank-and-file union members indicating their belief that their leaders ought to spend more time at their industrial tasks: leaders themselves have resented the amount of time they have had to spend on political issues.

George Woodcock, newly elected General Secretary of the T.U.C. in 1960, is said to dislike the 'political game', to be anxious that the T.U.C. should put its industrial interests first. A similar view was put very strongly by George Green, as General Secretary of the Civil Service Clerical Association, at the annual conference of the National Federation of Professional Workers in April 1961. Green said that it was time for the T.U.C. as a corporate body to depart from its close liaison with the Labour Party in its organizational links. The T.U.C. should leave those unions which wanted to preserve the direct link with the Labour Party to go and develop that connection at another time and in another place. If this could be done the T.U.C. would be able to embrace those organizations which wanted unity in pursuance of their economic and material wellbeing.

Green, a member of the T.U.C. General Council, said:

> The only indications of growth (in the T.U.C.) are in the field of organizations which do no necessarily desire the political expression which the older industrial trade unions have allowed to dictate their course. If the T.U.C.

is going to continue to grow by absorbing organizations which cater for non-manual workers it has, I think, to look at ways and means of persuading those organizations that in joining the T.U.C. they do not necessarily under-write the fortunes of a particular political party. It is a hard doctrine for many unions to face but I believe it is the answer in our time. (*The Guardian*, 1st May 1961.)

Elsewhere there have been suggestions that Labour's political side might benefit from a looser connection with the trade unions, such as exists between the unions and the Democrats in the United States. These suggestions relate to the unpopularity of trade unions with some sections of public opinion. (See Vol. II, p. 127.) At the moment, as part of the price it pays for the trade union connection, the Labour Party is blamed for unofficial strikes, although the strikers are not all Labour supporters.

It is difficult to contemplate the Labour Party in anything but its present form. From its very beginning the Party has been an alliance of political and industrial elements (see above, p. 4), linked together financially. To a significant extent the industrial and political elements are operated by a common personnel. One may begin to believe in the political independence of the Trades Union Congress when one sees Conservative and Liberal Parties sending representatives to the annual meetings.

4. *Party Politics: the Liberals*

The Liberals are a poor and struggling party. Their internal affairs have had less importance for the public than have those of the two major parties and, since the promise of office has not been for them, their disputes have not had the quality of earthquakes.

The 1958 Liberal Assembly was a fiasco—the platform and the floor could not hear each other, and the Chairman was deaf anyway. In debating Education, the Assembly reversed a decision and seemed to be unclear what it was voting for. The Liberals spent a long time discussing topics thought by many observers not to have much immediate political relevance—for example, Welsh devolution and co-ownership of industry. (Taxation of land values was debated—a subject of con-siderable immediate importance, then and now.) Skilled opponents were able to publicize the Assembly as an absurdity.

In 1960, 1100 Liberal delegates worked through an agenda which had been drastically cut, and was concrete and realistic: three principal debates took place—on Europe, the trade unions, and the Bomb. The Assembly also discussed tax incentives, the reform of company law, and redundancy and retraining in industry. The Assembly was quite disciplined, the programme went like clockwork, and the voting proceeded almost entirely as the party Executive wished. The younger delegates obviously wanted to get on with the job, the older ones were those who complained against the platform.

At the 1958 Assembly party administration was hotly attacked. It is relevant to say here that the Liberals have been woefully hampered by lack of funds. In its pamphlet, 'This is Your Party', published in September 1960, the Liberal Party declared that its annual budget was substantially below that of the Communist Party of Great Britain. Whereas Liberals spent £25,000 per annum, Labour spent £400,000— and Conservatives spent £450,000 on public relations alone. The party, said the pamphlet, needed at least £150,000 a year if it was to compete with its opponents. (Income in 1962 increased to £73,000 from £55,000 in the previous year.) In August 1963 Grimond launched a £500,000 election appeal.

As far as publicity is concerned the Liberals have strong competition from the Labour Party which receives technical assistance from the *Daily Mirror*, and from the Conservatives, who employ Messrs. Colman, Prentis and Varley. In January 1959 it was reported that Chorley Liberal Association was employing a firm of sales consultants —the first constituency party to do so.

In addition to attending to their publicity work at national and local levels, Liberals have had to make good the deficiencies of their ward and constituency organization. This organization is improving. On 9th January 1962 the party announced that its membership, after a three-month recruiting drive, had reached 243,600. (At this time the Conservatives estimated their membership at between two and two-and-a-half millions; Labour's individual membership was about 800,000; the Communists declared they had about 24,000 members.) In March 1964 Liberal membership had risen to 351,280.

In July 1963 there were 436 constituency associations affiliated to the Liberal Party. The party's 1963 report said that sixty-six full-time agents were employed, as compared with twenty-four a year previously. In addition, a further 162 known honorary agents had been chosen by constituencies. At national as well as local level a shortage of professional staff has thrown a tremendous burden onto the few officials and national leaders.

Aided by vigorous new lieutenants, Grimond has streamlined the Liberal Party's central organization. This has not been done without causing some dissension. In January 1960 it was announced that Herbert Harris would cease to be General Director—a Standing Committee and a Co-ordinating Secretary would do his work, and greater authority would devolve upon the various party headquarters departments. Harris subsequently complained about the manner of his dismissal—he felt he had been ostracized. The Editor of *Liberal News* resigned in sympathy. In April 1960, one of three Honorary Party Treasurers, Lieutenant-Colonel Lort-Phillips, resigned saying that his office had ceased to exist since the work was being done by the new Standing Committee.

Behind these events has been Grimond's desire to make the Liberals an efficient party. The allegation has been made that he has made it a less democratic party—the National Executive, replaced by the Standing Committee, has ceased to execute. Liberals as a whole may think that efficiency is worth the loss of a little democracy. (In 1960 the Standing Committee was enlarged to become the Organizing Committee, to remove suspicion that it was running the party.) Troubles continue, however: towards the end of 1963 there was a party squabble over the election of treasurers—the Executive and the constituencies being at odds.

Young Liberals have attracted some national attention by the energy of their activities. In October 1957, admitting that few people understood Liberal policies, they set out to 'put a face on Liberalism' by launching 'Operation Manifesto'. The ideas of two hundred Young Liberal branches were canvassed, embodied in a pamphlet, and discussed at a special conference in April 1959. In January 1961 the joint political committee of the National League of Young Liberals and the Union of Liberal Students launched the 'New Orbits' group, a focus for Liberal research projects.

5. *Local Government*

(i) *Local Authorities and Their Functions.* Local services to the public are performed by central government agencies such as the Post Offices and Labour Exchanges; by such statutory bodies as the National Coal Board, the Regional Hospital Boards, and the Milk Marketing Board; and, by the local authorities:

83	County Boroughs
61	County Councils
319	Non-County Boroughs
564	Urban District Councils
473	Rural District Councils

—and about 11,000 parishes. Additional to these local authorities is the London County Council, under which operate twenty-eight Metropolitan Borough Councils, and the Corporation of the City of London. Some 80,000 unpaid councillors direct the work of over 1,600,000 employees. (This is a pattern of government which is about to change —see below.)

It is possible to distinguish four broad groups of local authority functions:

Protective functions include policing proper and the regulation of such things as building and weights and measures.

Amenities provided by local authorities include care of roads, streets, bridges, lighting, baths, cleansing, sanitation and refuse removal.

Social Services managed locally embrace education, housing, public health and welfare services.

Trading is carried on by some authorities—in transport, water-supply, and markets.

Local government as we know it evolved from the need for local services and local regulation during the Industrial Revolution: by the end of the nineteenth century the civil service was organized in an efficient manner and the local authorities were no longer the only possible agents for the performance of local functions. There has, in fact, been much movement towards the centralization of government in Britain: there has been straightforward transfer of functions to the central government, and transfer to *ad hoc* authorities such as the Gas and Electricity Boards. The local authorities have lost passenger vehicle licensing, trunk roads, municipal hospitals, gas and electricity undertakings, the payment of public or national assistance, and rating valuation and assessment. Important (and costly) functions have been assumed: housing and slum clearance, welfare services for the old under the National Assistance Act of 1948, and the care of the young under the Children Act 1948 have helped to maintain the busyness, and costliness, of local government. While there has been much discussion of new ways of financing local government (see below) and relieving the local burden there have continued to be complaints about the decline of the local authority: in February 1964 the Chief Education Officer of Leeds wrote (*The Guardian*, 25th Feb. 1964) under the title, 'The dwindling local authority'—he was dealing with the question of the administration of teacher training colleges.

Within the framework of local government there has been a shift of power to the larger authorities who have taken on increased responsibility for such things as education, police, fire services, ambulance and personal health services, and town and country planning. Essential services—for example education, or policing—cannot be provided by small units. They need a considerable range of population and adequate financial resources to function properly. Large units are needed for town and country planning, sewage, and for housing.

Many of these functions were not thought of when our local government structure was laid down: as demand for them arose, local government structure was not reformed. Functions were either lost, because of inherent weakness of the local structure, or were given to the larger units of local government. Some people are not concerned about a decline of local self-government—they speak of the need for a National Education Service and a National Building Corporation. Others desire to prove that the local authorities can be efficient and administratively versatile—they wish to see the local authorities as partners and not mere agents of the central government.

Champions of local self-government claim that it is necessary to the working of a liberal democracy—it encourages people to take an active part in government, makes full use of their energy and vigour, and ensures a healthy division of powers between Whitehall and Market

Street. The public, however, is very apathetic towards local government and shows greater concern for national and international issues. Perhaps the local authorities are themselves to blame: they often neglect public relations. The National and Local Government Officers Association made a survey of town halls in 1959 and had many criticisms: accommodation was drab and there was a lack of central inquiry points, adequate signposting, proper facilities for interviews; there was a shortage of chairs and other simple amenities, and it was not an uncommon practice to leave inquirers to be dealt with by untrained juniors. Some local authorities publish bright broadsheets with local news, Cheltenham had the B.B.C. film a full council debate in 1960, but all too often the public is left in ignorance of the nature and significance of local government.

(ii) *Areas and Financial Resources.* The Local Government Act of 1888 laid down the main structure of our local authorities—it created sixty-two administrative counties, and sixty-one county boroughs. As far as the counties were concerned the 1888 boundaries were based on historic, traditional, and sentimental considerations, not wholly on considerations of administrative need. Boundaries did not always result in geographically ideal units and populations varied considerably—today the counties have populations varying between 20,000 and 1,000,000. County boroughs were to be created with a population of at least 50,000: twenty-two new county boroughs had been created by 1926, Doncaster being the last creation. In 1926, population requirements for the securing of borough status were raised—the figure of 50,000 was excessively low, even in 1888. Luton, Poole, and Ilford are among those towns which have failed to secure county borough status since 1926. Charles Hill, speaking during the debate on the Luton Bill in 1954, said that, of the existing eighty-three county boroughs, forty-three had smaller populations and smaller rateable values than Luton, and forty-four had a smaller penny-rate yield.

The desire for freedom from the county on the part of the rich borough has for many years caused much bitter controversy in local politics. Quite naturally, the counties have not wanted to be left with smaller populations, smaller areas, and greatly diminished incomes.

Lancashire, for example, has had to live with seventeen 'borough islands' within her boundaries. A second cause of conflict between the counties and the boroughs has been the question of the extension of borough boundaries. The 1888 Act provided for the extension of these boundaries: extensions have, in recent years, been on a restricted scale. To an increasing extent the boroughs have been short of land and have had to export their populations in some cases.

The conflicts between county and borough have absorbed much energy and have diverted attention from the important question of the reform of local government and have prevented fruitful co-operation in this direction.

The railways, the joint-stock banks, and the newspapers are among those institutions and industries which have, in the course of this century, grown into bigger units. In our social and economic life generally we are a group of densely populated geographical centres, the result of the coalescing of what were, earlier, separate and distinct industrial and economic units. In these large geographical growths— known conveniently as 'conurbations'—we have retained a haphazard pattern of local government. Only the London County Council, in part, has met the need for co-ordination. There has been a pressing need for the creation of properly sized units of local government, which might rule themselves more efficiently and secure greater freedom from Whitehall and Westminster.

In order to create 'areas of consciousness' reformers have said that boundaries should be redrawn according to the 'test of accessibility': observing the movements of population towards the larger shopping centres on Saturday or market day, they would designate particular towns and cities as local government centres, each of which would have its physical and demographic catchment area. The Manchester, Liverpool, Newcastle-on-Tyne areas, and so on, would then give us a reasonable network of local government. (See next section.)

The local authorities are of varied financial strength but, generally speaking, are poor. There has been an increasing dependence on central grants from the government and, in the early 'sixties, the ratio of grants to income from rates was 6:5. Expenditure continues to climb: this has been due, not only to inflation and the high cost of loans, but also to the increased amount of work asked of local authorities consequent on national programmes in education and welfare. A steep rise in local expenditure has been unavoidable.

In 1957 a political storm arose when the government announced an alteration of the method whereby exchequer aid was given to the local authorities. Circular 334 said that percentage grants for specific services—except police, housing and roads—were to be replaced by a general grant similar in total. The old percentage grant system ensured that the local authority received from the Treasury about 60 per cent. of the cost of approved projects whereas the new system of general, or 'block', grants fixed Treasury contributions, period by period. The new grant was to be distributed on a population basis, adjusted for numbers of children and old people: there was to be a method of reducing the government grant where rateable value was relatively high. (Part of the Rate Deficiency Grant was to be paid direct to the District Councils, instead of as previously through the County Councils, as one means of strengthening local government.)

Protests at the change came from many quarters, even from Conservative-controlled authorities. Since the main grant to each authority was no longer to be directly related to the local level of spending critics declared that the new system was an 'incentive to parsimony'. Particularly resented was the implication, seen in the Government's statement that the old system of grants had acted as an undiscriminating incentive to expenditure, that wasteful spending had occurred.

To try to ensure that future Treasury aid should be of a known figure and that percentage claims by local authorities should not bring unexpected burdens or importunate claims to Whitehall was perhaps a wise aim: the Government made its task much more difficult when it stated that the aim of the change was to give local authorities more freedom. Critics immediately pointed to the possibility of freedom in education leading to varying standards of provision. The control of exchequer aid, and not the enhancing of local democracy, was the aim of the Government. It should have stuck to this. (One must note that, after the 1958 Act and the introduction of the general grant system in the year 1959–60, an increase and not a decrease of government assistance to local authorities occurred.)

In January 1960 a Ratepayers' Party was formed in Manchester to wage war on the city's 'civic waste'. Experts have said that, as far as local government as a whole is concerned, efficiency and economy will be of only marginal help in solving the financial problem. They look instead to a change in the rating system. One problem has been the unjust incidence of rates. Lady Simon of Wythenshawe has written:

> The assessment of any property is the measure of that property's *liability* to contribute to public expenditure: it settles the proportionate payment to be made by the different classes of ratepayers in any area.

This, by itself, solves no problems. The Rating and Valuation Act 1961 included provision for the ending of industrial derating, and that of shops and offices. The purpose of revaluation, which came into force in April 1963, was to ensure that houses, industry, shops and offices would each pay rates at full current values. The 1963 change, however, was not radical.

Rates increases have lagged behind those of direct and indirect taxes, partly because the suggestion of a rise meets with strong local opposition, partly because revaluations have occurred at long and erratic intervals. Conservative and Labour Members jointly tabled a motion in the Commons in April 1962 demanding an inquiry into the rating system. The motion read:

> That this House, in view of the increasing amount of local government expenditure and the consequent dependence on the national exchequer for grants, urges Her Majesty's Government to appoint a committee to inquire into the rating system and the possibilities of alternative and more equitable ways of raising local revenue. (2nd April 1962.)

The Government had no ready answer: in 1957 a White Paper ('Local Government Finance', Cmnd 209) had rejected all currently discussed alternatives to the existing rating system. Reformers have suggested the taxation of site values, a local earnings tax, and a local tax of both real and personal property. Others have suggested a reduction of the total welfare burden on local funds: this could be done by imposing fees for education, and by removing subsidies from council rents. (There could be a relief of national funds by the imposition of a charge for visits to the doctor. See Volume Two, p. 227 and p. 232.)

(iii) *Local Government Reform.* The 1958 Local Government Act sought to give 'greater independence to local authorities in the spending of government grants' (see above). The most ambitious part of the

Act, however, concerned the review of local government areas. Two Commissions, for England and Wales, were to be set up, charged with the task of reviewing the organization of local government outside Greater London. The Commissions would review the areas of counties and county boroughs in 'General Review Areas', together with reviews of five 'Special Review Areas' in the Midlands and the North of England. In England the work of the Local Government Commission is proceeding in five main stages, the first having begun in January 1959. In the Commons on 4th December 1963 the Minister of Housing and Local Government reviewed progress:

> By April, 1965, we shall have Greater London [see below] and the West Midlands reorganized. We shall have a decision—I am not saying what that decision might be—on Tyneside, where an urban county has been proposed and perhaps the new arrangements in force. We shall have West Yorkshire settled, and Merseyside and South Lancashire well on the way. That covers, by April 1965, the six conurbations. In addition, Tees-side—where a single county borough has been proposed—should be settled by then. Again, I make no reference to what decision may be taken on that by the Government. In short, by April 1965, we shall have settled most of the business of local government reorganization and got much of it into operation.

In short, after years of government procrastination, the work of the Commissions represents what may be the beginning of the heroic period in local government reform.

In July 1957 there was announced in the Commons the setting up of a Royal Commission on Local Government in Greater London. Its terms of reference were:

> To examine the present system and working of local government in the Greater London area; to recommend whether any, and if so what, changes in the local government structure and the distribution of local authority functions in the area or any part of it would better secure effective and convenient local government; and to regard, for these purposes, local government as not including the administration of police, or of water.

The London County Council had been created in 1888 to administer a new county of London and eleven years later the county was divided into twenty-eight boroughs.

In October 1960 the Report of the Royal Commission recommended the extension of the County of London to take in the whole of Middlesex and parts of Surrey, Kent, Essex and Hertfordshire: the

Commission also recommended the creation of fifty-one Greater London boroughs of 100,000 to 250,000 inhabitants—this was to be effected by the amalgamation of the existing twenty-eight Metropolitan Boroughs with the sixty-six other local authorities in the area under review. The City of London would become the fifty-second borough. The 151-member London County Council would be replaced by a Council for Greater London with 155 members—one for each parliamentary constituency.

The Commission did not intend that the Council for Greater London should become a vast regional authority with concentrated powers: the new borough would be the primary unit of local government and would perform all functions except those which could be effectively performed only over the wider area—planning, education, traffic control, and fire and ambulance services.

The London Government Act 1963 allowed for the creation of fewer, and larger, boroughs than the Royal Commission had suggested —thirty-two instead of fifty-two. Their populations would range from 146,000 to 340,000. The Royal Commission had recommended that education should be the responsibility of the new boroughs and the Council for Greater London: the Bill gave responsibility to the new borough councils, save for a central area, corresponding to the old London County Council area, which was to be the responsibility of a special committee of the Greater London Council. (These educational arrangements in the central area were to be reviewed before 1970.)

The Press welcomed the 1962 London Government Bill: local authorities within the effected area were hostile. The Labour Party opposed the measures for various reasons: it objected to interference with the 'heart and centre of London's Government'. (Labour opposition, and popular opposition generally, led the Government to modify the Royal Commission's, and then its own White Paper (Cmnd 1562) proposals on education.) Labour's chief concern was, perhaps, that the change of boundaries threatened the party's firm control of the London County Council: in 'Twelve Wasted Years' (1963) it quotes the statement of a Bromley Borough Councillor:

> Frankly, and I speak as a Conservative, I wonder whether the whole underlying fact is not political, an attempt to correct by law something they have not been able to achieve by the ballot box. (p. 263.)

Councils for the new London Boroughs will come into being in May 1964 and the Greater London Council on 9th April 1964. For a transitional period until 1st April 1965 the new and old authorities will continue side-by-side. The plans may come to little: Labour has promised to halt the transfer of functions if it comes to power in 1964.

(iv) *Party Politics in Local Government.* Apathy towards local government can be explained by reference to the fact that local political debate covers only a narrow front, that local issues do not involve such major changes as those at national level, and that in local debate there is not a great deal of room for political manoeuvring, for violent clash on political principle. These suggestions are not wholly sound: in recent years the council chamber has been the forum for quite violent political debate—Nottingham has not been unique in attracting national attention to its council quarrels.

In pre-war days there was always more party control of the council chamber than was apparent to the public and it would be wrong to say that, in those days, all that mattered was free debate, the exercise of individual conscience and judgement, and co-operation between people of different parties. The power of majorities existed, in a less obvious and systematic manner than today, and on important political issues such as the Poor Law and Housing clashes of opinion could be as violent as clashes occurring today.

Party politics in local government cannot now be brushed aside as incidental to the administration of local affairs. Today, in many places, there has been a change in the way the council chamber is managed—party politics are dominant and we see parliamentary government in miniature, complete with whips, 'cabinets' of party leaderships, meaningless debates which follow the taking of decisions outside the chamber, and even party expulsions when councillors have not toed the party-line. The change came with Labour's post-war municipal successes. Labour did not originate caucus control in local government but began to practise it more thoroughly. In the allocation of offices in pre-war years, for example, practices varied: in some councils the majority party took all committee chairmanships, while in others there was a sharing according to the numerical strength of the parties. Coupled with the post-war development towards stricter party control of the local council chamber has been the taking by the majority party of a bigger share of offices—chairmanships, vice-chairmanships, aldermanic seats, and mayoralties:

> A new trend in local government theory can be drawn. . . . A majority of seats on a council, however small, is now taken to be a mandate for absolute control. It is the parliamentary outlook. Everything follows logically from this. It is seen at its most consistent in places like Bristol, where Labour takes full control even with a majority of four; but, when in a minority, moves into straight opposition. The idea is—no sharing of responsibility, no co-operation. (Roy Perrot, *The Guardian*, 6th Aug. 1959.)

Until Labour lost control of Nottingham in the spring of 1961 the city council's policy was virtually decided by a committee of eight, elected annually by the whole Labour group on the council. The Conservative opposition was not given a share of committee chairmanships and the practice of having, at any one time, a Conservative Lord Mayor with a Labour Sheriff (or vice versa) was no longer followed.

Commentators have objected to this kind of situation, to 'Tammany Hall' politics, on the grounds that it discredits local government, increases party bitterness unnecessarily, leads to the group in power disregarding public opinion (which would not occur if real debate still took place in the large council group), and to the displacement of experienced opponents from offices where their talents could well be used.

Apologists for the new system of local government declare that the use of words like 'Whips' and 'spoils' surrounds the subject of the place of party in local politics with an unnecessarily unpleasant atmosphere. There has been, they say, an enormous growth of local government work, particularly in the fields of education, health, welfare, and housing. Majority caucus control gets things done:

> The days of the independent member of the council raising an issue when and where he thought fit are over, and those of us who work and live in industrial areas know only to our cost what it means to rely upon the pre-war system as a means of achieving advances. . . . (*The Guardian*, letter, 18th Aug. 1959.)

Independent committees and departments are too unwieldy for speedy and radical decision-making: there is a definite need for a small political committee in local government—decisions have to be made by someone, better the majority's political committee than the un-elected officials. Where parties are weak, officials, and vested interests, are strong. Finally, say supporters of majority-party control in local affairs, a party will be judged on its record: power should thus go with responsibility. Under the pre-war system, blame could not be placed fairly and squarely where it belonged and the citizen's vote was less effective as an instrument of praise and blame.

II. JUSTICE: ADMINISTRATIVE LAW

6. *The Franks Report 1957*

Since the beginning of the century there has been a vast increase in the powers held by governments—for example in requisitioning, in their ability to grant agents rights of entry for the purposes of inspection, and in the granting of licences and foreign currency to traders. Some government powers have involved the exercise of unfettered discretion: the British Nationality Act 1948 gave to the Home Secretary the right to decide on applications for naturalization, there being no appeal from his decision; the Safeguarding of Employment (Northern Ireland) Act 1947 gave the Irish authorities power to exclude outsiders from the country, again with no provision for appeal. Some enactments have made way for government action which could result in unintended burdens and injustices: the Compensation (Defence) Act 1939 allowed for the payment by the Government of compensation for loss of rent on property taken over, but not for loss of goodwill. (On the question of market value and compulsory purchase see Town and Country Planning Act 1959.)

In the above cases the complaint is not that the Government will act beyond its powers or act unfairly, but that certain powers are not balanced by an acknowledged duty. A citizen might suffer, for example, because a government department had delayed the granting of import licences: he would have no remedy.

In the note sections below we examine various topics relating to the safeguarding of private rights: in this section we examine the proposition that we, in Britain, lack a regular system of administrative law to protect the citizens as a body from the arbitrary action of the State. Some optimists are undismayed by the increased powers of the State, they see the rise of administrative power as a useful instrument of planning in a period of rapid social change. The pessimists, on the other hand, have for many years thundered against the 'petty despots of Whitehall' and their 'impudent usurpations', and against the 'victories of public policy over private right'.

There exists today a real constitutional problem relating to the question as to how the individual citizen can be protected from the encroachments of the State, from the State's potential contempt for legal processes. Without forgetting those topics discussed in the notes below, one can say that British justice as far as criminal and civil disputes are concerned is good: we are deficient, however, in one field —administrative law. 'Our procedure for securing our personal freedom is efficient, but our procedure for preventing abuse of power is not' (Lord Denning). W. G. Friedmann says,

> Hostility to a systematic development of Administrative Law has not stopped administrative power, but has directed it away from legal control into a multitude of separate and unco-ordinated channels. ('Legal Theory', 3rd edition, 1953, p.418.)

British Administrative Tribunals—covering Transport, Lands, Rents, Military Service, Social Security, and so on—run into their thousands. They deal with objective questions relating to fair rents, appropriate rates of pensions, the degrees of injury caused by industrial accidents, the quality of people's farming: they are cheap and deal with a mass of specialist work with which the ordinary courts could not cope. The Rent Tribunals deal with about 15,000 cases per annum: the National Insurance and Injuries Tribunals with from 50,000 to 60,000.

Public Inquiries seek to obtain objective information—for example, about land suggested for requisitioning—but their findings are subject to policy decisions by a Minister or his agents. An Administrative Tribunal will ask if a particular rent is fair: a Public Inquiry will seek information relating to the application of a boat club to build a boat-house in a national park and a Minister or his agent will then decide, in the light of government policy, whether the boat-house would endanger public amenities. In the work of Tribunals there is a finding out of fact and a reference to regulations: in the work of Inquiries there is a similar search for fact but the reference is then to the balance of public and private interest—the Minister, in the last resort, is responsible to Parliament for his decision.

Parliament enacts laws and commits functions of adjudication to a Minister, which he performs by means of tribunals and inquiries. Tribunals have been of haphazard growth and this has had an adverse effect on their reputation for justice and fair dealing. They touch the citizen closely but, until recently, they have employed sketchy rules of evidence and have lacked generally recognized rules of procedure. They have also lacked an orderly system of appeal, and have not given reasoned decisions. Critics called for a decent standard of executive behaviour: they may have had in mind such anomalies as that relating to the decisions of the various Military Service Tribunals— in 1957 18 per cent. of Scottish applicants were granted exemption, only 0·6 per cent. of London applicants.

The Franks Committee on Administrative Tribunals and Inquiries was appointed in November 1955 and reported in July 1957 (Cmnd 218). The Report stated that Tribunals were essential to our society but went a long way to meet the criticism mentioned above. The Tribunals, said the Franks Committee, ought to be regarded as a machinery of adjudication rather than as part of the machinery of administration and to this end their work ought to be marked by 'openness, fairness and impartiality'. There ought to be room for appeal, and the chairmen ought to have legal qualifications.

As far as Inquiries were concerned there ought to be a standard code of procedure and the reports of Inspectors—who attend Inquiries and inform the Minister—ought to be published. Objectors should be allowed to correct Inspectors' reports. The Franks Committee recognized that the decisions flowing from Inquiries were matters of ministerial policy, and not judicial decisions: nevertheless, individuals might be injured by the ministerial decision—they should know why.

Following the Franks Report the Government asked departments to re-cast their system of tribunals and the Tribunals and Inquiries Act 1958 provided for the setting up of a Council on Tribunals to keep their constitutions and procedures under review.

In November 1958 there was an inquiry relating to a quarry at a site in Stansted, Essex. The Minister of Housing and Local Government refused to accept the recommendation of his inspector that chalk quarrying should not be allowed. After the public inquiry the Minister had received expert advice to the effect that the quarry would not produce chalk dust noxious to neighbouring farmland. The expert advice was not publicly available and the experts were not accessible for questioning. The Council on Tribunals, in 1962, extracted from the Government the undertaking that, where a Minister ignores his inspector's recommendations after receiving new evidence, he would reopen the inquiry. Said a *Guardian* leader:

> The civil servants have now given way to the increasing demand from the public that these public inquiries should more nearly approximate to judicial inquiries than to fact-finding missions by Ministers. The theoretical position, as evinced by the intention of Parliament in the various statutes setting up tribunals, is still that the public inquiries are nothing more than the right arm of the Minister stretching out to inform him how he should decide the particular issue. The public has willy-nilly distorted the statutory position and the Ministries have succumbed. They have recognized that administration will not, as they feared, become bogged down if the citizen is given the right to challenge ministerial decisions on issues vitally affecting the citizen. This concession should not lead the citizen for his part to regard the tribunals as courts of law; the decisions these tribunals have to make are still ultimately the responsibility of the Minister who in turn is answerable to Parliament. If both the civil servants and the public accept this position the new functioning of administrative tribunals should strike the right balance between State and citizen. (3rd April 1962.)

Lest one should feel too optimistic after reading the above, one should note that the 1962 and 1963 reports of the Council on Tribunals contained remarks which were, in effect, complaints that the Government was acting in such a way as to give rise to the belief that it wished to restrict the Council's activities. The Government has ignored the recommendation made in the Whyatt Report (see below) that the Council on Tribunals' functions should be extended.

7. *The Ombudsman*

The Government must get its way or cease to govern. With this injunction, and with further references to the need to preserve the sovereignty of Parliament, constitutional lawyers have long rejected the idea of a *conseil d'état*, on the French model, or a fourth division of the High Court (to join the Chancery, Queen's Bench, and Probate, Divorce and Admiralty Divisions), to stand between the State and the citizen.

In Britain, a citizen may seek to right a wrong in various ways. He can write to the Press but, conscious of its readers' demand for novelty, the Press may not carry through a sufficiently vigorous campaign. (See reference to *Sheffield Telegraph*, p. 192.) A citizen can approach his M.P., who may then put down a Question in the House: the M.P. may be fobbed-off, the Minister refusing to deliver up the facts. An unusually persistent M.P.—a Frank Allaun or a Gerald Nabarro—helped by a clamorous Press, may secure a remedy. The Government, in response to public pressure, may start an inquiry under the Tribunals of Inquiry (Evidence) Act of 1921. These inquiries are costly and cumbersome: the Waters Case inquiry (see p. 166) cost £8000 and was regarded by some as a sledge-hammer used to crack a nut. Finally, a citizen can seek to correct the 'errors' of the High Court by reference to the Court of Appeal, and ultimately to the House of Lords.

There exists in Britain, however, no institution which can deal with remedies for those cases involving a mixture of law and administrative policy—the Franks Committee did not examine all points of potential administrative abuse, nor does the Council on Tribunals which resulted from the Franks Inquiry. There is no regular forum where civil servants and lawyers meet.

Much interest has been generated recently by the suggestion that we should follow Sweden and Denmark by appointing an Ombudsman, or Warden of Rights, to supervize the observation of the law by public officials. The Ombudsman would be an independent officer with the right of access to courts, committees, public papers, prisons, mental homes, and so on, and he could initiate prosecutions after receiving and investigating complaints. Examples of the actions taken by the Scandinavian Ombudsmen make interesting reading. In Sweden in 1959 a judge was fined £100 for calling a witness a liar: other cases have related to the wrongful detention of an alcoholic; the wrongful confiscation of a fishing boat; the laxity of a foreign office worker which led to treachery; the method of granting licences to potato exporters, and, finally, academic nepotism.

Opponents of the idea of a British Ombudsman have pointed to the size of our population and have declared that he would be inundated by cases: even if there were selective handling of cases, or some kind of regional devolution (based on the areas of the nationalized industries, for example) the burdens of the new institution would be far heavier than in the Scandinavian countries with their smaller populations. (One might argue that the nation with the big population, the most business, is just the one to need an Ombudsman to check the trespasses of busy officials.) In British circumstances, say the critics, the office of Warden of Rights can be successful only in limited fields—for example, in the field of government finance, where the Comptroller and Auditor-General operates (but see p. 106).

In 1959 the Prime Minister, when asked a Question in the House, replied that he was reserving his judgement about an Ombudsman until a report by the all-party organization of lawyers, 'Justice', was published. In the autumn of 1961 'Justice' delivered up the Whyatt Report: it favoured the appointment of a Parliamentary Commissioner, an Ombudsman built into the parliamentary system. Acting along the lines of the Comptroller and Auditor-General, he would investigate complaints received by M.P.s. (Another plan to maintain the sovereignty of Parliament while having an Ombudsman was elaborated as follows: a Registrar would investigate complaints and, if a case seemed to exist, hand details to a High Court judge; the judge would investigate, for example, public documents and hear the explanations of the government departments involved, and would report the case with his findings to a Select Committee of the Commons—in this way the Ombudsman, the courts, and Parliament would work together.)

In June 1962 the Royal Commission on the Police Report carried an appendix which contained a proposal by three members of the Commission that a 'Commissioner of Rights' should be appointed. At this time Norway and New Zealand were appointing Ombudsmen. (In the first six months of the New Zealand Ombudsman's existence 334 complaints were received.) But, in June 1962, an ominous note was struck by the British representative at the United Nations seminar on judicial and other remedies against administrative abuse: he said that an Ombudsman on the Scandinavian model would not be acceptable to Britain.

In October 1962 the Government declined to adopt the Whyatt proposals, stating several reasons: it would be difficult to reconcile them with the principle of ministerial responsibility; an Ombudsman would seriously interfere with the prompt and efficient dispatch of public business; the M.P. was the guardian of the citizen's rights.

The principle of ministerial responsibility had been seen as a bar to a British Ombudsman before the Government's statement. According to our system Ministerial responsibility 'screens' the Civil Servant from direct blame, the Minister is accountable to Parliament for errors and abuses. It is true that the Swedes do not operate a system of Ministerial responsibility: their Civil Service departments receive only general directives from Cabinet Ministers and make their own independent administrative decisions. Here, the Ombudsman fills an obvious need for the exercise of control over officials. But, by contrast, the Danes do have a system of Ministerial responsibility similar to our own and they have been able to enjoy possession of an Ombudsman. Supporters of the Ombudsman idea in Britain have claimed that impartial investigation of a Civil Service department might well be welcomed by a Minister.

The respectable academic law journal *Public Law* was outraged by the Government's negative attitude to a British Warden of Rights— an editorial described the decision as almost unbelievable, the lack of reasoned argument disreputable:

> Here, in its simplest and purest form is revealed that attitude of mind which is at once so self-sufficient that it thinks a reasoned statement superfluous, so limited that it cannot free itself from the constraints of its private mythology and so obtuse that it will not see the effect of its own arrogance. (*The Guardian*, 14th Jan. 1963.)

Note (b). Law and Justice

(i) *English Law and Justice.* Law might be defined as man's whole system of enforceable rights and duties: justice, as freedom under law. Among those requirements necessary for the securing of justice is the limitation of authority—there must be absolute supremacy of absolute law uninfluenced by arbitrary power. While reading newspaper reports of the breakdown of law and justice in Turkey, Persia, or South Africa, the average Englishman tends to assume that law and justice need no defence at home—the battles have been fought and the victories won. Actually, yesterday's gains have to be defended and new battles over the redefinition of law and justice have to be fought.

To begin with, in England we labour under the difficulty of not always knowing what the law is. English courts operate under an uncodified (in the Continental sense) system of Common Law and Equity, a system of gradual growth described by Lord Radcliffe as 'too much precedent, too little principle'. In recent years study of our copious Common Law, our legal theory, has raised demands for rationalization. In R. S. W. Pollard's Fabian pamphlet of 1958, 'Speed up Law Reform', the writer draws attention to the deficiencies of our administrative law, the law of landlord and tenant, the state of the divorce laws, the judicial attitude to wills and bequests, and the need for the codification of statutes and common law decisions. In 1935 the Hanworth Committee first recommended that the Rules of the Supreme Court, which with explanatory notes fill 3000 pages, should be redrafted and simplified. This advice was repeated by the Evershed Committee in 1951.

Reform has been long neglected because there is no government department responsible for English justice and there is great reluctance to introduce anything in the nature of a Ministry of Justice. As the Haldane Committee reported in 1918, the responsibility for the administration of justice is shared between the Lord Chancellor (who has primary responsibility, but who is overburdened and under-staffed), the Home Secretary, the Attorney-General, and the Chancellor of the Duchy of Lancaster. It has been suggested that the Lord Chancellor's department might assume full responsibility—specifically charged with the duty of law reform, with the introduction of reform bills every year.

(ii) *Freedom: civil liberties.* The aim of the law is to balance personal freedom with the social good. Among the civil liberties we have come to take for granted are those connected with freedom of speech, of association, procession, person, contract, property, enterprise, mind and conscience. It is important that civil liberties be established and that grounds for interference with them be clearly known. This is not always easy—it is not always possible to say that the limits of freedom or the permissible occasions for interference are clearly defined.

The Incitement to Disaffection Act of 1934 was seen both as a useful safeguard against the Fascism then being publicized by the 'shirted organizations' and as a measure affording dangerous opportunities for interference with freedom. In the same way, the suppression of a post-war international peace-rally organized by the British Communist Party was regarded both as a wise and prudent measure and as a blow against free speech.

The debate which preceded the Public Order Act 1963 (which increased penalties for offensive words or behaviour at public meetings or in public places) and the visit of the King and Queen of Greece in the summer of 1963 concentrated attention once more on the right of peaceful demonstration. It was alleged that the Greek Queen had been assaulted a short time before on a previous visit: the Government were now taking extra care of the visitors. Tom Driberg, in the Commons on 9th July, declared that the police had suppressed peaceful demonstration.

The early 'sixties saw much discussion of obscene publications. In the nineteenth century the authorities had power to destroy books when their contents were seen to deprave or corrupt. This power was very far-reaching—it was applied to Annie Besant's books on birth control. More recently Doncaster police have taken exception to the 'Kinsey Report' (a book outlining the attitudes to sex and sex practices of American men), Swindon magistrates to Boccacio's 'Decameron'.

Many people considered, before recent legislation, that the law relating to obscenity was damaging to works of literary merit but reform of the law was slow in coming—one of the chief obstacles was the difficulty of deciding how to assess the effects of books on people. In April 1959 there was introduced into the Commons the Jenkins Bill. This resulted in the Obscene Publications Act 1959 which gave publishers a greater degree of freedom—'tendency to deprave and corrupt' in future may be a judgement applied to a whole book, not to passages taken out of context. Since 1959 the 'Lady Chatterley' and 'Fanny Hill' cases have received national attention.

It is not uncommon for foreign newspapers to print British news before our own papers do so. Our newspapers, for example, did not print news of the 1963 Profumo affair until Profumo's declaration freed them. At a meeting of the *Sunday Pictorial* shareholders in 1962

Cecil King said that the British Press was as censored as the most censored—though in an arbitrary and indeterminate way. There was Contempt of Court, the Official Secrets Act, 'D' (Security) Notices, and the laws of libel: the *Daily Mirror* employed three full-time, and eleven part-time barristers to help it keep out of trouble. (*The Guardian*, 5th June 1962.) (See also sections on Press and Broadcasting where the question of availability of information is dealt with at length.)

One interesting case, concerning freedom of mind, related to action against nuclear war. The Justices of the Peace Act of 1361 gave magistrates power to bind anyone over to keep the peace even if they had not committed an offence, provided there was reason to believe that the person's actions might lead to a breach of the peace. In December 1959 a case was brought to court, under this ancient act, which concerned six members of the Direct Action Committee against Nuclear War. They were kept in prison although they had committed no offence because they refused to be bound over to keep the peace. Many people probably thought that the magistrate had acted reasonably: Sidney Silverman, in a letter to the Home Secretary, alleged that the Statute of 1361 was being used as a kind of veto on political action.

To deprive a person of his liberty is a serious action. In recent years the extreme limit of the power of the authorities to detain a person was reached with the wartime Regulation 18b—under this regulation a person could be detained, not for what he had done, but for what he might do. The ancient remedy against unlawful detention is the power of the courts to issue a writ of *Habeas Corpus*—the power to call some official to bring forward a prisoner so that the court may know on what ground he is being confined.

In 1959 a former Kenya prison-warder sought a writ of *habeas corpus* in order to obtain his release from Brixton Prison, where he was being detained on the order of a Bow Street magistrate, awaiting his return to Kenya. The former warder alleged that the African authorities were seeking to prevent his making further disclosures about the ill-treatment of prisoners: the Kenya authorities made counter-allegations to the effect that the former warder had forged cheques in order to obtain credit.

An anomalous and unsatisfactory state of affairs relating to the remedy of *habeas corpus* had been revealed in a previous case, the Edward Thomas Hastings case in 1957:

> In July 1957 Hastings was convicted at Liverpool Crown Court on each of five counts of an indictment alleging various frauds, and was sentenced to four years' corrective training. The record of the conviction did not state that concurrent sentences had been passed on each count. Hastings appealed to the Court of Criminal Appeal, which quashed his conviction on one count only and left his sentence unaltered. Hastings then applied to a Divisional Court of the Queen's Bench Division for a writ of *habeas corpus* on the grounds that since only one sentence had been passed on him and since the conviction on one count had been quashed, there was no longer any lawful sentence upon him in existence and he was therefore unlawfully detained. The Divisional Court took the view that the Recorder in the Crown Court had clearly intended the sentence to be concurrent on each count, so that the quashing of the conviction on one count was immaterial, and it dismissed the application. ('Do the Habeas Corpus Acts Need Revision?' *The Listener*, 22nd Oct. 1959.)

Hastings appealed against the dismissal of his application but ran into difficulties: there was revealed an unsatisfactory position in respect of the ability of both prisoner and custodian to appeal against High Court decisions. The Administration of Justice Act 1960 made new provision for appeals.

Chief Enahoro's battle to avoid deportation to Nigeria, where he faced charges of treason, secured much newspaper space between December 1962 and June 1963. The case started with the Chief's committal to Brixton in December, charged with treasonable felony: it developed when he applied for a writ of *habeas corpus* in January. The case was debated in the Commons on at least six occasions before the Chief was deported. One newspaper report of this case was headed, 'The Law's Delay': a better title might have been, The 'Law's Safeguards'. The Government may have been wrong in denying Chief Enahoro political asylum, but at least the case was debated over a period of six months. (In April 1963 the South African Minister of Justice published a new security Bill which in effect nullified *habeas corpus* and suspended the rule of law for anyone suspected by the police of sabotage, terrorism, or subversion—as defined by the Government. One of the Bill's clauses made provision for the deten-

tion of a person for ninety days with no appeal. This period of detention could be repeated as often as the police wished.)

(iii) *Freedom: grounds for interference.* A citizen should be free from
arbitrary arrest. In Britain arrest must be on a warrant unless reasonable grounds for arrest without a warrant exist—for instance, if the
person is 'caught in the act', or clear suspicion of criminal intent arises
when there is no time to obtain a warrant. A person in custody has to
know the charge being made against him, and to seek legal help at the
earliest possible moment. While under arrest a person must be free
from oppression and his statements must be voluntary, not obtained
from him by either promise or threat.

In March 1961 the Home Secretary was asked what representations
he had received about the existing practice of recording and use, in
evidence, of statements made by accused persons when in police
stations or in police custody. In reply, Butler announced that there
would be a review of Judges' Rules (under which the police operate in
this matter). New Judges' Rules were announced in January 1964.

Enforcement of the law depends very much on the goodwill of the
public towards the police and yet the latter have seen an increase of
potential antagonists—among those who may commit traffic offences,
or may suffer because of out-of-date betting and licensing laws.
(The Licensing Act 1961 and the Betting and Gaming Act 1960 have
brought changes here.) The newspapers are always ready to seize
upon allegations of police misconduct. In the Waters Case of 1958,
when police brutality was alleged, a full-scale inquiry inflated the
issue greatly and attracted considerable public attention. The case
showed weakness and confusion in methods of investigating police
activities.

In the Nottingham Case of 1959 the police were again brought
before the public notice. Chief Constable Popkess had thought that
the receipt of gifts by certain councillors while visiting Germany
merited investigation as a possible breach of the Public Bodies Corrupt
Practices Act of 1889. This investigation, and previous clashes between
the Chief Constable and the Council, led to Popkess being suspended
by the Watch Committee. A national as well as local debate followed
as to who, in Britain, controls the police. Butler, the Home Secretary,

stated that a chief constable's duty was to enforce the criminal law, and in doing so he was not subject to the control of local authorities. Responsible to the Watch Committee in administrative matters, a chief constable has a free hand in law enforcement.

The *Garratt* v. *Eastmond* case followed an alleged assault by Eastmond in December 1958. A payment of £300 was made by the police, without admission of liability, and a debate arose as to the financial responsibility of police forces for the actions of their constables. The question was asked why, if the constable involved was not guilty of assault, public money had been paid over. If the constable was indeed guilty, it was asked, why had public money been spent to save him from the legal consequences of his own actions?

Butler defended the payment by asserting that a police constable would not be effective if he had to think about his personal liability all the time. An Opposition motion of censure, which followed the refusal by the Home Secretary of a Disciplinary Inquiry, was withdrawn when a Royal Commission on the Police was announced by the Government. The Commission was to investigate the constitution, functions, control, administration, status, accountability, pay and recruitment of the police. It was also to study the relations of the police with the public, as well as the question of the investigation of complaints made by the public.

The report of the Royal Commission was published on 31st May 1962 (Cmnd 1728). It called for a reduction of the number of our police forces; a chief inspector of constabulary for the whole of Great Britain; provision for powers to remove a chief constable who was inefficient; and changes in promotion procedures. The Commission said that the number of complaints against the police was very small, but detailed changes in the methods of handling complaints were proposed. The decision whether or not to prosecute a police officer ought to be taken by the Director of Public Prosecutions, in England, and not by chief constables. Towards the end of 1963 a Police Bill was introduced into the Commons to give effect to the recommendations of the Royal Commission's report.

In 1937 the Home Secretary and the Postmaster-General decided that telephone-tapping should be put on the same footing as the opening of letters—it should be allowed by written permission of the

Home Secretary. (This provision was embodied in the Post Office Act 1953, section 58.)

Following the passing by the police of telephone conversation recordings to a professional society which was taking proceedings against a barrister, the Birkett Committee was set up in 1957 to examine powers relating to the use of telephone-tapping. The committee of three condemned the passing of information to the Bar Council by the police but disagreed on the question of the proper use of tapping powers. Lords Birkett and Monckton said the powers of the Home Secretary should continue, to be used as in the past in a circumspect manner, but that there should be stricter Home Office control: Gordon-Walker declared that telephone-tapping and letter opening were so repugnant to public opinion that they should be voluntarily abandoned, save for occasional cases of extreme urgency.

The Reading Case of 1959 saw the issue discussed again. The police passed shorthand notes to the General Medical Council, which was inquiring into allegations that a doctor had had improper relations with a woman patient who had committed suicide. The Birkett Committee had recommended that transcripts of information secured from tapping should not be handed over to private bodies or persons. However, certain bodies, of which the General Medical Council is one, have power to subpoena (issue a writ commanding a person's attendance) and the question arose in the Reading Case as to whether the Birkett safeguard had been reduced to nothing.

In the 1959 case the police had not asked the Home Secretary's permission before tapping—the police had recorded information from a single conversation, with the permission of one of the parties to the conversation: it was, however, the Home Secretary's decision to pass on the information to the G.M.C. In December 1959 the Opposition put down a motion of censure in the Commons regretting the Home Secretary's failure,

> . . . to ensure that no telephone conversation should be intercepted without his express warrant and that materials obtained by interception should in no circumstances be made available to anybody or person whatever outside the public service.

There are several possible objections which can be made against the use of material derived from telephone conversations—recordings are unreliable since the tape can be so easily tampered with, it is often difficult to be sure of the identity of the voice heard, and it is easy to misinterpret what is heard or recorded. The passing of information to private courts is also open to objection since these courts do not have the strict rules of procedure used in the public courts and the individual 'on trial' is not fully protected.

During the debate on the Reading Case in December 1959 the Home Secretary announced the setting up of a Committee under the chairmanship of Lord Simonds to consider to what extent, and subject to what conditions subpoenas should be issued to outside disciplinary bodies, and in particular subpoenas to secure the production of evidence obtained by police officers in the course of criminal investigations. In May 1960 the Simonds Committee recommended that all statutory tribunals should have powers of subpoena and that the police should be required to give tribunals evidence acquired during criminal investigations.

The security measures taken by the Government sometimes require that reports on university students be obtained. A debate has occurred from time to time as to whether, while requests by an ordinary employer for a report on the character of a prospective employee are sensible and proper, government requests for information about those applying for the relatively few 'security' jobs constitute 'spying'. On the one hand it is held that, since recruits for security jobs come from the universities, enquiries have to be made there—there is nothing surreptitious about the inquiries. On the other hand, it has been alleged by Lord Chorley in the Lords (22nd May 1957) that security officers have invaded the universities. Fears have been expressed elsewhere that university teachers are being asked to act as 'listening-posts'. Professor J. L. Montrose of Belfast University said at a conference of the Association of University Teachers:

> We ought to make it clear that this Association is quite convinced that no person can with honour remain a university teacher and at the same time agree to be a secret agent for the government in this work. Our prime obligation is to discuss quite openly principles and politics and all sorts of things. . . . (*New Statesman*, 1st June 1957.)

Security-checks by the Government have reached back to applicants' sixth-form days. In 1960 there was some discussion of investigations, 'sixth-form screening', which had resulted in teachers warning their charges against the airing of dangerous opinions and the wearing of badges. (*Guardian* leader, 4th June 1960.)

The Radcliffe Committee's report on security procedures (Cmnd 1681) was published in April 1962. While it thought that a previous inquiry in 1956 (see p. 173 below) had attached undue importance to Communist Party membership in the Civil Service, it pointed out that the British Communist Party had a disproportionately large number of members and sympathizers among Civil Service trade union officials. (In June the Institution of Professional Civil Servants at its conference declared that it would welcome any investigation of its organization by the security services.) The Radcliffe Committee did say that most danger to Britain came from the activities of Russia's professional spies. The Radcliffe Committee was quickly followed by the Radcliffe Tribunal which investigated allegations relating to the Vassall spy case. Its report was published in April 1963 (Cmnd 2009). (See also p. 189.)

(iv) *The Machinery of Justice.* Certain institutional conditions are necessary for the securing of justice. There must be equality before the law; there must be the application of a body of legal rules or principles by a judicial mind in an institutional framework; there must be self-regulating courts free from outside interference, with free public access. Judges must be impartial, must be free from criticism, and must enjoy security of tenure—and thus have nothing to lose by doing right, nothing to gain by doing wrong. A judge's absolute privilege within his own domain is very much taken for granted in Britain: judicial independence, in respect of contempt of court, was modified to a degree in 1960 (see p. 194).

The lay magistracy recently celebrated its sexcentenary. Much criticism has been made of the unpaid justices who perform the bulk of our judicial work. J.P.s are appointed by nominating committees and objection has been taken to the fact that the membership of these committees is confidential, the names of the committee-members not being made public. It is open to any individual or organization to submit nominations for the magistracy: at the meeting of the Women's Liberal Federation at Fleetwood in May 1960 there was a call for an

inquiry into the nominating procedure—it was alleged that appointment often depended on the nominee being a member of a political
party.

Criticism has also been made of the fact that magistrates are usually
of the professional, employer, or managerial classes, rather than of the
salaried or wage-earning classes. In January 1962 the General Council
of the Trades Union Congress decided to press its view that J.P.s
should be paid subsistence allowances and compensation for loss of
earnings. The Magistrates' Association and the central council of the
Magistrates Courts' Committee were opposed to these measures but,

> As these bodies are dominated by people who are not wage-earners their
> opposition to the acceptance of proposals that would enable wage-earners
> to accept appointment as J.P.s 'neither surprises nor impresses the General
> Council', who have asked the Home Secretary to give a reasoned reply to
> the case they put forward in February 1959. (*The Guardian*, 9th Jan. 1962.)

An allied criticism is that the average age of magistrates is too high—
because the position is unpaid, many young people cannot afford to
become J.P.s. A Royal Commission on Justices of the Peace reported
in 1948 and there was a Justices of the Peace Act in 1949 which fixed
the retiring age of J.P.s at 75, 65 for those serving on the juvenile panel.
The Act also provided for a training scheme for newly appointed
magistrates but, unlike the Royal Commission Report, the Act did not
say that training should be compulsory.

The Bow Group pamphlet, 'Scales of Justice', published in April
1962 by the Conservative Political Centre, declared that the rigid rule
of non-payment of magistrates should be relaxed to the extent of
compensating, on a similar basis to that of councillors, for time lost
at work. The pamphlet also demanded extensive training for magistrates—every appointee to the lay bench should be required to attend
a ten-day residential course to begin with, with further courses to
follow.

The pamphlet said that the magistrates courts' civil work, notably
the matrimonial cases they dealt with, should be taken away from
them. However,

> The twentieth century technocrat, with his delight in specialization and his
> worship of the 'fully trained expert' may well regard our whole lay

magisterial system as a nightmare, but none the less it is a system which has the supreme merit that it works, and on the whole it works well. (*The Guardian*, 26th April 1962.)

Of the stipendiary (professional) magistracy the writers were less happy,

> A visit to some other courts of the same sort will reveal a very different state of affairs; sufficient to say that in them, both lay men and women are bullied and chivvied and treated in a way which sometimes ignores even the most elementary rules of civilized behaviour. The sentencing of offenders tends to be haphazard and sometimes almost savage. Fortunately such courts are rare, but no practititoner would deny their existence or think the picture painted a false one. One bad stipendiary magistrate sitting alone can do more harm than a dozen bad lay magistrates whose deficiencies will be tempered by right thinking colleagues. (*op. cit.*)

Under the English system a person is presumed innocent until proved guilty and he has the right of a speedy trial with adequate facilities for defence. A trial must proceed according to a known and established procedure, with the equal application of the law evident to all in an open court wherein takes place competitive cross-examination. These standards of judicial procedure are very high and, in various respects, we may not always achieve them.

In June 1959 'Justice', an all-party body of lawyers, criticized the anomalies occurring in the award of legal penalties, the tendency to punish offences against property rather more heavily than offences against the person—a situation owed to the enactment of laws in a period when there existed a different social climate. 'Justice', commenting on the varying maxima of punishments for similar crimes and the lack of a consistent standard of assessment, declared there was a need for a review of penalties.

The English legal system relies on parties to an action for the production of evidence on which the court can make a judgement. The administration of justice fails if the adducing of certain relevant material is not available to the court. At present certain immunities of the Crown—that is, the Executive—are sanctioned and these have caused legal theorists some concern.

Cases where Crown Privilege has been claimed include one which followed the sinking of a submarine. In the 1942 Thetis Case the

Admiralty directed the defendant company, during compensation proceedings, not to produce certain documents. A further case occurred after one prisoner had been assaulted by another in one of our prisons and the question arose as to whether prison officers had been negligent in letting the incident occur. Clearly much depended on whether it could be shown that the prison authorities knew that the assailant was unsafe but the Crown claimed privilege for police and medical records relating to him. Justice may have been done in the two cases just mentioned: it was not seen to have been done.

The basic rule operating in cases such as the above is that the public interest is paramount, and that only the Executive can judge whether the public disclosure of certain facts would be against public interest:

> Those who are responsible for the national security are the sole judges of what the national security requires. (Lord Parker.)

To this the objection has been made (J. E. S. Simon, Q.C., M.P., *Observer*, 13th Nov. 1955) that, while it is true that the Executive is solely responsible for the public security, Crown Privilege extends beyond this to the general consideration of the public interest, for which the Executive is not solely responsible.

In 1956 there was some relaxing of Crown Privilege, a decrease in the number of things for which secrecy was demanded, but lawyers were still concerned. Reformers have demanded that the task of determining whether public security is involved in any case should be given to an independent tribunal. At the moment the Crown Privilege system is very rigid—either evidence is allowed in open court, or is totally excluded. The demand has been made that some relaxation should be made by allowing the evidence in question to be heard in a closed court. In January 1959 the Attorney-General refused to set up an inquiry into Crown Privilege.

In July 1956 over a thousand people attended a protest meeting at the Caxton Hall, London. These people, differing in their politics, were uniting to express their disapproval of the attempt of security officials to deprive a certain John Lang, whose wife was an ex-Communist, of his job with the I.C.I. In 1955 a committee of Privy Counsellors had been set up following the defection of Burgess and McLean: in a White Paper published in March of the following year the Government announced that it intended to extend security measures so as to exclude from important security jobs in the government service Communist Party members, Communist sympathizers, those associating with Communists, and those likely to be subject to Communist Party pressure in such a way as to raise reasonable doubt as to their reliability. The Government also said it would, in dealing with applicants for certain posts, take into account defects of character and conduct, and would tilt the favour in the public interest when making selections.

The Government's security measures were held to be vague and opponents objected to the use in the White Paper of such loose expressions as 'reasonable doubts', 'Communist sympathizer', and 'association with Communists'. It was feared that the new measures would encourage tale-bearing in the Civil Service. A person might suffer in his career but never know the charge against him, there could be damage to a person's reputation without any adding to the national security: there was an absence in the new arrangements of the chance for an appellant before a tribunal (whose members might have no legal experience) to have the opportunity of being accompanied by a representative or friend.

The Campaign for the Limitation of Secret Police Powers is among those bodies which have objected to the imposition of penalties, not from due process of law, but out of deference to denunciation by unidentified informers and allegations made by the 'secret police'. (A publication of 1957 listed as members of the Campaign's sponsoring council: Lord Chorley, G. D. H. Cole, Tom Driberg, Gerald Gardiner, Q.C., Kingsley Martin, Earl Russell, and others.) This body has demanded certain protective procedures for those whose reliability for security work has been brought into question—the right of legal representation, the right to know charges and have full opportunity to refute them, and the right to be heard by a professional tribunal.

The Legal Aid and Advice Act 1949 went some way to modify that situation which has been summed up in the assertion that English justice is good because it is expensive. Legal aid was inadequate after 1949, partly because the service was not sufficiently publicized, but chiefly because that part of the 1949 Act relating to advice was not implemented—there was a great need for a system whereby a person could have an interview with a lawyer for a small fixed fee, to kill needless and vexatious disputes before they grew expensive. This was particularly true after the passing of the Rent Act in 1957. The Legal Aid Act 1960 raised the limits of capital and income which people could have without being disqualified from receipt of legal aid: in March 1959 the Government had brought in a nation-wide legal advice scheme, run by solicitors in ordinary practice, which entitled people to an interview; in April 1960 the capital and income limits under which people could qualify for free legal advice were raised also. Legal aid is a growing business: in 1961–2 £2,595,000 was spent, in 1962–3 £3,594,000. A bill extending the legal aid scheme was introduced into the Commons at the end of 1963.

A jury is a 'body of citizens sworn to draw logical conclusions from facts of which they have no personal knowledge'. When there is lack of unanimity in a jury as to a proper verdict the divided jury may cause the court some irritation. There have been recent cases where, because of the court's exasperation, directions to juries have been alleged to have contained an element of undue persuasion. One Nottingham jury was told by a judge in 1959 that he would have them locked up for the night if they did not arrive at a decision within ten minutes: his action caused a critical motion to be put down in the Commons. Following this and similar cases discussion has again arisen as to whether majority jury verdicts ought to be allowed in England, as they are in Scotland.

The Commons, on 20th March 1962, refused leave by a narrow majority for the introduction of a Private Member's Bill, the Jury Service Bill, which would have changed the basis of qualification for jury service. Mrs. Judith Hart, M.P., wished to remove the obsolete property qualification laid down by an Act of 1825 and substitute a provision that all those on the electoral register in an area for three successive years should be liable for service. Her opponents said that, if the change occurred, too many women, undoubtedly more emotional than men, and too many ill-educated people might serve on juries.

A person has a right to a speedy trial but people are kept in prison before conviction and a proportion of these are eventually acquitted of the charges against them. The authorities have been concerned to know the length of the periods people have had to await trial, the effect on the prison population, and the variation of waiting time according to magistrates' bailing policies. A new research unit in the Home Office, established in 1957, made these problems the subject of its first report, published in January 1960 ('Time Spent Awaiting Trial'). The Streatfield Committee Report (Cmnd 1289, February 1961) made a number of recommendations for ensuring that cases are disposed of expeditiously and that the courts have all the necessary information before passing sentence. The Criminal Justice Administration Act, 1962, brought some mitigation of the situation: the number of High Court judges was increased and some reallocation of court work was made possible.

On the 14th March 1960 the Court of Criminal Appeal, in the space of four hours, disposed of nine appeals and thirty-two applications for leave to appeal against convictions or sentences. This despatch of criminal appeal may have been too hasty: such speedy 'justice' is suspect. There may be need for greater facilities for appeals, with more time allowed for reasoned judgements.

A person may successfully defend himself in a court of law but leave the court a much poorer man: there has been discussion of the introduction of a scheme to meet the costs of the acquitted.

Other reformers have wanted to see our machinery of justice improved by the provision of compensation for victims of violence. The question was considered by a Working Party which reported in June 1961 (Cmnd 1406). It found that many difficulties would be involved if such a scheme were introduced. A committee of Conservative laymen and lawyers appointed by Butler as Home Secretary reported in favour of compensation for victims of violence in July 1962. 'Justice' (the British section of the International Commission of Jurists) published a report in November 1962. Lord Shawcross said in the preface:

> There are no great—certainly no insurmountable—practical or administrative difficulties; there is no great involvement of public funds. The time for governmental action on the matter is, therefore, now.

In March 1964 the Government announced details of an experimental scheme in a White Paper (Cmnd 2323): the Government intended to introduce the scheme, after debate, during the life of the existing Parliament.

(v) *Corporal Punishment and Capital Punishment.* Nineteenth century penal reformers were concerned to balance the interests of society with the good of the individual and they attacked unnecessary pain and suffering. Thus occurred a mitigation of the criminal law in relation to the whipping of women, the use of the pillory, the hanging of prisoners in chains, the reduction of capital offences, and the ending of public executions.

The deterrent element in punishment—the presenting of the potential offender with the risk of loss of liberty, separation from family, social shame and withdrawal of group support—is valid as a preventive measure but punishment should be the lesser of two evils—otherwise society would be everything and the individual nothing. Purely repressive punishment is neither necessary nor effective—the criminal is often the least mature of people, least able to reason—and detention should lead to rehabilitation, not merely be used for revenge. The prison conditions, mentioned elsewhere (see Vol. II, p. 207), often create an atmosphere of repression rather than reform. Thus argue many thinkers on penal reform.

However, people at large are not at one on the question of the proper balance of the deterrent, reformative, and retributive elements in punishment—perhaps they never will be. As far as legislation is concerned, the humanitarians appear to be succeeding against the disciplinarians of society, although the former are still faced with many signs of what has been described as the public's emotional need to punish.

The Criminal Justice Act of 1948 abolished flogging, except for grave offences against prison discipline, and also the birching of young offenders. The Cadogan Committee of 1938 had declared that the abolition of flogging would not affect the downward trend of crimes for which it was then applied and, since 1948, the validity of this judgement appears to have been maintained. Nevertheless, vociferous minorities, concerned about the significant rise in crime figures, and impatient of the idea that the criminal should be treated as sick, are calling continually for the reintroduction of corporal punishment—

the cane or birch, if not the 'cat'. Lord Chief Justice Parker, speaking to the Magistrates' Association in 1959, in reference to the use of the birch and the cane, asked his audience not to let anyone persuade them that there was no such thing as a deterrent sentence. In 1960 a Gallup survey revealed that 78 per cent. of those sampled were in favour of corporal punishment, a sanction also favoured by the police, the prison service, and the Bench.

David Renton, Minister of State at the Home Office, addressing a conference of Townswomen in 1959, said that there was no evidence that corporal punishment was better than a stiff prison sentence: in 1960 probation officers were almost nine to one against the reintroduction of corporal punishment. The whole question of judicial corporal punishment was examined by the Advisory Council on the Treatment of Offenders, which reported in November 1960 (Cmnd 1213). The Council was unanimous that judicial corporal punishment should not be re-introduced and the Government accepted its findings.

The Criminal Statistics for 1957 showed a rough similarity in the number of murders committed each year over the previous 50 years. Renton, at the meeting referred to in the preceding paragraph, said that there were no grounds for thinking that the number of murders had increased since the Homicide Act of 1957. The steadiness of the murder rate, in the 30 years before 1957 and in the 4 years after, was confirmed by the Home Office Research Unit in its report, 'Murder', published in 1961.

The 1957 Act was a compromise measure and, according to some, was evidence of an evasion of moral responsibility on the part of the Government. The Silverman Bill, seeking the abolition of capital punishment, passed through the Commons on a free vote but, in 1956, was rejected by the Lords. The 1957 Act did not allow for complete abolition of the death penalty, although drastic restrictions in its use were envisaged. In the first place, the Act made a distinction between capital and non-capital murders—the death penalty was to be restricted to types of murder which struck at law and order and for which death was considered to be particularly effective as a deterrent. In the second place, the Act introduced the defence of diminished responsibility which, if successful, reduced murder to manslaughter.

The unresolved issue of the 'sixties is whether more murderers should hang—for example, those of old people or children—or none at all. The 1957 Act has been attacked by the abolitionists and by the 'hanging and flogging' lobby. Critics of the 1957 compromise point to the illogicality of the distinction between capital and non-capital murders. Some murders commonly regarded as the most heinous escape the death penalty, while others, less heinous, still attract it. Murder in furtherance of theft—by shooting or by explosion—or by resisting arrest or while escaping from legal custody of police or prison officers is a capital offence: murder by poisoning, strangling, stabbing is not. The situation is even more difficult to understand when one realizes that about half those condemned to death are reprieved.

Some abolitionists believe that the Silverman Bill was deficient since the only alternative it left to the death penalty was the penalty of life imprisonment. They think that the problem of the murderer is insoluble, with or without capital punishment, until more is done to study the treatment of abnormality. (See Vol. II, p. 210.) The report mentioned above, 'Murder', gives a picture of murder as largely a family crime committed as a result of quarrels, violent rage, insanity or despair. More often than not the murderer subsequently commits suicide. The report observes:

> . . . it is clear that, from the point of view of saving life, and especially the lives of children, seeking a deterrent penalty is less important than investigating the kind of mental breakdown that leads to family murders.

The Government's position was defended by Butler at the 1961 Conservative Conference in the following terms:

> Under the Act of 1957, capital punishment is kept for those types of murder which strike especially at law and order, and for which capital punishment is likely to be particularly effective as a deterrent; murder by shooting, murder in the course of theft, and murder of a police or prison officer, or murder in resisting arrest. This compromise, which is what it is, I inherited when I got to the Home Office. It has only been working for a comparatively short time, and it was arrived at only after long debates in Parliament and controversy across party lines. I want to tell the Conference quite clearly that with the present composition of Parliament it is quite uncertain whether a majority in fact exists to restore capital punishment for all murders, and it would be difficult to justify unless it could be shown that the 1957 Act had resulted in an increase in murders, and there is no evidence of this. (Conservative 'Notes on Current Politics', 1st Jan. 1962, p. 9.)

III. POLITICAL INFORMATION

8. *The Press*

(i) *Respect for the Press: Triviality*. Adlai Stevenson is reported to have said that newspapers are for people who can read but not think. The quality and function of the Press is a subject of periodic debate in Britain. The Royal Commission on the Press (see below) said in its 1949 report that the newspapers catered overmuch for the lowest tastes: many other charges have been brought against newspapers— of distortion, sensationalism, mis-statement, narrow and undifferenti- ated presentation of news, of triviality, and of creating a 'candy-floss' world in which no real issues exist. The cause of these evils, very largely, is the financial need of the newspaper proprietors to attract advertising revenue through large circulations: thus, a debate on the National Health Service or on Pensions has to give way to 'flying- saucers' or, in summer, to the Loch Ness Monster.

Defenders of newspapers ask whether the situation is quite so bad as painted. They deny that the man in the street is lacking in ideas or awareness of the world and, further, attack the assumption—of those like the nobleman who would not read *printed* books, or Greek classics *in translation*—that to popularize is to debase, that a wide culture is bad. Both television and the popular Press provide education for those who do not find reading easy, bringing them sport, travel films, books, and archaeology in an easily assimilable form. What is highbrow is rendered comprehensible, although the highbrow is not necessarily best. In any case, the standards of the newspaper ought not to be laid down by decree: the critics of the popular Press are in the end critics of life.

First, say champions of the Press, it is not the function of the news- paper merely to inform: we all need to escape from the real world—in cowboy films, space-travel, and so on—and so the provision of entertainment is a second and valid function. Many readers of so- called 'quality' papers, it is claimed, often read a second paper for its entertainment value. (Malcolm Muggeridge has said that the difference between 'top' and 'bottom' people is that the former prefer their smut in Restoration costume.) Second, the popular Press does inform—in its own fashion. Such an argument came a few years ago from the

Editor of the 'Church of England Newspaper' who spoke of the educationally privileged critics in their ivory towers who did not understand the function of the popular newspaper. The question and answer columns of such a newspaper, said the editor, contained some of the best education on sex and marriage given anywhere in the country.

J. B. Priestley has said that the obscenity and sensationalism of the Press are not of prime importance—its increasing triviality is. The worst New York tabloids contain more worthwhile reading, more glimpses of the real world than British papers. Further, said Priestley, it is inadequate to argue that the Press merely reflects popular tastes— this is too simple. Newspapers create the tastes they cater for and are not just reflections of the mass mind.

Richard Hoggart ('Uses of Literacy') has claimed that popular publications and entertainments generally are deficient not by failing to be highbrow but by failing to be concrete—people are not led on to an idea, to an understanding of problems. Our taste for pleasure is outrunning our education:

> The strongest objection to the more trivial popular entertainments is not that they prevent their readers from becoming highbrow but that they make it more difficult for people who are not thinkers to become wise in their own way. (*op. cit.*, p. 276.)

Our chief concern here is not with the Press as cultural medium but with its ability to provide political information. The two cannot be wholly separated in discussion however. It is alleged that the Press has destroyed public confidence by irresponsibility and triviality:

> In the United States today the journalist is a member of the respected Fourth Estate. In Britain, though there is quite a lot of sympathy for him as a man who has to do a job of work, he is written off as the hireling of a singularly unattractive group of business men . Since the war, the press lords have managed to give the public the impression that their attitude to the papers they manage is not as dedicated as that of Charlie Clore to the properties he picks up in a take-over bid. In the view of the British people today, the popular newspaper has been degraded into a shoddy part of the entertainment industry, and the newspaper proprietor is rated the most cynical of all the big business tycoons. (Crossman, *The Guardian*, 15th March 1963.)

(ii) *The Royal Commission Report 1949: monopolies and economic crisis.* A review of the political history of the Press would take into account its freeing from state control, the lifting of the 'taxes on knowledge', the rise of the editor and the advent of the political correspondent. In the growth of the freedom of the Press the strong editor, the independent owner, and the fearless reporter were important factors, as was the assurance of a degree of independence from the State through the receipt of advertising revenue. Today, monopoly ownership, standards of reporting, and newspapers' dependence on advertising revenue are matters of concern.

In October 1946 a motion was placed before the Commons:

> That having regard to the increasing public concern at the growth of monopolistic tendencies in the control of the Press, and with the object of furthering the free expression of opinion through the Press and the greatest practicable accuracy in the presentation of the news, this House considers that a Royal Commission should be appointed to inquire into the finance, control, management and ownership of the Press.

The Report of the Royal Commission in 1949, while holding that local press monopolies should be brought within the scope of the Monopolies Commission, declared that nationally there was nothing approaching a monopoly of the Press in the existing degree of concentration of ownership. The concentration of ownership was not so great as to prejudice the free expression of opinion: there was biased reporting but an adequate representation of news. The decrease in the number of newspapers had not been so great as to prejudice the public interest—any further decrease, however, would be a matter for anxiety and any decrease in provincial morning newspapers would be a serious loss.

After the publication of the 1949 Report there was a further contraction of the number of our newspapers and there was constant talk of a crisis in the newspaper economy. Not only did provincial dailies disappear but also national dailies such as the *News Chronicle* and the *Daily Dispatch*. The demise of the *News Chronicle* at the end of 1960 was the cause of much political comment. On the 2nd December Kenneth Robinson placed the following motion before the House:

> That this House regrets the closure of the *News Chronicle* and *Star* newspapers, and methods by which it was effected; expresses anxiety at the increasing concentration of newspapers in fewer hands; and calls upon Her

Majesty's Government to institute an inquiry into the press with particlar reference to the monopolistic trends and its social implications.

The debate which followed was inconclusive.

There was no one cause of the sickness of the newspaper world. Variety of opinion is important to the community yet the value of a newspaper as an organ of opinion may not be the same as its value as an advertising medium. In recent years there has been a shift of advertising from newspapers in general to television, from certain mass daily newspapers, and to the 'quality' newspapers—leaving a number of journals with a diminished revenue from this source. Some serious political weeklies have been hurt by a lack of advertising revenue rather than any fall in sales: in May 1958 the *New Statesman* and the *Spectator* made a joint appeal to advertising agencies for more business. The printing unions in the newspaper industry are strong and maintain a strict control of staffing, thus ensuring that their members are among the highest paid of workers. On the other hand, the price of newspapers is very low compared with other products: the price is kept artificially low by those papers with mass circulations which attract the most advertising business. Newsprint has been very expensive because of the growth of American and Russian demand and, although the Fleet Street giants have links with newsprint producers, and are thus protected from price rises, the 'savage cost of newsprint' hits the smaller, progressive newspapers as well as provincial newspapers.

At the time of the first Royal Commission on the Press suggestions for the amelioration of the economic plight of newspapers included an inquiry into the supply of newsprint, a subsidy on newsprint, an inquiry into trade union restrictive practices, and self-help by the newspapers themselves—the smaller and less successful newspapers to improve their situation by convincing the public of their quality, of their 'strong editorial personality'.

The Report of the Royal Commission rejected the idea of any form of state control of newspapers: a free Press was linked with free enterprise. Free enterprise may not ensure a free Press, and advertising may interfere with the expression of a strong editorial personality: there have been complaints that newspapers insert material with the aim of buttressing their advertising columns. (The 1949 Report found that advertisers did not rule newspaper policy.)

(iii) *The Press Council 1953.* There was only one major recommendation by the Royal Commission—that a Press Council should be set up. In 1953 a Press Council was appointed to preserve the freedom and maintain the character of the Press, to maintain the free flow of information, to encourage the education and training of journalists, and to watch tendencies to monopoly.

Sir Linton Andrews, until the beginning of 1959 the Chairman of the Council, said in the Council's third annual report that, 'After three years of conscientious effort the Council is recognized by a large and increasing number of people as a professional court of honour, a safeguard of press freedom and press fairness.' Investigations by the Council have been made into allegations of unnecessary intrusions on grief, editorial mangling of reporters' signed articles, publicity of the activities of the royal family, and so on. An example of the type of case referred to the Council concerned a *Daily Sketch* allegation in 1959 that half-a-million copies of the Labour Party's pamphlet, 'The Future Labour Offers You,' were lying unwanted in Transport House: Morgan Phillips's denial and his complaint against this allegation had not been given space in the *Sketch*.

The Council has provided a channel of complaint against the Press, has proved false many complaints and has built up a body of 'case-law'. So far as complaints against the Press are concerned, however, it has been regretted that the strictures of the Council carry weight only with those editors unlikely to deserve them. A major weakness of the Council is that, unlike the General Medical Council, it is denied statutory powers and has not even the power to call the witnesses it needs. With this situation has been compared that obtaining in Sweden where the profession's own Comprehensive Code of Conduct is supplemented by the Press Law of 1949. Disputes are referred to a Fair Practices Commission which has a judge as chairman. (It should be noted that there is less violent competition among Swedish newspapers than here: many Swedish papers are provincial, and among city newspapers there is little casual sale—six out of ten copies go to subscribers.)

By 1962 the catalogue of complaints against the Press Council was large: it had done nothing to help train journalists; it was ineffective in investigating and reporting on complaints; and it had carried out no technical research. H. A. Taylor, formerly President of the Institute of Journalists, has made some pungent criticisms of the Press Council ('The British Press' 1961): the 1955 strike of electricians silenced the national newspapers and London evening newspapers for 26 days; in the Press Council annual report published 8 months later not one of its 20,000 words related to the stoppage, 'one of the most significant events for the Press for years'. In 1962 the Council had an income of only £4,100 and a paid staff of two: lack of income and facilities could account for some of the Council's inadequacies, but not all.

(iv) *The Royal Commission Report 1962.* The terms of reference of the second post-war Royal Commission on the Press appointed at the beginning of 1961 were:

> To examine the economic and financial factors affecting the production and sales of newspapers, magazines, and other periodicals in the United Kingdom, including:
> (a) Manufacturing, printing, distribution, and other costs;
> (b) Efficiency of production; and
> (c) Advertising and other revenue, including any revenue derived from interests in television.
> To consider whether these factors tend to diminish the diversity of ownership and control or the number or variety of such publications, having regard to the importance, in the public interest, of the accurate presentation of news and the free expression of opinion; and to report.

The Report of the Royal Commission, published in September 1962, recommended several important changes: an Amalgamations Court should be established to examine certain acquisitions of controlling interests in newspaper companies; the Press Council should be reconstituted to comply with the recommendation of the 1949 Commission that there should be a lay chairman and a substantial lay membership; the control of commercial television interests by newspaper undertakings should end; and, the 'gravely inefficient' production methods of national newspaper offices should be altered. (Cmnd 1811.)

In January 1964 Lord Devlin took up the chairmanship of a newly reformed Press Council—he was joined by five new lay members, appointed in the previous November. The Council's income was to be £15,000 in the year—still quite inadequate.

(v) *Political Reporting*. The story of the Press as a vehicle of political news is not entirely happy. As seen above, many references have been made to the triviality of our newspapers: the following quotation shows the link of triviality with the lack of adequate reporting:

> The press bears almost the same relation to news as the American drugstore to pharmacy; it is possible to get a prescription filled at a drugstore, but drugs are a very small part of its business, and most of its customers are attracted by the soda fountain, the book-racks, the tobacco counter, the fountain pens, rubber goods, etc. etc. There are still a few old firms which confine themselves strictly to pharmaceutical business, but they are in a dwindling minority. It's the same with the press; it sells news more and more as a sideline, and attracts its customers mainly by its soda fountains, pipe-racks and 'biologicals'. ('The Sugar Pill' T. S. Matthews, quoted Muggeridge, *New Statesman*, 2nd Nov. 1957.)

The earnest and diligent student in Britain may secure much, if not all, of the political information he requires; the average intelligent reader of the more serious newspapers is adequately provided for; the population at large, however, gain a very deficient and distorted picture of political events from their chosen newspapers.

Even during the four-week General Election campaign the popular Press allocates relatively little space to politics and at this time its methods include the concentration on personalities rather than on issues, and the neglect of straight reporting and the giving of unembellished political material to readers from which they can make their own judgements. During the 1959 Election one newspaper thought fit to report that a certain Labour candidate owed money to his grocer while another suggested the murderer Podola was a Socialist ally.

The right-wing enjoys the weight of newspaper support in Britain and the left is not very well served by journals allegedly friendly towards it. Macmillan is said to have remarked recently that, nowadays, he could never find any politics in the *Daily Herald*, although the illustrations were sometimes quite good: these remarks have been matched by the Labour complaint that the only way to get news into the *Herald* would be to tattoo it on the back of a bathing beauty. Since August 1960 the *Daily Herald* has been formally free of obligations to Labour and trade union opinion. (In September 1964 the *Herald* disappeared and was replaced by the *Sun*.) In

November 1959 Roy Thomson, the newspaper owner, said that half the British people were Labour supporters and there ought to be more Labour newspapers. It was pointed out that Thomson did not own a national daily paper to convert to Socialism.

It has been argued that the political influence of the Press is very small—in the United States, the majority of American newspapers were against Roosevelt in every election campaign he fought—and that the right-wing nature of the British Press does not matter. The success of Conservatives in mobilizing sentiment against nationalization, to take only one issue, makes one doubt this.

In 1959 the International Press Institute reported on the Press in totalitarian countries and noted that among the sanctions used by governments against the newspaper world were imprisonment of journalists, the censorship of material, the allocation of newsprint and the forbidding of editorials. Journalists were trained by some governments. In 1956 the I.P.I. had revealed that the Press of the 'free' world was not so free—that the controls exercised in freedom's name often came uncomfortably close in purpose to those of totalitarian countries. Again, in 1962, the director of I.P.I. said that it had been a grim year for press freedom—in many countries, editors and publishers striving to tell the truth to their communities had been silenced or dispossessed. The director was particularly critical of the newly independent states of Africa:

> Under one pretext or another, the press has either been bullied into a narrowly subservient Government line, or emasculated of all crucial comment throughout most of North Africa and West Africa.

Even in the United States (see below), 'the strongest of all bastions of liberty, the Cuban crises produced suggestions of a major breach in the traditional independence of the American press'.

In Britain it is commonly assumed that the free flow of political information is part of our tradition—even during the Second World War newspaper censorship, save on outgoing cables, was voluntary. One cause of complaint against the wartime government attached to its suppression of the *Daily Worker*. Under the Defence Regulations it was an 'offence for anyone to publish or convey to the enemy information likely to be of value in carrying on the war as was the 'systematic

8

publication of matter calculated to foment opposition to the war'. Section 2d (Additional Powers) of the Defence Regulations allowed for the immediate suppression of a newspaper in an emergency, on the Home Secretary's personal edict, where opinions expressed were likely to undermine the will to resist. The closing down of the *Daily Worker*, from January 1941 to August 1942, and the threat against the *Daily Mirror* in 1942, have been condemned on the grounds that there was no need for immediate and urgent action as provided for under Section 2d:

> The case against the *Daily Worker* was a serious and well-founded one, but the paper should properly have been charged before a court of law instead of being dealt with by administrative action. However, most people were agreed that the *Daily Worker* was guilty and that if different methods might have been used nevertheless justice had been done and there was little general complaint—perhaps too little! (F. Williams, 'Press, Parliament, and People', p. 34.)

Delane, editor of *The Times* from 1841 to 1877, once declared that the duty of the Press was to obtain the earliest and most correct intelligence of the events of the time and, instantly, by disclosing them, to make them the common property of the nation. The British Press is perhaps in danger of shirking its duty, as laid down by Delane. Newspapers, free though they may be from the legal pressures discussed above, face danger from more subtle pressures. Ideally, the Press might regard government as a 'conspiracy against the people': in practice it may fail by submitting to the public relations techniques of government, heeding the blackmailing appeals to 'responsibility', being silenced by the 'off-the-record' briefing.

Sir William Haley, in his Haldane Memorial Lecture of 1958, referred to the dangers of serious papers 'addressing themselves to the grapevine of well-informed opinion'. Of the Suez period *The Guardian* has said:

> Between August and October 1956, a constant spate of rumour and reassurance was put out from Government sources. It had its effect in persuading editors not to tell the public how far the Government was moving towards a war-like policy—the more so when they were rightly reluctant to do anything that might endanger the lives of British soldiers. Similarly, in Hitler's day, there were constant efforts on the part of those who believed

in an Anglo–German rapprochement to prevent 'insults to a friendly Power' from appearing in the British press. Discretion served the public interest in neither instance, but that will not prevent Government departments from trying the same tactics again. . . . Appeals for 'trust' from politicians and officials need to be treated at times with a measure of suspicion. The danger of talking too much to top people is that a grapevine may easily turn into an octopus. (12th March 1958.)

Angus Maude, a Conservative, has referred to the pathetic eagerness of Tory papers to act as government propagandists, which has caused them repeatedly to overplay their hand and which has caused the Government to suffer from 'unconscious sabotage'. ('The Public Relations Machine', *Spectator*, 7th Feb. 1958.)

(vi) *Private Sources of News: Foster and Mulholland.* In April 1963 Parliament received the report of the Radcliffe Tribunal on the Vassall Spy Case (Cmnd 2009). One of the report's main findings was that most of the press criticism of the Government's security network were either 'pure comment expressed in the form of assertion of fact' or conjectures. (T. G. Galbraith, who resigned from the Government, was acquitted of any impropriety in his relationship with Vassall: Lord Carrington, First Lord, was acquitted of having known, for 18 months before Vassall was caught, that there was a spy in the Admiralty.)

The Radcliffe Report said that it had not been able to exhaust its lines of inquiry because two (originally three) journalists, whose frankness was important, refused to reveal sources of information:

Since, without being able to know who these informants were and thus to examine them for ourselves, we were unable to obtain direct information and so satisfy ourselves as to the truth or falsity of the statements made, we could not accept these claims to professional privilege except so far as the law governing the proceedings of our tribunal would itself admit them, and this, as we understood the matter, it did not do.

The two journalists, Foster and Mulholland, were gaoled for contempt and a vigorous debate on the ethics of journalists commenced.

The journalists had defended officialdom: officialdom had punished the journalists. This was the essence of much of the Press comment. No one in Whitehall or Westminster should have complained about the journalists' professional reticence because 'off the record' briefings, which assured the anonymity of the donor of news, had long been an established part of government.

There are several reasons why anonymous briefings occur in all branches of government and administration. Some politicians desire to gain political advantage, some to help guide and shape public opinion, some to be friendly to their journalist contacts. Some officials have a contempt for secrecy, some do not want to seem to be courting the Press by open statements, some wish to right an abuse which would, otherwise, remain hidden. John Cole ('Why Private News Sources Matter', *The Guardian*, 22nd March 1963) gives this information and declares that the Press cannot be like the B.B.C., contenting itself to make an efficient and fair presentation of information generally available. *The Guardian* had printed an important National Economic Development Council document which had been intended for internal circulation only—this had been to the public advantage. (See Vol. II, p. 94.)

Crossman summarized the battle which must occur between a free Press and government as follows:

> If a newspaper is fulfilling its main functions within the democratic community, by collecting and printing accurate news, its staff will nearly always be looking for facts which some interested party wants to suppress. And when this interested party is the Government there must arise a conflict between the determination of a free press to get at the truth and the State to prevent revelations which it considers injurious to public security. The fact that Mr. Mulholland and Mr. Foster have been sent to prison, therefore, is no evidence that the freedom of the press is endangered by the state of the law.

One must accept this but there remains the suggestion that, if a means of investigation other than the tribunal established on the basis of the 1921 Act (see also p. 159), perhaps a parliamentary committee or tribunal, had been used in the Vassall case, the two journalists would not have been sent to prison. There also remains the suggestion that editors, and not journalists, should have been punished in this case, since theirs was the final responsibility for publishing the various allegations investigated by Radcliffe.

(vii) *The American Press.* In the United States in 1955 a 'Freedom of the Press Sunday' was arranged to precede a meeting of the House of Representatives Subcommittee on Government Information Practices. Before this subcommittee the American Civil Liberties Union complained that 'abuses of the power of federal agencies to suppress information of value and interest to the nation had never been so rampant', while the chairman of the subcommittee expressed concern that government news had to be obtained from 'designated officials' instead of being freely available at 'pick-and-shovel level'. Specific causes of complaint against the Government were: Eisenhower's order of May 1954 forbidding executive departments to disclose confidential matter; a directive from the Defence Department forbidding contractors to release information of possible value to a potential enemy; the failure of the Defence Department to publish promptly a prominent general's critical letter of resignation.

In the 'sixties, in complaints against Kennedy, the assertion was again being made that there must be something wrong with policies that cannot endure the test of publicity. The Administration has been charged with placing unnecessary restraints on reporters.

The status of the American Press is high: the freedom of the Press grew along with self-government and in the United States democracy is equated with publicity. Because of the loose structure of American government and the absence of parties of a monolithic nature, American newspapers have a distinct function in carrying forward national debate, and a sense of obligation and responsibility stemming from the provision relating to the freedom of the Press written into the First Amendment to the Constitution. The journalist, who may study his craft at university, is regarded as a professional, while newspapers, being of a more local character than in Britain, are more aware of public disapproval and the need for responsibility. In the United States the laws of criminal libel are less strict than in Britain, and the charge of contempt of court is less used (see below, p. 193), and the Press is not restrained by any Official Secrets Act. These facts lead many commentators to compare the British Press unfavourably with the American—some of the discontent has already been noted.

However, the British system in regard to the publication of political news is not without its champions. Some Americans have commented on our 'good fortune' in possessing 'institutional solidarity', a hierarchical society, an 'Establishment', and a cohesive ruling-class. (See

Shils, 'The Torment of Secrecy', 1957.) In Britain the Press and the people hold the State in awe, there is trust on the part of the ruled for the rulers, and a really effective call for democratic 'open government' is absent. Thus, goes the argument, whereas in Britain the attempt to balance publicity with security has succeeded, in the United States it has failed—there is a lack of trust in the government and an inadequately developed sense of national solidarity which causes the American people to look to publicity for constant reassurance.

> If American experience is any guide, the national interest is better served by the existence of a cohesive, if secretive, governing class than by the daily revelations of well-placed journalists on the inside who satisfy curiosity among the masses only by weakening mutual trust among the few. (Peregrine Worsthorne, *Daily Telegraph*, 17th Feb. 1957.)

The effectiveness of the American Press and the cohesiveness of the American Government during the McCarthy period have been subjects of unfavourable political comment. In the prevailing anti-Communist atmosphere, the American governmental élite failed to rally against the Senator's attacks while the Press, despite what has been said above, may be judged to have failed the nation. McCarthy made headline news: it has been said that the fact that he was a liar was not printed by American newspapers in headlines because no one 'quotable' declared the fact. Adverse comments by editors were published, but the fact that there never developed a newspaper counter-attack on McCarthy may, in some eyes, have reduced the claims of the American Press to a special status:

> The role of the American Press during McCarthy's days was an unhappy one, and none of the journalists involved would contend that their newspapers solved the problems or covered themselves with glory. (Alfred Friendly, Editor, *Washington Post*, quoted *Observer* 27th March 1960.)

However, after our own *Sheffield Telegraph*, between March and November 1963, had investigated allegations of police brutality within its city it was credited with having secured a 'rare American-type exposure': we are still deferential towards the American Press.

(viii) *Court Proceedings and the Reporting of Debates*. The right to report Parliamentary debates was one of the historic achievements in the story of the freedom of the Press. The Press is not free, however, to report all activities at Westminster and there exists between the newspaper world and the House of Commons (as opposed to the Government) a 'love–hate' relationship. In 1947 an M.P. was expelled from the Commons for selling confidential information of a Parliamentary Labour Party meeting to a newspaper. On 10th December of that year the House of Commons passed a resolution:

> That, if in any case hereafter a Member shall have been found guilty by this House of corruptly accepting payment for the disclosure and publication of confidential information about matters to be proceeded with in Parliament, any person responsible for offering such payment shall incur the grave displeasure of this House; and this House will take such action as it may, in the circumstances, think fit. (Herd, 'The March of Journalism,' pp. 317–320.)

Earl Winterton described the motion as most dangerous and unnecessary. By passing it the House would extend privilege in a way in which it had never hitherto existed. The dangerous resolution might be used by a subsequent Government as 'an engine of suppression' against the Press or members of the House.

In 1957 an editor was called to the Bar of the House for making allusions to the system of allocation of petrol to M.P.s—petrol at this time being rationed. J. P. W. Mallalieu, on this occasion, thought that the House might be taking itself too seriously. The most recent cases relating to the reporting of debates have occurred in the field of local government. During 1959, from feelings of solidarity with printers who were on strike, some local councils sought to interfere with the free reporting of their proceedings. They were able to do this because the Local Authorities (Admission of the Press to Meetings) Act 1908 provided for the exclusion of the Press on grounds of 'public interest', and did not make provision for entry of the Press where councils chose to 'go into committee'. The Public Bodies (Admission of the Press to Meetings) Act 1960, which began life as a Private Member's Bill, ensured greater freedom for the Press.

In 1957 Messrs. W. H. Smith and Son and the Rolls House Publishing Company were each fined £50 for selling copies of *Newsweek* which contained matter which might have prejudiced the trial of Dr. Bodkin Adams. It was held that, 'since foreign publications imported here have no responsible editor or manager in this country' the distributors had to be punished as 'the only persons who can in these circumstances be made amenable in the courts of the country'. The judgement raised the question as to how Messrs. Smith's could possibly censor the 300 publications they imported, and, perhaps more serious, the question of possible change in the law of contempt of court, with its 'medieval refusal of right of appeal'. A resolution had been passed 50 years previously in the Commons:

> The jurisdiction of the judges in dealing with comtempt of court is practically arbitrary and calls for the action of Parliament with a view to its definition and limitation. (Quoted, *Spectator*, 17th Jan. 1958.)

The Administration of Justice Act 1960 provided for the right of appeal in cases of criminal contempt of court and extended to the Press a greater degree of freedom. Discontent was still left since no precise definition of contempt was given.

9. *Broadcasting*

(i) *The B.B.C.: record of Social and Political Orthodoxy.* A few years ago Lord Simon of Wythenshawe, Chairman of the B.B.C. between 1947 and 1952, outlined the policy of the B.B.C. in regard to the broadcasting of opinion. ('The B.B.C. from Within', 1953, pp. 305–314.) In practice, various degrees of partiality and impartiality were observed. Where public opinion was practically unanimous—for example, in respect of the royal family, the Christian religion, the recent war—the Corporation showed no impartiality whatever and took the purely national view. Where public opinion was overwhelming, but where active minorities existed, the Corporation observed a degree of impartiality: it accepted the majority view but with reservation—for example, while the general character of programmes was anti-Communist, nevertheless such programmes as the 'Soviet View', and 'Soviet Affairs' were broadcast. In matters of public controversy, in particular with regard to party politics, the Corporation observed complete impartiality. The greater part of broadcasting time in politics and religion was given to the more powerful existing groups and organizations: on the whole, the B.B.C. had to be a stabilizing force.

The social orthodoxy of the B.B.C., as illustrated by the expounding of a conventional middle-class outlook in such programmes as Woman's

Hour, Mrs. Dale's Diary, and so on, has been strongly condemned in the past. One may still regret that the B.B.C. does not give more time to unconventional views, to the humanism or rationalism of the Mrs. Margaret Knights of the world: however, under the impact of competition from independent television, the B.B.C. has shown a greater regard recently for the investigation of such topics as prostitution, birth control, A.I.D., and for social commentary of the more searching kind. One hears less criticism today on the score that the B.B.C.'s social conservatism is political Conservatism in disguise.

(ii) *Formal and Informal Controls.* As far as the broadcasting of political opinion is concerned, the B.B.C. operates under certain legal restrictions. The Royal Charter, which is renewed at intervals, lays down that the B.B.C. shall be impartial in the presentation of news, and shall broadcast no editorial opinion of its own. The Corporation should broadcast for the information, education and entertainment of the people; it is free to approach controversial matters, including politics, from a balanced and objective point of view; the reporting of proceedings in Parliament is a duty.

The Licence granted to the Corporation by the Postmaster-General covers the financial arrangements between the Corporation and the Government: Clause 15 (iv) of the Licence gives the Government of the day absolute formal power of veto over the programmes of the B.B.C. if these are not liked. (B.B.C. Handbook 1963, pp. 111). This power has never been exercised in peacetime.

The Independent Television Authority operates under the Television Act 1954, which enjoins accuracy and impartiality of news presentation, impartiality in programmes covering matters of political and industrial controversy, or relating to current public policy. No matter designed to serve the interests of any political party is to be included in programmes—save relays of B.B.C. party political broadcasts, and properly balanced discussions or debates.

Both B.B.C. and I.T.A. have, in addition, to observe the provisions of the Representation of the People Act 1949, which limits expenditure for election purposes to candidates and election agents. No expenditure must be incurred by others for the promotion of a candidate—this covers meetings, public displays, the issuing of advertisements, circulars or publications, or the presenting to the electors of the candidate or his views by other means. (See p. 45 for note on the control of electoral spending.)

Less formally, political broadcasting also depends on agreements between the political parties and the broadcasting organizations. The Ullswater Committee of 1935 recommended close co-operation and consultation between the B.B.C. and the authorized spokesmen of the political parties—not meaning to imply that the treatment of all political broadcasting should be controlled by the party organizations. Lord Simon has said that the tolerant and reasonable attitude of party leaders has facilitated the B.B.C.'s task.

The 1947 agreement between the B.B.C. and the leaders of the three main parties provided for several types of political broadcast: Ministerial broadcasts would permit the publication of factual government statements, to explain legislation for example; party political broadcasts would be made each year, the time allotted to the parties depending on the ratio of votes at the previous election; political broadcasts would be made by the parties at the time of General Elections—the parties would decide the allocation of these broadcasts according to the number of candidates of each party, the B.B.C. would decide the total number of broadcasts to be made. In addition there would be occasions when the B.B.C. would itself put on round-table controversial broadcasts or when it would invite a member of the Government or Opposition to broadcast. No discussion or statement on any issue would be broadcast when the issue was within a fortnight of being debated in the House.

The B.B.C. has a meeting with party leaders about once a year to discuss the agreements reached from time to time and to examine proposed changes. Normally there is an additional meeting before a General Election.

The B.B.C.'s Charter and the I.T.A.'s Licence Agreement were renewed on a temporary basis so that they would both expire at the end of July 1964. In June 1960 the Government decided to appoint an independent committee to survey the whole field of broadcasting. The Pilkington Committee reported in June 1962 (Cmnd 1753). Shortly afterwards the Government issued a White Paper (Cmnd 1770, July 1962) setting out its views. A second White Paper (Cmnd

1893) was published in December 1962. The Pilkington Report recommended that there should be additional party political broadcasts for Scotland and Wales, and that minor political parties should be given fair opportunity to take part in controversial broadcasts. (See below.) The Government, in the White Paper, promised to discuss political broadcasting with all the parties concerned.

(iii) *Impartiality: party suspicions of political broadcasting.* In the past the B.B.C. has regarded political broadcasting as an audience-loser and has interpreted the concept of impartiality very strictly by keeping political broadcasting to a minimum. From the first, the parties themselves were suspicious and distrustful of political broadcasting, jealous for the independence and impartiality of the B.B.C., and these feelings were magnified as audiences grew and with them the potential influence of political broadcasting.

At the time of Suez, doubts were expressed about the contacts between the B.B.C. and government information offices and concern expressed for the disturbing tendency of these contacts to expand. Reference was made to the unprecedented number of 'guidance' hints from official quarters and to the seconding of a Foreign Office official to the Corporation, for liaison duties. Complaints of bias in the reporting of political news came from both left and right.

In November 1956 Conservatives took objection to the broadcasting of newspaper debate on the Suez invasion and called for an inquiry into the B.B.C.'s impartiality. It was wrong, they felt, that our troops in Cyprus should hear that *The Guardian* had described the operation as an 'act of folly without justification'. At the same time a complaint was made from the Opposition side of the House that the B.B.C. was being made subject to censorship—no mention had been made over the air of Britain's breach of mutual security agreements and her 'embezzlement' of equipment supplied for the purposes of collective security. George Wigg declared that, ever since the beginning of the crisis, the B.B.C. had gone out of its way to withhold the truth from the public.

In the Middle East crisis of 1958, when the Foreign Office again sent an adviser to Broadcasting House, commentators found the B.B.C.'s Parliamentary reports objective and noted that some airing was given to anti-Government views and that an Egyptian journalist was given the freedom of the air. On the other hand, some objection was taken to the tone of patriotism with which the views of Lloyd and Dulles were reported and the derisive treatment accorded to the views of Khrushchev and Nasser.

In February 1959 a programme about the 'thirties, 'The Hungry Years', coincided with a debate on unemployment in the House and some Conservatives complained.

Some jealousy has been occasioned within the political parties by the B.B.C.'s use of the 'smooth expositors', the Members who can hold forth on any topic at short notice. The Corporation, it has been said, has depended on too small a circle of broadcasting M.P.s. (In the first hundred editions of the programme 'Ten O'clock' sixty-three M.P.s appeared—roughly a tenth of the Commons.)

In May 1960 Lord Teviot asked the Government to appoint an inquiry to consider the advisability of permitting B.B.C. staff (and especially the 'Panorama' staff), which had no authority or responsibility, to discuss matters which were the concern of the Government. He was refused.

(iv) *The Freeing of the Political Air: the chronology of derestriction.* While much of the history of political broadcasting in Britain is concerned with restrictions, recent events have concerned the freeing of the political air. The freedom of the B.B.C. and I.T.A. to broadcast politics has been greatly enlarged in the recent past.

A directive from the Postmaster-General in July 1955 reaffirmed the 'Fourteen-day Rule' enunciated in the 1948 agreement between the political parties and the B.B.C. No one could arrange discussions for radio or television relating to any issue during the fourteen days preceding a parliamentary debate on that issue, or while debate was proceeding. The theory behind the rule, it would seem, was that Members should have their judgement unclouded by external contention. The rule was strongly criticized as a fussy restriction, and as the first formal act of political censorship for over a hundred years.

After a Select Committee Report published in May 1956, the rule was suspended temporarily in December, indefinitely in July 1957, and has not since been reintroduced.

At the 1958 Rochdale by-election Granada Television gained a limited, but historic, success. Some progress was made towards the establishing of the right of the television services to treat their viewers as the Press, without impediment, treats its readers. The I.T.A., the party H.Q., and the Law Officers, on the initiative of Granada Television, studied, in relation to the Representation of the People Act, the question of the televising of the by-election. It was allowed.

In November 1922 2LO broadcast the results of the General Election; in 1935 results were broadcast under a restrictive agreement which delayed the Corporation's publishing them until the evening newspapers had appeared; in 1945 the B.B.C. broadcast continuous election results, and in 1955 results were accompanied by analysis. Despite this progress severe restrictions were still observed in 1955 in respect of the election campaign itself. Between the dissolution of Parliament and polling-day nothing was broadcast which could influence the voter, party political broadcasts excepted. During the three days immediately before polling-day there was a complete close-down as far as domestic political news was concerned. It was then forbidden to report, even in normal objective terms, a political speech of any kind. Oxford Union debates and comedians' jokes were censored. All current affairs programmes were dropped and no reports of the election campaign given.

Much discontent was expressed over the curious unreality of broadcasting during the General Election, and the policy of 'leaving the voter to the processes of calm thought' was derided. Politics at this time became a matter, not of issues, but of slide-rules, lists of marginal boroughs, and of results. At the only time the electorate became supreme an important source of information dried up and the power of the less responsible newspapers was enhanced.

The negative conception of neutrality shown in the policy of the broadcasting organizations stemmed from their weakness in relations with the political parties. To a far greater degree than the Press, they depended, and still depend, on the benevolence of the two major parties which, when in power, grant and renew charters. In spite of Lord Simon's tribute to the party leaders, mentioned above, frequent complaints were made until very recently about the grudging co-operation of politicians in the question of political broadcasting. Like the politicians of the nineteenth century who did not easily come to terms with a free Press, twentieth century politicians were shy of new electoral techniques, frightened that innovations might work against them and give opponents unforeseen advantages.

Along with comments on the negative neutralism shown in political broadcasting went other criticism. In 1955 there was no provision for the broadcasting of regional politics—perhaps because it would have been difficult for the major parties to exclude Scottish and Welsh Nationalists, and other minorities. In 1955 broadcasting was confined to party statements by a few important political figures. Party spokesmen were chosen for 'safeness', and Conservative and Labour speakers were alike liberals. Radical voices, like that of Bevan, were not heard. In sum, criticism was made of the parties' 'gentlemen's agreement' to keep broadcast politics neutral and sterile, to pursue a safety-first policy, of the many barriers to dissenting opinions, and of the powerful party machines. In the sterility of broadcast politics was a further excuse for the electorate to become cynical towards politics.

Between 1955 and 1959 significant changes were occurring, as we have seen. There was a change in straight political reporting. Whereas during the Suez crisis only set political speeches were broadcast, during the Jordan landings in 1958 there were dozens of controversial political discussions, talks by experts on subjects imminently to be debated in Parliament, films of the landings and of the Security Council debate.

In the 1959 General Election a change was also seen. The B.B.C. assumed a new freedom in news reporting—no attempt was made in individual bulletins to provide an exact balance of 'left' and 'right' news. Granada, which broadcast feature programmes on the machinery of elections, the development of the constitution, and so on, also gave about 150 northern candidates an opportunity to speak on television and to participate in debate. The 'B.B.C. Hustings' was a series of programmes, 40 minutes in length, from a dozen regional centres. These changes were important since they gave the electorate a broader picture of the election than they had ever previously had and they gave a picture of the general level of party forces rather than of the top leadership alone. The broadcasting companies displayed varying degrees of enterprise and caution: Tyne–Tees Television, out of respect for the Representation of the People Act, presented no political feature programmes. However, the electorate as a whole had a picture of the election which was not of the parties' own choosing.

Obviously one must enquire why these changes occurred. The changes which came over political broadcasting between 1955 and 1959 stemmed from a variety of causes. The parties were faced with a decline of public interest in orthodox political talks; Independent Television had introduced an element of competition into broadcast reporting; the parties' experiences at by-elections and party conferences had given them experience of television techniques. Grimond, in February 1959, spoke out for a greater freedom in political broadcasting and contrasted the frankness of the Kennan (Reith) lectures with the refusals of British politicians really to debate. (The Kennan lectures were anti-Cold War in tone and examined the failings of the West as well as those of Russia. The lectures were delivered in 1957 and printed in 1958 under the same title, 'Russia, the Atom, and the West'.)

Academic lobbying must also be taken into account in explaining derestriction. Nuffield College Oxford, concerned with the question of the parties' timidity in political broadcasting and with the question of the fashioning of democracy, initiated in January 1958 a private conference of leading figures from all three parties and from the two broadcasting authorities.

The freeing of the political air is not yet completed. The so-called 'South Ealing formula' still inhibits broadcasting at the time of parliamentary elections. Any candidate can veto political broadcasts by his opponents: if broadcasts are agreed upon, brief set-speeches are given before a strictly bi-partisan audience, and questions, submitted in advance, can be rejected by any candidate.

Early in 1959, at Harrow East, South West Norfolk, and Galloway by-elections, the Conservative candidates vetoed the televising of the election proceedings. Their policy was, apparently, to use the veto where a third candidate was standing.

In March 1959 Labour M.P.s campaigned for the televising of by-elections where a majority of candidates taking part were willing. In his reply to these Members in the House, Butler rested on the Representation of the People Act: there had to be compliance with the rule that all candidates should signify their agreement to broadcasting.

A development occurred in October 1963 when the Prime Minister fought the Kinross By-election: Independent Television News interviewed six of the candidates and gave a report on the Liberal abstainer, thus challenging the view of the law which enjoined the strictest interpretation of impartiality.

The allocation of broadcasting time is also a live issue. In 1945 any party nominating twenty candidates was allowed a broadcast and the Communists were thus included in the allocation. In 1955 the minimum number of candidates needed to qualify for a party political broadcast was raised to fifty and the Communists were excluded. The question in debate here is whether the allocation of broadcasting time should reinforce the bigger parties' existing advantages. In 1959 the Welsh Nationalist Party protested because it was not allowed a party political broadcast on radio or television during the election campaign. The 'three English Parties' were allowed a total of 915 minutes broadcasting time, the Welsh Nationalists, contesting twenty out of thirty-six Welsh seats, none at all.

In the March 1964 announcement regarding election broadcasts Pilkington seemed to have been ignored. Parties had to field at least fifty candidates to qualify for broadcasting time. The Communist Party held a protest march, and threatened to take proceedings under the Representation of the People Act if opponents in those constituencies where it had candidates standing were given favoured treatment.

(v) *The Impact of Television.* Sir Robert Fraser, as head of I.T.A., said that television should be ashamed of itself if it did not contribute to the democratic process. Compared with the Press, it could present both sides of an argument at the same time: television could cater for the readers of a single newspaper who were 'under-exposed' to the full range of democratic argument. Other writers have noted that the broadcasting of politics over television means that the public receives fairer, more objective news. Some have suggested that the provision of more political education to replace political propaganda will be an additional step towards a fall in the political temperature, towards the neutralizing of politics. The political parties have been accused of giving dull, respectable broadcasts from which controversy, attack and counter-attack are carefully excluded. Electoral politics may well be further neutralized unless the political parties exploit to the full the possibilities presented to them by television:

> I have the feeling that in both our countries the politicians are unduly fascinated by the mechanics of this new method of communication—a little too inclined to make political television a competition between film cutters and producers, rather than a competition of ideas and convictions. There is, I suggest, no substitute for the man who has at least a mild fire in his belly, and is able to pierce that screen with his own conviction. (Ed. Murrow, Granada Lecture, quoted *The Guardian*, 20th Oct. 1959.)

It is difficult to assess the impact of political television on the British electorate during the last seven or eight years. In 1955 the highest number of viewers watching a political broadcast was less than a seventh the estimated total viewers in the country: in 1959 a typical broadcast was seen by only 30 per cent. of those with sets. Except for sound radio's Home Service, it is a fact that audiences decline when a political broadcast begins and that the size of the audience remaining for this broadcast is often determined by the popularity of the preceding programme. The fact that a political broadcast is not switched off may only mean that the owner of the set is unwilling to risk damage by switching off too often.

One of the successes of political television has been to show that mass assemblies are still worth while. At the last General Election there was an increased attendance at political meetings—people turned out to see political leaders in person. It will be interesting to see what part political television can play in securing a higher turnout at future elections.

Trenamon and McQuail ('Television and the Political Image' 1961), made a study of the impact of television in West Leeds and Pudsey constituencies at the time of the 1959 General Election—taking a random sample of 700 of the 112,000 electors. They found that television had enlarged political knowledge but, with slight exceptions, had not changed attitudes: people had picked up a lot of information but had screened themselves from direct persuasion. The effect of television will be long-term: it has not yet been used to capacity.

BIBLIOGRAPHY: VOLUME ONE

INTRODUCTION

HISTORICAL BACKGROUND TO THE POLITICAL DEBATE

DICEY, A. V.	*Law and Public Opinion in England during the Nineteenth Century*	Macmillan	1962
GINSBERG, M. (ED.)	*Law and Opinion in England in the Twentieth Century*	Stevens	1959
SOMERVELL, D. C.	*English Thought in the Nineteenth Century*	Methuen	1929
BRINTON, C.	*English Political Thought in the Nineteenth Century*	Benn	1949
MACCOBY, S.	*The English Radical Tradition (1763–1914)*	Black	1952
EMDEN, C. S.	*The People and the Constitution*	Oxford	1956
WOODWARD, E. L.	*The Age of Reform*	Oxford	1962
ENSOR, R. C. K.	*England, 1870–1914*	Oxford	1936
THOMSON, D.	*England in the Nineteenth Century (1815–1914)*	Penguin	1950
THOMAS, N. P.	*British Politics from the Year 1900*	Jenkins	1956
COLE, G. D. H. } POSTGATE, R. }	*The Common People, 1746–1946*	Methuen	1946
GRAVES, R. } HODGE, A. }	*The Long Week-End (A Social History of Great Britain 1918–39)*	Faber	1941
BUTLER, D. } FREEMAN, J. }	*British Political Facts 1900–60*	Macmillan	1963
—	*Britain: An Official Handbook* (See also lists of material on home and overseas affairs published by the Reference Division of the Central Office of Information)	H.M.S.O.	Annual

205

BIRNIE, A.	*An Economic History of the British Isles*	Methuen	1955
COURT, W. B.	*Concise Economic History of Modern Britain from 1750 to Recent Times*	Cambridge	1954
ASHTON, T. S.	*The Industrial Revolution 1760–1830*	Oxford	1948
ROLL, E.	*A History of Economic Thought*	Faber	1961
ROBINSON, J.	*Economic Philosophy*	Watts	1962
GROVE, J. W.	*Government and Industry in Britain*	Longmans	1962
HEARNSHAW, F. J. C.	*Conservatism in England*	Macmillan	1933
WOODS, M. C.	*A History of the Tory Party*	Hodder and Stoughton	1924
BIRCH, N.	*The Conservative Party*	Collins	1949
McDOWELL, R. B.	*British Conservatism 1832–1914*	Faber	1959
JONES, W. D.	*Lord Derby and Victorian Conservatism*	Blackwell	
MACLEOD, IAIN	*Neville Chamberlain*	Muller	1961
COLE, G. D. H.	*British Working Class Politics 1832–1914*	Routledge & Kegan Paul	1941
COLE, G. D. H.	*A History of the Labour Party since 1914*	Routledge & Kegan Paul	1948
PELLING, H.	*Origins of the Labour Party, 1880–90*	Macmillan	1954
POIRIER, P. P.	*The Advent of the Labour Party*	Allen & Unwin	1958
BEALEY, F. ⎫ PELLING, H. ⎭	*Labour and Politics 1900–06*	Macmillan	1958
McBRIAR, A. M.	*Fabian Socialism and English Politics, 1884–1918*	Cambridge	1960
CLINE, C. A.	*Recruits to Labour: the British Labour Party, 1914–31*	Syracuse	1963
LYMAN, R. W.	*The First Labour Government*	Chapman Hall	1957
SYMONDS, J.	*The General Strike*	Cresset	1957
BASSETT, R.	*The 1931 Political Crisis*	Macmillan	1958
FYFE, H. H.	*The British Liberal Party: a historical sketch*	Allen & Unwin	1928
SLESSOR, SIR H.	*A History of the Liberal Party*	Hutchinson	1944
CRUIKSHANK, R. J.	*The Liberal Party*	Collins	1948
MORGAN, K.	*David Lloyd George*	University of Wales	1963
McCORMICK, D.	*The Mask of Merlin*	Macdonald	1963
BEVERIDGE, J.	*Beveridge and His Plan*	Hodder & Stoughton	1954

McElwee, W.	*Britain's Locust Years*	Faber	1962
Watkins, E.	*The Cautious Revolution*	Secker & Warburg	1951
Sissons, M.⎱ French, P.⎰	*The Age of Austerity*	Hodder & Stoughton	1963
Mitchell, J.	*Crisis in Britain, 1951*	Secker & Warburg	1963
de Jouvenel, B.	*Problems of Socialist England*	Batchworth	1949
Hoffman, D.	*The Conservative Party in Opposition*	McGibbon & Kee	1964

CONSERVATISM IN THEORY AND PRACTICE

Block, G. D. M.	*A Source Book of Conservatism*	Conservative Political Centre	1964
White, R. J.	*The Conservative Tradition*	Black	1950
Goldman, P.	*Some Principles of Conservatism*	Conservative Political Centre	1956
—	*Conservatism 1945–50*	Conservative Political Centre	1950
—	*One Nation: a Tory approach to Social Problems*	Conservative Political Centre	1950
—	*One Nation: The Responsible Society*	Conservative Political Centre	1959
Bow Group	*Toryism Revived*	Crossbow Jan.–March	1964
Home, Sir A.	*Peaceful Change*	Barker	1964
Raison, T.	*Why Conservative?*	Penguin	1964

SOCIALISM AND THE LABOUR PARTY

Pelling, H.	*The Challenge of Socialism*	Black	1954
Beer, M.	*History of British Socialism*	Allen & Unwin	1953
Cole, M.	*The Story of Fabian Socialism*	Heinemann	1961

McBRIAR, A. M.	*Fabian Socialism and British Politics, 1884–1914*	Cambridge	1962
CROSLAND, C. A. R.	*The Future of Socialism*	Cape	1956
CROSSMAN, R.	*Socialism and the New Despotism*	Fabian Society	1956
STRACHEY, J.	*Contemporary Capitalism*	Gollancz	1956
AMIS, K.	*Socialism and the Intellectuals*	Fabian Society	1957
McKENZIE, N. (Ed.)	*Conviction*		1958
CONNELL, J.	*Death on the Left*	Pall Mall	1958
BEVAN, A. CASTLE, B. GAITSKELL, H.	*Main Speeches: 1959 Blackpool Conference*	Labour Party	1959
—	*The Future Labour Offers You*	Labour Party	1959
VARIOUS	*Where? Five views on Labour's future*	Fabian Society	1959
CROSLAND, C. A. R.	*Can Labour Win?*	Fabian Society	1960
UNIVERSITIES AND LEFT REVIEW	*Out of Apathy*	Stevens	1960
POTTER, D.	*The Glittering Coffin*	Gollancz	1960
CROSSMAN, R.	*Labour in the Affluent Society*	Fabian Society	1960
ABRAMS, M. ROSE, R. HINTON, R.	*Must Labour Lose?*	Penguin	1960
CROSLAND, C. A. R.	*The Conservative Enemy*		1962
SMITH, H.	*The Economics of Socialism Reconsidered*	Oxford	1962
JAY, D.	*Socialism in the New Society*	Longmans	1963
RODGERS, W. T.	*Hugh Gaitskell*	Thames & Hudson	1964
HALL, P. (etc.)	*Labour's New Frontiers*	Deutsch	1964
NORTHCOTT, J.	*Why Labour?*	Penguin	1964
WILSON, H.	*Purpose in Politics*	Weidenfeld & Nicolson	1964
WILSON, H.	*The Relevance of British Socialism*	Weldenfeld & Nicolson	1964
WILSON, H.	*The New Britain*	Penguin	1964

THE NEW LIBERALISM

BULLOCK A. SHOCK, M.	*The Liberal Tradition* (From Fox to Keynes)	Black	1956
FULFORD, R.	*The Liberal Case*	Penguin	1959
GRIMOND, J.	*The Liberal Future*	Faber	1959
GRIMOND, J.	*The Liberal Challenge*	Hollis & Carter	1963
WATKINS, G. (ED.)	*The Unservile State*	Allen & Unwin	1957
—	*Partners in a New Britain*	Liberal Party	1963
—	*New Orbits*	Young Liberals & Liberal Students	1959
COWIE, H.	*Why Liberal?*	Penguin	1964
McCALLUM, R. B. READMAN, A.	*The British General Election of 1945*	Cumberlege	1947
NICHOLAS, H. G.	*The British General Election of 1950*	Macmillan	1951
BUTLER, D. E.	*The British General Election of 1951*	Macmillan	1952
BUTLER, D. E.	*The British General Election of 1955*	Macmillan	1955
BUTLER, D. E. ROSE, R.	*The British General Election of 1959*	Macmillan	1960

THE POLITICAL DIVIDE

ALLEN, A. J.	*The English Voter*	English Universities Press	1964
—	*British Attitudes to Politics*	Political Quarterly	Jan.–Mar. 1959
MARTIN, C.	*The Bored Electors*	Darton, Longman and Todd	1961
SAMPSON, A.	*Anatomy of Britain*	Hodder & Stoughton	1962
BLONDEL, J.	*Voters, Parties, and Leaders: the social fabric of British politics*	Penguin	1963
FINER, S. E.	*Anonymous Empire*	Pall Mall	1958

FINER, S. E.	*Private Industry and Political Power*	Pall Mall	1958
STEWART, J. D.	*British Pressure Groups*	Oxford	1958
ECKSTEIN, H.	*Pressure Group Politics: the B.M.A.*	Allen & Unwin	1959
WILSON, H. H.	*Pressure Group*	Secker & Warburg	1961
POTTER, A. M.	*Organized Groups in British National Politics*	Faber	1961

ONE: POLITICAL

I. GOVERNMENT AND PARTIES

Chapter 1 and Note (a): Parliament

JENNINGS, SIR I.	*Parliament*	Cambridge	1958
HARRISON, W.	*The Government of Britain*	Hutchinson	1960 (7th ed.)
MORRISON, LORD	*Government and Parliament*	Oxford	1964 (3rd ed.)
HANSON, A. H. WISEMAN, H. V.	*Parliament: A Casebook of Parliamentary Procedure*	Stevens	1962
MACKENZIE, W. J. M. GROVE, J. W.	*Central Administration in Britain*	Longman	1957
KEETON, G. W.	*Passing of Parliament*	Benn	1952
NICOLSON, N.	*People and Parliament*	Weidenfeld & Nicolson	1958
PETER, P. G.	*Honourable Members: A Study of the British Back-bencher*	Faber	1959
—	*Report of the Select Committee on Procedure* (H.C.92 of 1958–9)	H.M.S.O.	1959 (March)
HANSARD SOCIETY	*Parliamentary Reform, 1933–60*	Cassell	1961
FINER, S. E. BERRINGTON, H. B. BARTHOLOMEW, D. J.	*Backbench Opinion in the House of Commons, 1955–59*	Pergamon	1962
BOW GROUP	*Parliament and Party*	Crossbow	Issue Oct.–Dec. 1963

BIRCH, A. H.	*Representative and Responsible Government*	Allen & Unwin	1963
CRICK, B.	*The Reform of Parliament*	Weidenfeld & Nicolson	1964
WILSON, H. } GRIMOND, J. } POWELL, E. } BRIDGES, Ld }	*Whitehall and Beyond*	British Broadcasting Corporation	1964
FABIAN GROUP	*The Administrators*	Fabian	1964
HILL, A. } WHICHELOW, A. }	*What's Wrong with Parliament?*	Penguin	1964

Chapters 2, 3, and 4: Party Politics

—	*The Organization of Political Parties in Britain* (R4243)	Central Office of Information	1960
MCKENZIE, R. T.	*British Political Parties: the distribution of power within the Conservative and Labour Parties*	Heinemann (2nd ed.)	1963
JENNINGS, SIR I.	*Party Politics*		
	Vol. 1 *Appeal to the People*	Cambridge	1960
	Vol. 2 *The Growth of Parties*	Cambridge	1961
	Vol. 3 *The Stuff of Politics*	Cambridge	1961
MAXWELL-FYFE, D. P.	*Report of the Committee on Party Organization*	National Union of Conservatives	1949
LLOYD, SELWYN	*Report of Enquiry into the Party Organization*	National Union of Conservatives	1963
CHURCHILL, R.	*The Fight for the Tory Leadership* (See also comment by Iain Macleod, *Spectator*, 10th Jan. 1964)	Heineman	1964
NICOLSON, NIGEL	See above. *People and Parliament* contains chapter dealing with Conservative constituency action during the Suez episode		
HARRISON, M.	*Trade Unions and the Labour Party since 1945*	Allen & Unwin	1960
LABOUR PARTY	*Party Constitution and Standing Orders* (Amended 1962)		

LABOUR PARTY	*Labour's Aims* (National Executive Committee statement on Clause IV)		March 1960
LABOUR PARTY	*Labour in the Sixties* (Part 2, The Party and the Unions). National Executive report to Conference		July 1960
LABOUR PARTY	*Constituton of the Labour Party* (Executive statement)		August 1960
WILSON, H. (Committee)	*Interim Report of the Sub-Committee on Party Organization*	Labour Party	1955
LIBERAL PARTY ORGANIZATION	Annual Reports		

Chapter 5: Local Government

WEBB, S. and B.	*The Development of English Local Government, 1689–1835*	Oxford	1963
SMELLIE, K. B. S.	*A History of Local Government*	Allen & Unwin	1957
CENTRAL OFFICE OF INFORMATION	*Local Government in Britain* (RF.P.4945)	H.M.S.O.	1961
CLARKE, J. J.	*Outlines of Local Government of the United Kingdom*	Pitman	1960 (13th ed.)
ROYAL INSTITUTE OF PUBLIC ADMINISTRATION	*New Sources of Local Revenue*	Allen & Unwin	1956
—	White Paper: *Local Government Finance in England and Wales* (Cmnd 209)	H.M.S.O.	1957
HERSIC, A. R.	*Relief for Ratepayers*	Institute Economic Affairs	1963
—	*Local Government Act*, 1958	H.M.S.O.	
—	*Report of the Royal Commission on Local Goverment in Greater London*	H.M.S.O.	1960
—	*London Government Act, 1963*	H.M.S.O.	
—	White Paper: *London—Employment: Housing: Land* (Cmnd 1952)	H.M.S.O.	1963
BOYDEN, H. T.	*Councils and Their Public*	Fabian Society	1951
KEITH-LUCAS, B.	*The Mayor, Aldermen and Councillors*	Liberals/ Unservile State	1961

II. JUSTICE: ADMINISTRATIVE LAW

Chapters 6 and 7: Franks Report and the Ombudsman

CHRIMES, S. B.	*English Constitutional History*	Oxford	1948
JENNINGS, SIR I.	*Cabinet Government*	Cambridge (3rd ed.)	1959
BAGEHOT, W.	*The English Constitution* (with introduction by R. H. S. Crossman)	Fontana	1963
DICEY, A. V.	*Law of the Constitution*	Macmillan	1959
CURTIS, M. R.	*Central Government*	Pitman	1958
—	*The Growth of Government*	Political and Economic Planning	1957
—	*Government by Appointment*	Political and Economic Planning	1960
HEWART,	*The New Despotism*	Benn	1929
BROWN, E. D.	*The Battle of Crichel Down*	Lane	1954
KEETON, G. W.	*Trial by Tribunal*	Museum	1960
DENNING, LORD	*Freedom Under Law*	Stevens	
MACDERMOTT, LORD	*Protection from Power under English Law*	Stevens	1957
KERSELL, J. E.	*Parliamentary Supervision of Delegated Legislation*	Stevens	1960
—	*Report of the* (Franks) *Committee on Administrative Tribunals and Enquiries* (Cmnd 218)	H.M.S.O.	1957
JUSTICE	*The Citizen and the Administration: the redress of grievances* (Whyatt Report)	Stevens	1961
UTLEY, T. E.	*Occasion for Ombudsman*	Christopher Johnson	1961

Note (b). Law and Justice

POLLARD, R. S. W.	*Speed Up Law Reform*	Fabian Society	1958
GARDIER, G. A. } MARTIN, A }	*Law Reform Now*	Gollancz	1963

STREET, H.	*Freedom, the Individual, and the Law*	Penguin	1964
—	*Report of the Royal Commission on the Police* (Cmnd 1728)	H.M.S.O.	1962
—	*Report of the (Radcliffe) Committee on Security Procedures* (Cmnd 1681)	H.M.S.O.	1962
HOME OFFICE RESEARCH UNIT	*Time Spent Awaiting Trial*	H.M.S.O.	1960
HOME OFFICE RESEARCH UNIT	*Report of the (Streatfield) Committee on the Business of the Criminal Courts* (Cmnd 1289)	H.M.S.O.	1961
—	*Report of the Working Party on Victims of Violence* (Cmnd 1406)	H.M.S.O.	1961
—	*Victims of Violence*	Conservative Political Centre	1962
—	*Scales of Justice*	Conservative Political Centre	1962
HOOD, R.	*Sentencing in Magistrates' Courts: A Study in Variations of Policy*	Stevens	1962
NEW ORBITS GROUP	*Summary Justice*	Liberals	1963
GILES, F. T.	*The Magistrates' Courts*	Stevens	1963
EDDY, J. P.	*Justice of the Peace*	Cassell	1963
GARDINER, G.	*Capital Punishment as a Deterrent: and the Alternative*	Gollancz	1956
KOESTLER, A.	*Reflections on Hanging*	Gollancz	1956
GRIMSHAW, E. JONES, G.	*Lord Goddard: His Career and Cases*	Wingate	1958
HOME OFFICE RESEARCH UNIT	*Murder*	H.M.S.O.	1961
CHRISTOPH, J. B.	*Capital Punishment and British Politics*	Allen & Unwin	1962
MORRIS, T. BLOM-COOPER, L.	*A Calendar of Murder*	Michael Joseph	1964
TIDMARSH, M. HALLORAN, J.	*Capital Punishment: The Case for Abolition*	Sheed & Ward	1964
—	*Report (Barry) of the Advisory Council on the Treatment of Offenders* (on Judicial Corporal Punishment) (Cmnd 1213)	H.M.S.O.	1960

III. POLITICAL INFORMATION

Chapter 8: The Press

HERD, H.	*The March of Journalism*	Allen & Unwin	1952
CENTRAL OFFICE OF INFORMATION	*The British Press* (RFP.5572)	H.M.S.O.	1963
WILLIAMS, F.	*Dangerous Estate*	Longmans	1957
TAYLOR, H. A.	*The British Press*	Barker	1961
HOGGART, R.	*Uses of Literacy*	Chatto & Windus	1957
		Penguin	1958
MATTHEWS, T. S.	*The Sugar Pill*	Gollancz	1957
COCKBURN, C.	*In Time of Trouble*	Hart-Davis	1956
WILLIAMS, F.	*Press, Parliament and People*	Heinemann	1946
SHILS, E.	*Torment of Secrecy*	Heinemann	1957
BENENSON, P.	*A Free Press*	Fabian Society	1961
—	*Report of the* (Radcliffe) *Tribunal on the Vassall Case* (Cmnd 2009)	H.M.S.O.	1963

Chapter 9: Broadcasting

SIMON, LORD	*The B.B.C. from Within*	Gollancz	1953
BRIGGS, A.	*The History of Broadcasting in the United Kingdom:* (1) *The Birth of Broadcasting*	Oxford	1961
BRIGGS, A.	*The Twenties to the Sixties* (Review of the first forty years of the B.B.C.)	British Broadcasting Corporation	1962
PAULU, B.	*British Broadcasting: Radio and Television in the United Kingdom*	Oxford	1957
CROZIER, M.	*Broadcasting* (Sound and Television)	Oxford	1958
—	*Report of the Select Committee on Broadcasting* (Anticipation of Debates)	H.M.S.O.	1956
—	*Granada Goes to Rochdale*	Granada Television	1958
TRENAMON, J. McQUAIL, D.	*Television and the Political Image*	Methuen	1961
—	*Report of the* (Pilkington) *Committee on Broadcasting* (Cmnd 1770)	H.M.S.O.	1962

INDEX: VOLUME ONE

Please see also **annotated table of contents**.
Acts of Parliament, White Papers, and **Reports, Official** are listed together under these headings.